Ravishing Maidens

University of Pennsylvania Press
NEW CULTURAL STUDIES SERIES

Joan DeJean, Carroll Smith-Rosenberg,
and Peter Stallybrass, Editors

A complete listing of the books in this series appears at the end of the volume

Ravishing Maidens

Writing Rape in Medieval French Literature and Law

Kathryn Gravdal

upp

University of Pennsylvania Press

Philadelphia

Printed in the United States of America

Library of Congress Cataloging-in-Publication Data

Gravdal, Kathryn.
Ravishing maidens : writing rape in medieval French literature and law / Kathryn Gravdal.
p. cm.—(New cultural studies series)
Includes bibliographical references and index.
ISBN 0-8122-8247-7 (cloth).—ISBN 0-8122-1315-7 (pbk)
1. French literature—To 1500—History and criticism. 2. Women—France—History—Middle Ages, 500–1500. 3. Rape—Law and legislation—France—History. 4. Women—France—Crimes against—History. 5. Women and literature—France—History. 6. France—Social conditions—987–1515. 7. Rape victims in literature. 8. Sex crimes in literature. 9. Rape in literature. 10. Law, Medieval. I. Title. II. Series.
PQ155.W6G7 1991
840.9′355′0902—dc20 90-26337
CIP

To my daughter

Contents

Acknowledgments

I wish to thank the National Endowment for the Humanities as well as the Columbia University Council for Research in the Humanities for the liberal grants that afforded me the time to complete this book. To Jonathan Z. Fallet of the Columbia Office of Projects and Grants, I owe an inordinate debt of thanks for his unstinting efforts on behalf of this project and for his painstaking comments as it took shape.

My thanks to the Medieval and Renaissance Collegium of the University of Michigan, and especially to Guy Mermier, for the travel grants that enabled me to participate in James Brundage's seminar and carry out research at the Newberry Library. I wish to acknowledge with sincere appreciation Michael Riffaterre, who took this project seriously from the very outset, lending his support at several key points.

Parts of Chapters 4 and 5 were published in an earlier form in "Camouflaging Rape: The Rhetoric of Sexual Violence in the Medieval Pastourelle," *The Romanic Review* 74, 4 (November 1985): 361–73, and "The Poetics of Rape Law in Medieval France," in *Rape and Representation*, edited by Lynn Higgins and Brenda Silver (New York: Columbia University Press, 1991), and are reprinted with permission. The cover illustration is reprinted courtesy of the Bibliothèque Nationale, with the special assistance of Gabriel Haddad and Peter Schulman, who trudged across Paris several times to obtain it.

I am indebted to Daniel Alter, Renate Blumenfeld-Kosinski, Cynthia Hahn, Geoff Loftus, and Eugene Vance for generously sharing their insights at critical moments in the elaboration of this book. My students are always an unfailing source of inspiration and I want to name Lynne Huffer in particular, who posed the liminal question of this study. Disa Gamberi, Lynn Higgins, Roberta Krueger, Richard Lockwood, Wendy Peek, Gale Sigal, and Brenda Silver extended gracious invitations to lecture and publish, which I was thankful to accept. Andrew Andersen, Laurie Postlewate, and E. B. Vitz were privileged interlocutors, perhaps especially when our interpretations differed.

This book could not have been written without the careful recommendations of many colleagues, who read these chapters in various states of disarray. Caroline Walker Bynum and Robert Somerville patiently guided me through vexed questions of legal history. Matilda Bruckner, Sylvia Huot, and Terese Lyons rescued me from tangled critical thickets on more than one occasion. Susan A. Manning and Mary Shaw gave crucial suggestions on the subject of theater performance. Katharine Jensen and Margaret Waller shared invaluable lessons in the practice of feminist criticism. My heartfelt appreciation goes to Stephen Harkavy, the kindest of partners, and to Christine Clements, the kindest of friends.

Every writer should have the privilege of working with an editor like Patricia Smith, whose enthusiasm was irresistible and infectious. I thank Ross Chambers for being my gentle reader—in both senses of the term. Nancy K. Miller's support of these ideas and her steadfast faith in my ability to express them have meant more to me than I can say. The patron saint of my apprenticeship as a medievalist has been Nancy Freeman Regalado, whose scholarly standards and lifesaving sense of humor have guided me through many drafts. James A. Brundage extended his help most freely over the past five years and I cannot express sufficient gratitude for his inspiring teaching, thought-provoking comments, and precious bibliographical assistance. Finally, I owe to Joan DeJean a debt that cannot be measured, for her wise and gentle counsel, and for the energetic alacrity that saw me through the final stages of this project.

This book was written for my sisters, Judith, Naomi, Jan, and Lori. It is dedicated to Nina Victoria, with all the love and hope in my heart.

Introduction: The Archeology of Rape in Medieval Literature and Law

Between the image of a Middle Ages in which men are so brutal they see nothing wrong with sexual violence and that of a Middle Ages dominated by powerful women who enjoy sexual freedom, this book traces the contours of something less sensational, perhaps less appealing, but more complex. It studies the naturalization of the subordination of women in medieval French culture by examining representations of rape in different discursive genres, both literary and legal.

This book is not a history of rape. Its first purpose is to scrutinize the cultural ideology that supports rape as a stock narrative device in various medieval genres. In the course of that examination, it explores the relations between signifier and signified, between text and society, from a new vantage. My initial question was not whether medieval poets were proponents of sexual violence, but that of the relation between rape and literary genre: how does it happen that the representation of sexual violence is built into a variety of medieval genres and what purpose does it serve?

Literary critics from various fields are today engaged in a polemic over the function and meaning of rape in its textual representation.[1] Depicting, narrating, or representing rape certainly does not constitute an unambiguous gesture of endorsement.[2] But it is crucial to ask of a historical period whose literature is enthusiastically given over to the idea of Woman: why then is rape a stock device in so many genres and what is the relation genre bears to gender? Annette Kolodny describes a critical position that corresponds to my point of departure in the following chapters: "The power relations inscribed in the form of conventions within our literary inheritance . . . reify the encodings of those same power relations in the culture at large."[3]

Medieval culture itself is anything but silent on the topic of rape.[4] The absence of a literary history of rape in medievalist criticism may reveal more about modern attitudes toward sexual violence than it does about the supposed medieval indifference to it. It definitely reveals that certain ambiguous ways of discoursing on rape, forged in the Middle Ages, still function effectively (and invisibly) today.

What is rape? Its signification in written discourse is not a given. The idea of rape bears many meanings. The discursive field around the topic of rape still needs to be constituted, whether in literature, philosophy, or biology, whether in ancient Greece or modern popular culture:

> Each usage of the term seems to capture some relevant aspect of the problem even if none encompasses them all. To favour any particular usage or usages would therefore foreclose insights into the question of rape and force us to come down on one side or the other of the issue before we have actually settled its nature.[5]

By the same token, the word "rape" bears many linguistic meanings in a broad semantic field. One of the hallmarks of medieval studies is the importance it assigns to philology. Medieval vernacular languages were in constant flux; and no modern scholar can safely assume that any medieval signifier refers to the same signified, or signifies in the same way, as its modern "translation." The importance of language studies to medievalists in no way conflicts with the importance of linguistics for feminists, who seek to study "language as a symbolic system closely tied to a patriarchal social structure."[6] Philology can show how language founds and grounds an asymmetrical relationship between women and men, coding sexual violence in ways that make it culturally acceptable. Or, in the well-known formulation of Hélène Cixous, "Language conceals an invincible adversary because it is the language of men and their grammar. We mustn't leave them a single place that's any more theirs alone than we are."[7]

Is it possible that Old French is a language of men? In Old French there is no word that corresponds to the modern French *viol* to designate rape. Medieval culture does not search to find one term to denote forced coitus. The Old French language favors periphrasis, metaphor, and slippery lexematic exchanges, as opposed to a clear and unambiguous signifier of sexual assault. Such periphrastic expressions include *fame esforcer* (to force a woman), *faire sa volonté* (to do as one will), *faire son plaisir* (to take one's pleasure), or *faire son buen* (to do as one sees fit). The interpretive codes through which sexual violence is both concealed and revealed are tangled in three etymological fields, where meanings converge, shift, and displace one another across the centuries of the French Middle Ages.[8]

The most frequent medieval locution for rape is *fame esforcer* (with its many orthographic variants, such as *esforcier, efforcier*, or *esforchier*). Philippe de Beaumanoir, the famous thirteenth-century jurist, uses this expression in the legal definition of the crime of rape:

> Femme efforcier si est quant aucuns prent a force carnele compaignie a feme contre la volonté de le feme, et sor ce qu'ele fet tout son pooir du deffendre soi.[9]

> Forcing a woman is when one has carnal knowledge of a woman against the will of that woman and despite the fact that she does everything in her power to resist him.

To understand the medieval specificity of this periphrastic euphemism, it is necessary to begin with the resonances that *esforcer* brings from the vulgar or popular Latin lexeme, **fortiare* (ablative of **fortia*). Both derive from the classical Latin adjective *fortis*: strong, powerful, mighty. *Fortis* bears distinctly positive connotations of military heroism: courageous, manly, brave, bold, impetuous. The Latinate nuances of manly strength and bravura survive when, in approximately 1080, the adjective *esforcié* (powerful, strong, impressive) surfaces in the epic *Chanson de Roland*.

In the twelfth century many Old French romances use the term *esforcer* to mean "to strive" or "to make a great effort": the hero spurs himself on to realize his full knightly valor. It is noteworthy that *esforcer* in the sense of "admirable striving" coexists, in twelfth-century romances such as Chrétien de Troyes's *Erec et Enide, Le Chevalier au Lion, Le Chevalier de la Charrette*, and *Le Conte du Graal*, with *esforcer* in the sense of rape. In *Le* Chevalier de la Charrette and *Le Conte du Graal* we find both meanings within one and the same romance.[10]

By the end of the twelfth century, the adjective "esforcible" signifies valiant, formidable, powerful. Within this chivalric rubric of admirable strength and heroic efforts appears, also in the late twelfth century, the word *esforcement*, denoting effort, power, military force, bravura, and rape. From the notion of strength, manliness, and bravery, we move to the knight's striving after heroism, and then to the idea of forced coitus. This specifically medieval *glissement* suggests that rape is part of the feudal hegemony, built into the military culture in which force is applauded in most of its forms.

It is significant that *esforcer* denotes sexual violence only in the medieval period. In the sixteenth century, the term gradually loses the meaning of forced coitus and leaves only the sense of *s'efforcer à*: to strive mightily to do something, or to do violence to oneself (in a figurative or moral way). As the official signifier of rape, *efforcer* would be eclipsed in the seventeenth century by the term *viol*, a more technical, legal word. The positive nuances of strength and manliness in *esforcer* triumphed, causing the idea of sexual criminality to fall away.

Philippe de Beaumanoir marks the important connection betweeen *femme esforcer* and *raptus* in the thirteenth century, making it official and *legal* in his somewhat circular definition of sexual violence: "on apele rat feme efforcier" (forcing a woman is called *raptus*). The study of medieval law reveals how confusing and tangled the legal notion of the crime of *raptus* can be. Its family of linguistic signifiers contains the marks of this cultural ambiguity.

The classical Latin *rapere* bears the seeds of an ambiguousness that will be fully developed in Old French. Some of the more common meanings of *rapere* are to carry off or seize; to snatch, pluck, or drag off; to hurry, impel, hasten; to rob, plunder; and, finally, to abduct (a virgin). The key semes are those of movement or transportation, appropriation or theft, and speed or haste. From *rapere* is derived the popular Latin **rapire*, which gives the Old French *ravir*. By the end of the twelfth century, *ravir* can mean to run at great speed; to carry off by force; or to be carried off at great speed. *Ravissant* designates, in the twelfth century, some one or thing that carries others off by force. But as early as 1155, the Latin *raptus* in the sense of abduction brings about the shift toward a sexual meaning: *rap* (c. 1155) or *rat* (c. 1235) designates abduction by violence or by seduction, for the purposes of forced coitus. The connotation of swiftness is coupled with that of force:

Jamès fame n'oseroit dire
De bouch cen que tant desire;
Mès mont li plest que nen la prenge
Mal gré soen, comment qu'il avienge.
Pucele soudement ravie
A grant joie, que qu'ele die.

(*La Clef d'Amours*)[11]

Never would a woman dare say with her own mouth what she desires so much; but it pleases her greatly when someone takes her against her will, regardless of how it comes about. A maiden suddenly ravished has great joy, no matter what she says.

In the thirteenth century also appears *ravissement*, a term that introduces a new etymological spin in the French history of *ravir*. When it first appears, *ravissement* means the action of carrying off a woman, but by the fourteenth century it comes to have a spiritual or religious sense: the action of carrying a soul to heaven. From this religious meaning develops a more secular, affective one: the state of a soul transported by enthusiasm, joy, or extreme happiness. *Ravissement* now, in the fourteenth century, refers to the state of being "carried away" emotionally, a state of exaltation. From this psychological troping comes a sexual trope: the state of sexual pleasure or rapture. *Ravir* is to bring someone to a state of sexual joy.

The slippage or *glissement* from violent abduction to sexual pleasure is as breathtaking as it is telling. The shift reveals the assumption that whatever is attractive begs to be ravished: carried off, seized, or raped. The ideas of a woman's attractiveness and a man's desire to rape are conflated in *ravissant*.

As the legal idea of rape gradually changes to exclude the requirement (which originates in Roman law) of abduction, *ravir* and *ravissant* are free to become wholly figurative: to be carried away emotionally or sexually. This transformation is inflected by a shift in gender coding: when *ravir* was literal, it was the male who ravished (carried away or abducted) the female. When the term soars off into the realm of the figurative, it is the female who is ravishing, who causes the male to be "carried away" and is responsible for any ensuing sexual acts. The moving force behind rape becomes the beautiful woman. The female reader cannot help but note the irony that, in modern French as in English, "ravishing" is intended to be the height of flattery, a compliment in which the male speaker implies that the female, object of his admiration, has captured his power. A man is overpowered by a ravishing woman. It is no coincidence that this linguistic "blurring" occurs in the Middle Ages. The French language conflates rape and ravishment as early as the thirteenth century, and the literal meaning of sexual violence is erased behind the romantic troping of ravishment.

What causes the word *viol* to take on the new meaning of forced coitus (not found in the Latin *violare*, to injure, outrage, dishonor) in classical French? *Esforcer* was emptied of its sexual connotation by the end of the

Middle Ages, probably owing to the dominance of the positive meanings of "force." *Ravir* and *ravissement* hold sway in the late medieval and Renaissance vernaculars. But as those lexemes shift into the figurative—spiritual, erotic, or sentimental—classical French seeks a more literal signifier to designate the act of sexual violence. It turns to a technical, legal term: to violate. This final choice (still in place today after three centuries) expresses a view of the female body as a place protected by law, an object to be respected, a site that is set apart and must not be invaded.

* * *

The semantic *mouvance* we find in the Old French language is not without points of correspondence in medieval law. The history of legal opinion on rape, like the term itself, follows a shifting line, with spiderlike detours, difficult to trace across the early medieval centuries. It is often buried in the complexities of adultery, marriage, or abduction laws.

The abduction of women was a common medieval practice, deeply engrained in the customs of pre-Christian Europe. The formulation and elaboration of abduction and rape statutes first began during the Christianization of Europe. The legal term for the abduction of a woman was *raptus*, and it is crucial that we begin this discussion with an explanation of that term, so confusing to the modern reader. *Raptus* refers to noncontractual marriage by abduction and/or to forced coitus (modern rape). The word is used in different ways at different times, but its standard meaning in medieval law is marriage by abduction:

> Rape, in the predominant sense of sexual relations forced on a woman, with some degree of violence against her person, is certainly not present as a subject in the penitential and non-penitential literature before Gratian.[12]

In early medieval Europe, secular law on *raptus* (abduction of a woman) followed Roman law, in which it was a serious crime. *Raptus* was not a public crime, however, but a kind of theft, a wrong against the man under whose authority the female victim lived. Roman law was hostile to an older (Germanic and Jewish) legal solution, which accepted marriage between the rapist and victim as a reparation of the crime.[13]

It was Constantine (311–77) who made *raptus* a public crime and instituted the death penalty. At the same time, however, he legislated that a woman found complicitous in the abduction was subject to the death penalty, as was the *raptor*.

In the sixth century, Justinian significantly rewrote previous law on *raptus*:

> Justinian specifically described *raptus* as a sexual crime against unmarried women, widows, or nuns. This was significant since at least temporarily it was not only a crime against property but against an individual woman.[14]

Subsequently, strict sanctions against abduction existed throughout Europe. Childebert II tried to impose death or exile as the punishment for the capture of a woman.[15] The secular penalty was a stiff fine of fifty-two and one half solidi, or the amount of the brideprice. Doubtless the severe fines imposed at this time were a measure for protecting not only women's bodies but also patriarchal family honor.

Ecclesiastic or canon law legislated against *raptus* primarily in the context of a long-standing cultural controversy over two models of marriage: marriage legally negotiated between the fiancé and the father of the bride, as opposed to marriage by abduction without the knowledge of the bride's family.[16] The latter practice is what canon law refers to in legislating on *raptus*. Marriage is viewed as a matter of social order, while forced coitus falls under the category of fornication.[17] The Church's chief concern was to decide whether or in what cases marriage by abduction is legal or can be legalized. The complicated and contradictory debates over this point continued for centuries.

In the eighth century, the Roman legal principle that mutual consent is required for a valid union was no longer upheld in Merovingian legislation.[18] By the ninth century, the secular governments of Europe had more important concerns than sexual behavior. Without their support, the Church had to accommodate age-old customs. As a result, the Frankish Church softened its earlier policy on rape and abduction. In 818, Louis the Pious showed lenience to rapists of betrothed virgins. They could avoid the death penalty by paying a fine to both the groom and the king.[19] In a landmark decision, the council of Meaux-Paris (845–46) relaxed legislation against marriages resulting from *raptus*. If the ravisher performed a penance, the couple could remain together. It is true that Hincmar (c. 806–82), archbishop of Reims, wrote a famous ninth-century treatise

De coercendis raptu.[20] Its essential goal, however, is not the protection of women against sexual violence but rather the restoration of law and order:

> [I]t was necessary to strengthen the "marriage pact," which allowed women to be shared out peacefully among men, and so to lend as much prestige as possible to the civil and secular rites by which this agreement was concluded. . . . Neither Hincmar nor his contemporaries gave any space to the need for consent, attributing no superior importance to the exchange of vows as distinct from the physical union.[21]

The early medieval laws on *raptus*, whether strict or lenient, whether for or against, share one overriding concern: that of maintaining peace among men.

A new interest in the legal question of rape arose in the early days of the courtly period, when the idea of courtly love and the literary genre of romance were born in northern France. Canon laws on *raptus* underwent major revision. While secular law in France continued to maintain the death penalty for forced coitus (following Roman law), the Christian church began to promote a new attitude and new legislation.

Gratian, the canonist and jurist, was chiefly responsible for the new policy, in his *Decretum* (c. 1140).[22] Drawing on the work of Isidore of Seville (560–636), Gratian states, "*Ait enim Ysidorus in II. lib. Ethimol. c. 33.4: C. I. Quid sit raptus.* Raptus quoque est illicitus coitus a corrumpendo dictus; unde qui rapto potitur stupro fruitur" (For Isidore says in the second book of his *Etymology* c.33.4:C.I. What is *raptus*? *Raptus* is also illegal sexual intercourse, so called because corruption takes place: hence whoever takes possession of a woman by *raptus* performs a debauchery) (C. 36. q. 1, c. 1). Gratian then redefines *raptus* in a still more restricted way: "Cum ergo hec illicito coitu sit corrupta, cumque ita sit abducta, id est a domo patris ducta, quod de eius nuptiis nichil actum ante fuerit, raptam appellandam negari non potest" (Since therefore this woman was corrupted by illegal sexual intercourse, and since she was abducted in this manner, that is to say taken from her father's house, and because nothing had been previously settled concerning her marriage, it cannot be denied that she is to be termed *rapta*) (C. 36, q. 1, d.p.c. 2). The crime consists of four necessary elements: there has been unlawful coitus; the woman has been abducted from the house of her father; the rape was accomplished by violence; and a marriage agreement has not been negotiated previously between the victim and the ravisher. Gratian's new specification that the victim was protected only when abducted from the house of her father underscored the patriarchal nature of this medieval law: it was concerned primarily with the protection of the father's rights, not those of his daughter. In this respect, Gratian took a step backward from the sixth-century laws of Justinian. Gratian's focus on the house of the father implies a return to the view of *raptus* as a crime against male property. Canon law also disallowed the punishment of forced coitus in marriage, since consent was given at the time of marriage, and further disallowed the prosecution of forced coitus with a prostitute, since a prostitute was not considered to be an honest woman.[23]

Gratian makes an eloquent appeal for the softening of ravishment laws, in the name of Christian love. Obeying the tradition that the Church should not shed blood, he rejects the death penalty. When committed by a layman, *raptus* is now punishable by excommunication, social and spiritual isolation for a defined period (often as brief as a year or two):[24] "si uero laici, excommunizentur" (but if they are laymen, let them be excommunicated) (C. 36, q. 2, c. 4). Furthermore, if the ravisher can flee to a church, he is promised immunity from secular prosecution: "Sed si ad ecclesiam cum rapta cunfugerit, priuilegio ecclesiae mortis inpunitatem promeretur" (But if he takes refuge in a church with the *rapta*, by privilege of the church he deserves impunity from the death penalty) (C. 36, q. 1, d.p.c. 2). When *raptus* is committed by a churchman, the provision for sentencing remains vague: "si quidem clerici sunt, *decidant a proprio gradu*" (if they are clerics, let them fall from their rank) (C. 36, q. 2, c. 4; emphasis added). The results of this legal leeway will be studied when we look at the rape trials of churchmen in Chapter 5.

The softening influence of Christian love appears to soften only the fate of the *raptor*. Many ecclesiastic decretalists followed Gratian and returned, ironically, after centuries of controversial debate, to the influence of Germanic law: they ruled that the ravisher, by way of penance for his crime, could simply marry his victim, if she consented. In other words, *raptus* becomes once more a way to contract a legal marriage. In 1200, Pope Innocent III allowed marriage subsequent to rape, if the victim consented.[25]

Some historians interpret Gratian's policies as influenced by, or an expression of, courtly love, "securing greater personal autonomy . . . for the woman in late medieval society."[26] Do such interpretations blur what is in fact a return to the legitimization of male force in socially approved relations between men and women? Simon Kalifa has argued that medieval society's acceptance of marriages between a ravisher and his victim does not reveal a new notion of the legal personality of women.[27] Rather it reveals, as Georges Duby has demonstrated, that the Church was eager to avoid private warfare between families: "The essential thing was to prevent the defrauded family of the intended bridegroom from attacking the family of the abductor."[28] It also shows that the Church was increasingly eager to bring marriage, a secular institution, under its porch and make it a religious sacrament.[29]

> In Carolingian France the institution of matrimony was still relegated to the margins of what was considered sacred. But because it was the main foundation of public peace, and because, through the structures of the State, the bishops were closely involved in the preservation of that peace, the leaders of the Church had to pay more attention to it than had their predecessors, and they had to do so with a lesser show of repugnance. It was then that the gradual sacralization of marriage began.[30]

For the female reader of medieval law, one crucial question remains. In these centuries of debate over the legality of ravishment, what became of the issue of forced coitus (rape in the modern sense)? The act of forced intercourse was not considered a canonical problem. Pure and simple rape was not a crime in Church law. This indifference to the legal personality of individual women (for already Justinian recognized there existed rape victims who were either not virgins, not abducted, not engaged to be married, or not living in their fathers' houses) could be explained on the grounds that the Church's principal effort was to codify marriage. It is only the abduction of a virgin engaged to be married that fell within the territory the Church claimed as its own. While forced coitus may not always fall under the heading of marriage law, however, there is another territory which the Church clearly claimed as its own in the Middle Ages: sexual behavior. It is startling to realize that while the Church devoted vast pages to the codification of sexual behavior in canon law, it did not study, comment on, or codify simple rape.

When Pierre Payer explains that rape, in the modern sense of "sexual relations forced on a woman," does not exist in penitential or nonpenitential literature before Gratian, he goes on to raise an important question: "Violence against persons is censured; illicit sexual relations are censured. Why these two notions were not brought together before the time of Gratian would be worthy of further study."[31] Equally worthy of further study are the specific, limited ways in which Gratian brought the ideas of violence and sex together in the twelfth century and the manner in which he created a legal space that, under certain conditions, could expand to accommodate their reconciliation. Gratian labored to codify marriage; Gratian strove to regulate sexual behavior, such as bigamy, sodomy, and prostitution.[32] But forced coitus, while it may have been a crime, was not a sin.

In twelfth-century canon law, as in literary texts, we see a blurring of distinctions between forced and voluntary sex, between love and violence. If, in the legal text, *raptus* can be the legal prelude to marriage, and if the victim could conceivably consent to marry her rapist, just how serious was this crime? If, in the literary text, the violence of the *raptor* can be construed as an expression of conflicted desire, the rape plot can become the basis of a romantic narrative.

* * *

Since the nineteenth century, medievalists' conceptions of the status of women in medieval French society had been derived primarily from studies of the literature of "courtly love." It was commonly held that in these poems and romances the feminine constituted a new cultural ideal according to which female characters were empowered and revered. What was left unsaid was that courtly love literature is not only obsessed with an idea called "Woman,"[33] it is also obsessed with an idea called "Ravishment." Medieval literature ceaselessly repeats the moment in which an act of violence makes sexual difference into subordination.[34]

Early studies of women in medieval literature and history were deficient in at least four important regards. First, despite frequently occurring representations of rape, rarely was it said that the literature of courtly love (or any other medieval vein) depicts sexual violence. In addition, the tendency to draw conclusions regarding medieval attitudes toward women only from courtly love literature excluded other fertile literary genres, such as hagiography or comic literature. Third, the gender position presented as dominant in courtly fiction, the feminine, was treated as the dominant position in the historical real. Literary history has been written as if the normative positions of male and female in fiction were the historical product of unanimous social consensus, rather than of conflict.[35] Finally, there was little effort to consider literature in the light of other discourses or to compare the literary fictionalization of rape to its construction in legal texts.

Revisionist studies of courtly love in the French Middle Ages first appeared in the 1960s.[36] During the 1970s, feminists began to unmask the fiction of the medieval "cult of the lady" and inspired a promising wave of new studies, both historical and literary, of women in the Middle Ages.[37]

By broadening the field of investigation to the study of societal relations in medieval France, particularly the institutions of marriage and of chivalry, scholars now reveal courtly love to be a mystification.[38] Historians have begun to treat the opposition between male and female as problematic rather than fixed, as contextually defined and repeatedly constructed.[39] This book argues that the critical paradigm of "courtly love" has blinded us to essential aspects of medieval French literature. Courtly love discourse constituted an attentiveness to emotional states of feeling. But this discursive examination of inner states was an expression of male culture that had little if anything to do with female roles in society or with changes in the masculine perception of female psychology or sexuality. Courtly discourse is a locus in which the feminine figures as an empty sign that can be filled with the reflections of masculine hegemony on itself. The methodology used in the following chapters draws on these revisionist studies of courtly love.

This book is informed by three practices in feminist theory: the Franco-feminist critique of male discourse; the revisionist study of women writers; and the Anglo-American tradition of historicist materialism.[40] The apparent anachronism of these complementary modern methodologies may disconcert fellow medievalists. Indeed, medieval studies and twentieth-century theory do not form an easy marriage. Many medievalists are reluctant to "force" modern grids on texts produced by a culture dramatically different from our own, texts that require a very specific historical grounding. At the same time, the work of the past twenty years has taught us that modern models can illuminate texts of all periods without betraying their cultural specificity. Aware of both the dangers of anachronism and the great promise of new epistemological insights, I want to proceed by foregrounding the theoretical assumptions and models at work in this book.

* * *

One of the important trends in feminist critical practice is the study of women writers. The question of the woman writer, the specificity of her work, and the need to reevaluate or at least understand the maleness of the canon is raised in Chapter 1, "Plotting Rape in the Female Saints' Lives." Hrotsvitha, a tenth-century playwright and author of hagiography, has truly been "brushed aside at the scene of inheritances."[41] Unlike the other writers studied in this book, she writes in Latin and her work predates the high Middle Ages. I include her work because it offers the earliest example of a European woman writing rape scenes and also because it can be studied for the ways it disrupts the rules of the male-established hagiographic genre.[42]

Modern readers may be taken aback to learn that fictions of sexual violence appear early in medieval religious literature. Chapter 1 demonstrates that the *vitae* or lives of women saints trope rape in a range of complex ways. By "trope" I mean a literary device that presents an event in such a way that it heightens figurative elements and manipulates the reader's ordinary response by suspending or interrupting that response in order to displace the reader's focus onto other formal or thematic elements. The mimesis of rape is made tolerable when the poet tropes it as moral, comic, heroic, spiritual, or erotic. Hrotsvitha's texts both maintain the patristic lesson on the importance of virginity and subvert the traditional troping of rape. Rather than use rape scenes to titillate her audience, she shapes them such that they disassociate female sexuality from male lust.

Much feminist work has constituted revisionist readings of the female literary tradition, both to show that such a tradition exists and to highlight its specific markers, its difference from the male-authored tradition.[43] Recent feminist challenges to the very notion of the canon as a measure of universal aesthetic and moral worth can pave the way for a revisionist view of women writers. The question is by now familiar: have "marginal" women writers been excluded from the canon because they are indeed inferior or because the standards imposed as transcendental criteria of quality are inflected by the specific values and judgments of male culture? In Kolodny's view, "male readers who find themselves outside of and unfamiliar with the symbolic systems that constitute female experience in women's writings will necessarily dismiss those systems as undecipherable, meaningless, or trivial. And male professors will find no reasons to include such works in the canons of 'major authors.' "[44]

When we compare Hrotsvitha's rape scenes to that of another tenth-century Latin hagiographer, the author of a *Life of Saint Margaret*, we are struck by the difference in writerly agendas.[45] While Hrotsvitha tropes sexual violence as a dilemma that must be resisted courageously by Christian women, the Latin author presents it as a mystical "swallowing." By the twelfth century, another change occurs in hagiographic depictions of sexual violence. Wace, an important and prolific Old French writer, appears, in his *Vie de Sainte Marguerite*, to draw on the romantic tropes of secular literature.[46] Overt references to force disappear. The villain threatens not to assault but to *marry* the unwilling virgin. The rape plot is transformed into a love plot or a marriage plot. The idea of courtly love impinges even on hagiography in its troping of sexual assault.

Chapter 2 mines another important vein in the recent explorations of feminists: the critique of canonical male writers. Many critics now argue that often the Great Books are considered great because they constitute literary reifications of the structures upon which male civilization and ideology are built. The classics are much loved by women readers, too, because those texts, and those who teach them, subtly "immasculate" women readers, training them to read like men, to enjoy and value ideas that alienate women from their own female difference.[47] In the field of medieval studies, resisting readers of history such as Georges Duby have taught us that some of our most cherished beliefs about medieval culture, such as our ideas about courtly love, support and sometimes even create the values of male culture.

One of the great canonical genres of twelfth-century France, and of the European Middle Ages in general, is courtly romance. Chapter 2, "The Poetics of Rape Law: Chrétien de Troyes's Arthurian Romance," shows that sexual violence is a powerful motor in the romance genre, both in plot and in audience interest, just as it was in female saints' lives. In romance, "ravishment" becomes aestheticized and moralized.

In studying Old French romance, we identify a key but unstated and invisible meaning of the word "romantic," a term much used to describe the new sentimentalization of literature in the twelfth century, the period to which the birth of romantic love in Western civilization has been traced.[48] In its invisible meaning I would define the romantic as that which blurs the distinction between seduction and aggression. The medieval romanticization of ravishment has left its clear imprint on modern literary critics as well as modern genres:

> I hope to read romances forever. Flowers with a fond note from an anonymous admirer; an invitation to the dance penned hastily on cream-colored parchment; gray eyes watching me across the ballroom floor; a light touch on my silk-covered arm; the final kiss as he bends my slight body to his own, and the flush of my face at the magic of it all; *and rape, ah, rape.*[49] (emphasis added)

The "rape, ah, rape" Helen Hazen invokes here is the poetic inscription of rape in romance. In arguing against any meaningful relation between the fictional representation and the act it fictionalizes, Hazen is certainly not alone. To critics belonging to this school of thought, it is naive and unscholarly to connect real rape to its literary portrayal. My own position in this book is that we must examine the crucial connection between a historical institution and its literary depiction and seek to understand the complex and varied cultural meanings borne by that representation.

Analogous work done by feminists in other areas has encouraged me in this project. Janice Radway, for example, has looked at the meanings of "ravishment" in twentieth-century popular romance.[50] In a comparable study of a different time and tradition, Leslie Rabine's book, *Reading the Romantic Heroine*, deftly reveals the invisible codes of interpretation already internalized by readers of nineteenth-century romantic literature.[51]

As a result of this examination, we can reread the work of one canonical medieval author, Chrétien de Troyes, and ask why he has long been viewed as a beloved master of medieval literature and an expert in the representation of feminine psychology. A close reading of female sensuality and male brutality in Chrétien discloses the essence of the power play behind "romantic love." The resistant reader of medieval romance perceives the ways in which male domination and female submission are coded as emotionally satisfying and aesthetically pleasing. Chrétien's troping of rape leads the audience to ignore its physicality and its literal consequences and to focus instead on the ideology of chivalry. Chrétien interrupts the immediacy of violence with a moral reflection on chivalric codes. The ultimate effect of romance "ravishment" is to shift the gaze away from the physical suffering of the female body to the chivalric dilemmas of men.

Chrétien de Troyes often links his representations of sexual violence to fictional rape laws, laws which he invents and which are ultimately laws of literary genre. Every chapter of this book studies the archeological dimensions of fictional discourse in its relation to the legal thought of medieval culture. Probing the cultural layering of images of sexual violence yields illuminating insights about medieval attitudes as they articulate themselves in literature and offers a necessary background for all the readings in this book.

Another twelfth-century Old French *roman* relies heavily on genuine legal discourse in its inscription of rape. Chapter 3, "Replaying Rape: Feudal Law on Trial in *Le Roman de Renart*," takes up the study of a medieval literary work that explicitly frames rape as a legal issue. In rereading the *Roman de Renart*, I draw on a critical model that examines the complex ways in which medieval literature and law impinge on one another. The materialist historicism practiced by feminists is not unrelated to a recent trend in scholarship which involves examining the intimate connections between these two types of discourse.[52] Practitioners of literary theory and members of the critical legal studies movement have begun to chart new fields of investigation.[53] Many of the theoretical premises of the law-and-literature movement in the past two decades have been drawn from post-structuralism. France's "new epistemology" has yielded rich insights as it has informed both of the dominant research trends in law-and-literature. Jacques Derrida's notion of a general, cultural textuality, in which all discourse is decentered and none is privileged, gave impetus to many of the initial attempts to read law and literature together.[54] The legal text is as artful as the poetic; these scholars conclude that literary discourse is not ontologically different from other forms of discourse.

The work of Michel Foucault has been central to the new historicism as well as to the law-and-literature movement, especially because of Foucault's keen historical understanding of the unity of discourse. In any given historical period, all forms of discourse are continuous, for they share profound common structures and are unified in their contingency.[55] The concurrent study of literary texts, of judicial norms affecting women, and of the writerly practices of courtroom notaries, affords greater insight into refracting notions of "fiction" and "reality" in the medieval representation of women.

One area of investigation in the law-and-literature movement is the study of literary representations of law: literary texts that take law as their subject matter, including trials, courtrooms, and legal themes. Medieval literature itself presents us with a rationale for the use of this approach. European literature of the Middle Ages, English and German as well as French, bears the imprint of a marked preoccupation with law.[56] Trial scenes are a staple of much European literature, and certainly that of the Middle Ages.[57] Medievalists have studied such literary mirrorings of law since the nineteenth century.[58]

A series of three trial scenes is found in the twelfth- and thirteenth-century *Roman de Renart*. This cycle of animal stories transforms the beast fable genre into a mimesis of community forum in which feudal rape law and procedure are debated, a feature never before discussed by critics. We learn from the *Renart* texts that the medieval public is well-versed and interested in the legal controversies surrounding rape as a social problem for the community.

Chapter 4 demonstrates that the medieval genre of the pastourelle is analogous to *Le Roman de Renart* in that both create a space in which it is permissible to laugh at rape. Moreover, both use the female sexual body as a pretext for reflecting on law, social class, and order in feudal society. How do these pastourelle authors make their audience comfortable in its enjoyment of literary rape? Chapter 4, "The Game of Rape: Sexual Violence and Social Class in the Pastourelle," takes up the crucial question of audience, to study the ways that pastourelle authors manage the audience response.[59] In *The Dynamics of Literary Response*, Norman Holland offers psychoanalytic models of literary analysis that presuppose male writers and audiences.[60] Such an assumption is quite appropriate for a study of the male medieval tradition. Holland shows how a male audience enjoys watching forbidden scenes of erotic pleasure but can only take pleasure in such contemplation if the text manages the taboo in an acceptable way. Through highly formalized, esthetic devices such as meter or music, through the use of character and narrative as intellectual defenses, and through the formulation of moral and political problems, the pastourelle authors allow the audience to overcome their own inner censors or scruples and to contemplate rape with pleasure.

The timing of the humor in the pastourelle is key to its troping of sexual violence. Just as the text reaches the point at which the harshness of a literal depiction of rape could disconcert or culpabilize the listener and inspire sympathy for the female character, it veers off, changing tone to undercut the violence. In a slapstick ending, the panting shepherdess thanks the knight for raping her and asks him to return soon. The listener is never allowed to stop and contemplate the violation in any literal way. The joyous verses that follow the assault confuse the reader and render the rape scene wholly ambiguous.

Feminist literary criticism highlights the implications about women's power that male-authored texts attempt to deny.[61] In the pastourelle, fictional seduction and rape are staged as a struggle between the powerful (the male knight) and the powerless (the female peasant) to give expression to conflicts between social classes. The pastourelle genre displaces class conflict onto a sexual axis where its violence can be directed at the figure of the woman and made comic. The construction of gender conflict can then be viewed as a mere cipher in a comic allegory of medieval society, a formal play that encourages the reader to ignore the violence that underlies the rape sequences. The genre transforms the political anxieties that fuel thirteenth-century social discourse into comic erotic conflicts.[62]

Freudian criticism has given rise to another issue in the study of literary rape, that of the female audience. What are we to make of women readers who contemplate, perhaps with fascination, scenes of sexual violence? This question brings to mind Hazen's argument that there is no connection between literary and real rape. Hazen, like others, claims that the fantasy of rape is a salutary female wish, a sign of an unrepressed woman's libido.[63] Many medievalists believe that the literary representation of rape enabled female listeners to revel in the contemplation of the forbidden, to indulge in a guilty wish without fear of punishment or consequence.

There are at least two other ways of understanding the presence of the female audience listening to rape scenes. The first is to recognize that women, like men, have been taught to view male aggressiveness as flattering. Hazen's assumption is that rape is a frustrated man's attempt to express true love. In life as in literature, male force and female submission have for centuries been coded and internalized as erotically appealing.

In claiming that female audiences enjoy and even create the market for rape scenes, critics have adopted the psychoanalytic model of reading as a wish-fulfillment fantasy. A second way of comprehending the interest of a female audience in the artistic representation of rape, however, is through the other type of fantasy in the psychoanalytic model, the anxiety-mastery fantasy. Rape "fantasies" may indeed enable women to contemplate sexual violence without fear of consequence . . . not because they wish to be victims of rape but rather because they can, in the safe space of imagination, explore violent conflicts between men and women and rehearse strategies for living with male aggression.[64] The frequency of sexual violence in medieval literature intended for mixed audiences may suggest that medieval listeners took the text as an imaginary locus in which they could stage their anxieties about living in a world in which rape was a daily reality and perhaps achieve a sense of mastery, however fleeting, over their fears.[65] The representation of rape in feudal France of the twelfth and thirteenth centuries allowed women listeners, as well as male poets and audiences, to examine attitudes about sexual violence and the relation of gender to power in their society.

In Chapter 5, "The Complicity of Law and Literature," the study of the medieval pastourelle and its management of rape scenes brings me once again to the question of literature's relations to law. The implicit question underlying this final chapter is that of the hierarchical nature of discourse and the way in which scholars privilege certain documents by assuming they are more objective than literary works.[66] The authority of a legal text, although different from that of a literary text, is nonetheless established through writing.[67] The modern law-and-literature movement examines the literary or poetic aspects of legal writing, such as opinions, statutes, or constitutional treatises. Legal writing is not without its own poetics. Judges and lawyers use literary strategies to strengthen the affective charge of their arguments and to move their audience.[68] Susan Estrich's study of modern rape law, *Real Rape*, is one example of an analysis that unveils the art of the legal theorist, the judge, and the prosecutor in the nineteenth and twentieth centuries. Estrich shows how those authors argue eloquently and with art that what a woman may call rape is not necessarily *real* rape.

Like legal historians and scholars, medievalists usually deal with texts whose temporal remoteness makes any original meaning impossible to recover: the poet, the audience, and the linguistic context have disappeared.[69] We must then *interpret* legal as well as fictional texts. Medieval law itself authorizes such an activity. Gratian, the foremost jurist of the high Middle Ages, author of the canonical *Decretum* (c. 1140), did nothing if not interpret the discourse of previous writers.

Chapter 5 analyzes representations of sexual violence in medieval law, both canon and civil, legal theory, and courtroom records of rape trials in northern France. The language and composition of archival texts, as well as their content, deserve analysis. Scholars must examine the "fictive elements" in medieval documents. Analogous work in other periods and countries has encouraged me in this undertaking. Natalie Zemon Davis has studied the fictional or literary qualities of sixteenth-century French pardon letters to discover the extent to which authors give narrative shape to the events of a crime.[70] In similar work on records of sex crimes in thirteenth- and fourteenth-century Italy, Guido Ruggiero finds that rape is treated as an extension of the customary victimization of women: a fact of life that is inscribed in the clinical language of court records.[71]

Among the earliest pertinent documents in France, the *Registre de l'Officialité de Cerisy* is the court register of the Abbey of Cerisy in Normandy.[72] The records maintain a technical and cursory tone in their description of rape trials, a tone of clinical distance. Their vagueness is so uniform that it raises a suspicion that the resulting ambiguity is deliberate. Their discourse on sexual violence is almost as elliptical as romance allusions to ravishment: it is difficult for the reader to determine what exactly took place and whether it was malicious violence or a private (romantic) misunderstanding.

In contrast, the professional secretaries who transcribe the secular trials in the *Registre Criminel de la Justice de Saint-Martin-des-Champs à Paris* linger with complaisance over the erotic details and violent drama of the crime in rape cases.[73] Echoes of the pastourelle in trial records suggest that popular song offered the preexisting linguistic materials with which the court scribe constructed his own text. The Saint-Martin records reveal a poetic troping of rape reminiscent of the pastourelles. The spectacle of violence against women is made tolerable as it is made literary. Medieval law patterns itself after medieval literature in the cultivation of textual practices that rationalize male violence against women.

* * *

The discourse on women and sexual violence in medieval France, whether in courtly or noncourtly literature, legal theory or case history, has long been roped off as an archeological site that is inappropriate for excavation by the right-minded medievalist. The incautious explorer who digs there will find a rough terrain of fragmented layers. Discontinuity is the rule in this site and meanings are elusive. Some fragments resist all analysis by turning to dust at the critic's touch. Others are so thickly overlaid with palimpsests that they remain undecipherable. Despite the precariousness of the evidence brought to light in this study, the reader will recognize a consistent feature in all the shards: the cultural habit of conceptualizing male violence against women as a positive expression of love is both evoked and grounded in these texts.[74]

1. Plotting Rape in the Female Saints' Lives

The specifically Christian transformation of sexual difference into subordination occurs in slow and complicated patterns. Out of the early Christian rejection of corporal experience comes a new asceticism that grounds itself in an ideological subordination of women and a misogynist construction of femininity.[1] Pauline doctrine on sexuality informs the patristic theology that legitimizes the gradual exclusion of women from ecclesiastic structures, from sanctity, from the intellectual centers of monasticism, and eventually from the political spheres of daily life.[2]

Ironically, the period known as the "Dark Ages," the nadir of European male civilization, constituted a time of great fecundity, promise, and power in medieval female culture. In the early Middle Ages, women were vitally necessary for the creation of a new society. They experienced legal, social, and intellectual advancement. As female roles expanded, medieval women exercised greater power than their counterparts in classical society.[3] But the empowerment could not last in the Januslike face of Christian patriarchy. As the looser structures of early medieval society became better organized, as the strength of the Church and monarchic hegemony grew, women lost their brief moment of opportunity. When the millennium arrived, women had been excluded from the mainstream of monasticism, education, and government.[4] The "renaissance" of female culture which Joan Kelly boldly pushed from the sixteenth back to the twelfth century had in fact long perished by that time.[5]

Hagiographic discourse constitutes one of the few remaining traces available to study European culture in the first millennium.[6] In the hagiography of the early Middle Ages, the saint's martyrdom constitutes the apex of the narrative paradigm. Death is the climactic episode in the hagiographic text of the first millennium. Torture, hanging, burning, crucifixion, starvation, or decapitation are the points of interest in the narration of the saint's legend.

The patristic understanding of female sexuality makes itself apparent in the *vitae*. The female saint's life of the early Middle Ages contains a gender-specific narrative structure. Before the climactic death episode, the story of the female saint may spin off onto its own narrative trajectory: sexual violence. There is a sexual plot peculiar to the female saint's legend. Rape, prostitution, seduction, and forced marriage are the signal variations in this gendered plot. The construction of sexual assault runs through hagiography like a shining thread in a tapestry, highly valued and useful. The sexual violence in female *vitae* has received little critical attention. Scholars have noted that the early ideal of the virgin-martyr saint gives way to other paradigms in the high and late Middle Ages (notably the queen or empress saint, and then the visionary or contemplative saint), but few have investigated the meanings of these generic paths to female sanctity.[7]

The obvious explanation for the importance of rape in early Christian hagiography is that it corresponds to the new ideal of feminine virginity. The Church fathers are well known for calling women to a virginal life.[8] Most patristic thinkers propounded the idea that woman is the objective correlative both of the sexual body and of human sinfulness. A woman could be saved from her inferior female nature only by renouncing sexuality and becoming like a man, *vir*, through virginity.[9] A woman accedes to sanctity by prizing her chastity so highly that she dies for it. Sexual assault is one of the preferred methods of promotion to female martyrdom in early Christian hagiography.

Sexual violence takes a variety of forms and functions in the female *vitae*. Four types of plots are most common in the literary shaping of feminine sanctity in early hagiography. The category of *vitae* in which the threat of rape is made explicit demonstrates that there does exist a language for rape in the hagiographic text. The heathen loses patience with the trappings of love-talk or marriage proposals and verbalizes his intention to violate the heroine. Such direct representation of rape is less common than sex forced through marriage or ravishment by a third party in a house of prostitution. But *vitae* referring openly to rape exist, such as the lives of Saints Lucia, Anastasia, and Euphemia.[10]

The topos of forced prostitution, with its potential for sensational eroticism and voyeurism, is a familiar choice in female *vitae* and is greatly prized by Christian hagiographers. In order to persuade the reluctant virgin to yield to his sexual demands, the heathen paints a menacing picture of life in a brothel. He hands the Christian convert over to the debauched mistresses of a house of sin that she may be corrupted by them. Or he opens the doors of the brothel to any young ruffian who wants a try at the virgin. Divine intervention, commonly in the form of an angel, a blinding light, or a shining garment that cannot be stripped from the virgin's body, prevents the heroine from any harm; and she ascends untouched to delight in the embraces of Christ. The plots of marriage, seduction, and prostitution can overlap and combine, as in the story of Saint Agnes, but the threat underlying all the plots is that of the unwilling loss of chastity: forced sex. The house of prostitution figures prominently in the stories of Saints Agnes, Agatha, and Daria.[11]

In the seduction plot, the male heathen lusts after a beautiful Christian convert. She may be a consecrated virgin or a chaste wife. The seducer attempts to inflame the female character with passion. In rare instances the heroine gives in to temptation and then enters a convent or dies. Failing to elicit consent, the antagonist often turns to violence, imprisonment, or torture. The convert is only too joyful to embrace death rather than suffer repulsive sexual congress with a man and a non-Christian. The lives of Saints Crisart, Eugenia, Justine, and Theodora belong to this paradigm.[12]

Forced marriage, with its attendant (if tacit) component of sexual violation, is a popular plot. A heathen man, wealthy or powerful in government, makes the acquaintance of a beautiful convert to Christianity. The heroine is typically a young virgin of noble birth who wishes to sacrifice her worldly advantages in order to become the bride of Christ. Infuriated when he cannot marry the pious maiden, the heathen tries various methods of coercion, humiliation, imprisonment, and torture, to force her to accept him as husband. The heroine prefers death to the loss of her virginity and thus acquires sainthood. The medieval legends of Saints Margaret, Ursula, and Petronille actualize this plot.[13]

The hagiographer addresses a varying audience: sometimes an exclusively male or exclusively female religious group, sometimes a mixed group of laity. The rape plot is versatile, charged with didactic possibilities for such a mixed public. With it, the Christian poet can highlight more than one point of religious dogma for the female audience, as well as achieve some unwonted literary effects aimed at male listeners. For women, the rape plot glorifies virginity through the medieval topos of the *miles Christi* or "soldier of Christ" and makes that literary motif available to female personages. Under physical assault, the female saint becomes a soldier of Christ in the early days of Christian militancy. The threat of rape thus opens a space for female heroism.

A second narrative function of sexual violence is that it exalts the life of the virgin as a specifically female form of *imitatio Christi*: this hagiographic topos was traditionally reserved for male saints who chose an ascetic life of renunciation, as in the legend of Alexis.[14] When the heathen seducer plays the role of diabolic tempter, the *vita* establishes an analogy between the female virgin and Christ, who underwent temptation by the devil.[15] Through the agony of sexual seduction, a woman can become Christlike.

A third didactic function of sexual violation in the female *vita*, a lesson for both men and women, is that it posits and celebrates the eternal justice of God. In hagiography, no rape is ever completed. Even if the saint dies, she dies sexually pure. The wicked seducers are always thwarted and punished, the faithful protected and rewarded.

In focusing on sexual plots the female saint's life creates and offers the female audience a discourse that glorifies the sublimation of female sexuality. As she resists the attacks of the heathen seducer, the female saint may indulge in sensual love language, expressing her desire to be held in Christ's arms or her yearning to receive his kisses. Models of this approved channeling of sanctioned female sexuality were available from patristic texts.[16] Medieval hagiographers incorporate this discourse in the biography of the female saint in order to glorify feminine virginity.[17]

Intertwined with the didactic aims accomplished by plotting rape is another less pious although equally time-honored function, doubtless aimed at male listeners: the representation of seduction or assault opens a licit space that permits the audience to enjoy sexual language and contemplate the naked female body. The *vitae* authors do not hesitate to indulge in descriptions of the nubile attractiveness of thirteen-year-old virgins; their smooth, tender flesh as they are stripped bare in public before a crowd; the debauched but beautiful prostitutes who seek to tease young maidens into licentious acts; or the sight of snow-white female breasts being twisted and pulled by heathen torturers. Hagiography affords a sanctioned space in which eroticism can flourish and in which male voyeurism becomes licit, if not advocated. Suggestive evocations of the female body were not uncommon in patristic diatribes against the wiles of women.[18] In hagiography, the discourse of the Church fathers is reconverted to a new end.

The voyeurism made possible by the performance of a literary text belongs to the realm of the imagination: a mental spectacle, a linguistic contemplation. But let me open a brief parenthesis on the visual arts and hagiography. The few manuscript illustrations remaining today suggest that my speculation is not unfounded and that part of the attraction these stories held lay in the contemplation of violence against the female body. In the iconography of the legend of Saint Agatha, one of the most important female martyrs, the best-known image of her passion is that of her mutilation: the removal of her breast.[19] Of the seven illustrations in a French manuscript of the story of Saint Agatha, belonging to the late tenth or early eleventh century, no fewer than three represent violence against Agatha: one depicts her in a brothel with nine prostitutes, one portrays her suspended from a rack, and one represents the removal of her breast. The medieval artist offers pictorial images of the scenes he must have deemed most significant in the narrative: the sexual seduction and torture of the female saint.

* * *

Most *vitae* authors were anonymous and, given the male orientation of education and writing in the Middle Ages, the likelihood is that they were male. But the early Middle Ages also admired the work of several female hagiographers (Baudonivia, Hugeburc, Lioba, the Chelles nun who wrote Saint Balthild's A *Vita*, and perhaps the author of Aldegund's *Vita*), not to mention the accomplished female scribes who copied *vitae* in manuscripts (the nine nuns of the Chelles scriptorium, the women of Dulcia's scriptorium at Laon, Madalberta of Meaux, Abirhilt of Würzburg, Caecilia of the scriptorium at Remiremont, and Eugenia).[20] The "golden age" of women authors in early medieval Europe was the seventh and eighth centuries.[21] At the end of this rich tradition, at the moment of its extinction, a prolific hagiographer appears. In her corpus we can examine the specificity of sexual violence as a plot in the work of a woman writer.

Hrotsvitha was a tenth-century intellectual who trained and wrote her substantial *oeuvre* in the Ottonian convent of Gandersheim. It is believed that she was of aristocratic family and a canoness, that is a woman vowed to a monastic life of chastity and obedience but, unlike a nun, not to poverty.[22] Gandersheim was a community of well-educated, powerful, and wealthy noblewomen leading the contemplative life. They retained their wealth, their libraries of Greek and Latin classics, their freedom to come and go, and their servants. They also retained their close connections with the Ottonian court. Directly related to the royal family, the abbesses of Gandersheim enjoyed political independence within the realm.[23] In this privileged female space, this millennial *cité des dames*, the erudite Hrotsvitha wrote eight hagiographic legends, six plays, and two epic histories.[24]

Her work may have been destined for the primarily male audience of the court as well as for the female audience of the Gandersheim convent.

The prefaces to Hrotsvitha's *opera* reveal that she has a clear vision of her singular vocation as a woman writer in male culture. Punning on her own praenomen in the "Praefatio" to her *Liber Secundus*, she proclaims herself the "loud voice of Gandersheim": *Unde ego, Clamor Validus Gandeshemensis.*[25] The imaginative etymology plays on the Old Saxon *hruot*, "voice," and *suid*, "strong."[26] Despite her heavy use of the clerkly topoi of *humilitas*, which Hrotsvitha strategically couches in the form of *excusatio* because of her *sexu feminae*, the poet is openly confident of her talent and craft, of her classical education, and of the fact that she was assembling an impressive literary corpus.[27]

From the sixteenth century on, Hrotsvitha's literary fortune has declined steadily. By the nineteenth century, she was dismissed as an elaborate joke: Joseph von Aschbach affirmed, in 1867, that she was a historical absurdity because a woman of her literary education and taste could not have existed in the tenth century. He explained her away as the creation of her sixteenth-century editor, Conrad Celtes.[28] In the twentieth century she is considered something of a mediocre scribbler. Modern readers have taken up (and put down) her work with the idea that it is both minor and marginal. Katharina Wilson notes that "the history of critical thinking about the poetic and dramatic merits of Hrotsvitha's works has oscillated between the poles of euphoric praise and fastidious disparagement." Peter Dronke's tongue-in-cheek summary of her critical fate accurately conveys the condescension of most critics:

> Discussion of Hrotsvitha has seldom wholly escaped the assumptions that her existence was "cloistered" and that her talent was naïve. The stereotype still most widely encountered is that of a woman (usually thought of as a nun) immured in her convent, who unaccountably took it into her head to read the plays of Terence and to "imitate" them by writing edifying Christian counterparts.[29]

The circular justification of Hrotsvitha's artistic inferiority has been her exclusion from the canon, from anthologies, and from courses on the history of theater. It has taken critics one thousand years to name her as the first female playwright in western Europe.

Recent feminist challenges to the very notion of the canon as a measure of some transcendent aesthetic worth can pave the way for a revisionist view of Hrotsvitha's work. Hrotsvitha's eight legends and six plays, which she refers to as *dramatica vinctam serie* or *dramatica serie contextus*, recount the lives of Christian saints. In them her goal is twofold. Above all, she writes to preach the story of Christ's salvation. Hrotsvitha's other goal, misunderstood by scholars from the sixteenth to the twentieth century, is a defense of women.[30] It is this aspect of her writerly agenda, her desire to situate herself in medieval female culture (however nonexistent it may seem to us today, doubtless because of its unofficial and oral character), that has escaped the grasp of critics and readers.[31] As Hrotsvitha states in her "Praefatio," she wants to show: "cum feminea fragilitas vinceret et virilis robur confusioni subiaceret" (Female weakness triumphs and male strength is defeated in confusion [Homeyer, 234, 5]). The critical failure to perceive Hrotsvitha's protofeminist strategies has helped to seal her fate as an *illustre inconnue*: "When viewed from an asexual or male perspective, she appears to be a rather average medieval theologian exploring standard concepts of sin and salvation illustrated in the lives of martyrs and virgins. . . . She emerges as a minor eulogist of ordinary Christian heroes."[32] But if we reread these plays as Hrotsvitha presented them, as plays about women and their specific struggles in a male world, their ingenuity and creativity rise from the ashes of standard literary history.

Like the Church fathers, Hrotsvitha ardently supports the ideal of virginity. It is perhaps difficult for a modern reader to see this religious celebration of chastity as anything other than patriarchal oppression. But for some medieval audiences virginity was a positive sexual category. It represented the choice to remain outside male desire and the refusal to circulate as an object of male possession.[33] To refuse to go to the marriage market is, in the Middle Ages, one path to female autonomy, however limited and narrow.[34] Hrotsvitha's meditations on virginity are an exploration of female sexuality and power in light of women's real roles at the time:

> 1) the young girl who chooses virginity over marriage; 2) the virgin whose desire to remain unmarried is not accepted by those in power over her; 3) the woman who marries but emulates the life of a nun in her marriage; 4) the nun who falls into sin and loses her faith, her religious profession, and her virginity; 5) the whore who willingly adopts a life of vice and wantonness; and 6) the woman who surrenders her virginity for the vocation of Christian motherhood.[35]

How does a woman writer use rape in her exploration of female culture and roles? Hrotsvitha takes up the rape plot in her stories of women saints, but it is sexual violence with a difference. Hrotsvitha transforms the rape plot to combat the contradictions of patristic thought: that woman is sexuality because she is sinful, and sinful because she is sexuality.[36] The paradox of Hrotsvitha's dogma is that she fiercely defends the patristic ideal of virginity, but does so to demonstrate the strength and purity of female nature, rather than any corruption that must be overcome.[37] Hrotsvitha depicts male aggression and violence against women, then focuses on the alternatives of women as they respond to such objectification.[38] In her *opera*, the troping of sexual assault becomes a way to represent female power, virtue, courage, and superiority.

Hrotsvitha frequently feminizes the *miles Christi* motif. In *Agnes*, the play entitled *Passio Sanctarum Virginum Agapis, Chioniae, et Hirenae*, and the epic history of her convent, *Primordia Coenobii Gandeshemensis*, the author uses attempted ravishment to underscore and develop her apology of female strength.[39] All these female characters are depicted as staunch militants for Christ and for virginity, "weak women who confound strong men."

In her version of the legend of Agnes, Hrotsvitha exploits the popular hagiographic motif of the virgin's imprisonment in a brothel to illustrate female purity and divine justice. Hrotsvitha paints sin in vivid colors, the better to portray the heroism of female virtue. Hrotsvitha does not hesitate to represent the whorehouse:

His dictis saeva praeses commotior ira
Caelestis sponsam regis iussit venerandam
Vestibus exutam, toto quoque corpore nudam,
Concurrente trahi conventiculo populari
Inque lupanaris nigrum concludier antrum,
In quo lascivi iuvenes rationis egeni
Colloquio scelerosarum gaudent mulierum.
Sed Christus, propriae praebens solamina sponsae,
Illam conviciis tangi non sustinet ullis.
Ast ubi distracto nudatur tegmine toto,
Continuo bene densati crevere capilli,
Qui, ductu longo lapsi de vertice summo,
Descendendo pedum plantas tetigere tenellas,
Corpus et omne comis tegitur ceu tegmine vestis.

(Homeyer, 206–19)

These words inflamed the savage rage of the prefect still more, and he commanded the esteemed spouse of the Celestial King to be deprived of her garments and with body entirely exposed to be dragged in the midst of a great concourse of people that had gathered, and to be shut up in the dark den of a brothel, in which wanton youths, maddened with passion, delighted in association with evil women. But Christ, bringing consolation to his own spouse, did not suffer her to be touched by any one of these revilers. For when she was thus exposed, deprived of her garments, immediately the luxuriant hair, which hung in long tresses from her head, grew longer, and in its descent reached the tender soles of her feet so that her entire body was covered with the tresses as with a protecting garment.

Hrotsvitha's Agnes articulately defends herself against the charge that she caused the death of Simphronius, indirectly refuting the Christian doctrine that posits female responsibility for male lust.[40]

"Non ego causa necis iuveni fueram pereunti,
Sed magis ipse sibi fuit incensor moriendi,
Glorificare deum stultus quia spreverat illum,
Gloria tristifico cuius praefulget in antro."

(Homeyer, 289–92)

"I was not the cause of the death which destroyed this youth; but rather he himself was the author of his own death, because stupidly he spurned to glorify the true God, whose glory radiates in this sullen dungeon."

The closure of Hrotsvitha's plots dramatizes her supreme confidence in divine justice. This optimistic assurance that all Christians will come to a good end is characteristic of Hrotsvitha's texts. The wicked either perish or convert.

Hrotsvitha's corpus does not construct a simple, gender-coded roster of female victims and male persecutors. From her legends to her plays, she shows that women as well as men reject God and abuse their worldly authority.[41] This avoidance of programmatic polemics is part of Hrotsvitha's strategy in making her defense of women acceptable to a mixed audience. The *vita* of Saint Pelagius shows Hrotsvitha's inclusion of male suffering. It also brings us to an analysis of the erotic potential of hagiography, for it best illustrates the author's grasp of human sensuality and her compassion for all Christians.

Pelagius is the only *vita* that Hrotsvitha draws not from traditional sources but from contemporary history, perhaps an eyewitness account, as she claims.[42] It is the story of a young Christian man in Muslim Spain. Pelagius, thirteen years old and strikingly beautiful, inflames the local Arab governor with lust:

Aspectu primo quoque rex suspensus in illo
Ardebat formam regalis stirpis amandam.
Tandem Pelagium nimium mandavit amandum
In solio regni secum iam forte locari,
Ignis ut ipsius fieret sibi sedulo iunctus;
Fronteque summisso libaverat oscula caro
Affectus causa, complectens utpote colla.

(Homeyer, 231–37)

The king also, attracted to him at first sight, was passionately inflamed by the amiable beauty of that royal youth. At length he ordered that Pelagius, for whom he entertained such an excessive infatuation, be now placed on the throne of the realm with him, so that he might give expression to his affection. And then he sought in his frenzy to bend his head and to kiss the youth he loved, embracing him the while.

The Muslim ruler becomes caricatural as he fawns over the unwilling boy in front of the entire court, covering Pelagius's neck with kisses and breathing promises of devotion.

Haec ait, et dextra compressit martiris ora,
Astrictim laeva complectens colla sacrata,
Quo sic oscillum saltem configeret unum.
Callida sed testis confudit ludicra regis
Osque petit subito pugno regale vibrato
Intulit et tantum pronis obtutibus ictum,

(Homeyer, 268–73)

This he said, and with his right hand he held firmly the face of the martyr, embracing with his left that hallowed neck, that thus he might imprint at least one kiss. But the martyr confounded the crafty pleasantry of the king and speedily directed against the royal countenance a swinging fist, dealing such a blow to that downturned face.

Enraged by this vigorous resistance, the king has Pelagius tortured and put to death.

Pelagius is the only text in which Hrotsvitha uses sensual language and imagery to portray the sexual attractiveness of the protagonist. Is it purely coincidental that the object of sexual desire in *Pelagius* is male, not female? In choosing a homosexual seduction, Hrotsvitha is not interested in condemning homosexuality. As John Boswell notes: "Hrotswitha meant to make no theological statement about homosexual acts. . . . [She] seems to feel that the major issue in her story is that of bearing witness to the Christian faith and not cooperating with lustful pagans."[43] By using male characters only, Hrotsvitha conveys her understanding of the undeniable pull of youthful beauty. More important, she communicates this in a narrative situation from which all female characters are absent, thus opposing—however indirectly—the Christian theological tendency to locate the cause of sexual transgression in the female.

Like other hagiographers, Hrotsvitha uses sexual violence as a vehicle for *imitatio Christi*: the pure virgin becomes Christlike in her resistance to temptation.[44] In the play entitled *Resuscitatio Drusianae et Calimachi*, commonly known as *Calimachus*, the poet refuses the traditional patristic inscription of woman as naturally lascivious and shows her to be naturally chaste. A married woman, Drusiana resists the sexual siege of Calimachus, a prestigious and attractive Roman. Displaying the ultimate form of resistance, Drusiana dies rather than be seduced. Hrotsvitha shows here the female power to petition and the eternal and perfect justice of the Christian God who unfailingly rewards the faithful.[45] In a scene deliberately reminiscent of the Easter story, Drusiana is resurrected from the tomb.

In *Resuscitatio Drusianae*, Hrotsvitha makes another attempt to situate concupiscence in men rather than in women by staging a scene of attempted necrophilia. Mad with grief, Calimachus bribes Fortunatus to open Drusiana's tomb so that he can violate her corpse.

FORTUNATUS: Ecce corpus: nec facies cadaverosa, nec membra sunt tabida. Abutere, ut libet.

CALIMACHUS: O Drusiana, Drusiana, quo affectu cordis te colui, que sinceritate dilectionis te visceratenus amplexatus fui, et tu semper abiecisti, meis votis contradixisti! Nunc in mea situm est potestate, quantislibet iniuriis te velim lacessere.

(Homeyer, 7:1)

FORTUNATUS: There's the body—she looks asleep. Her face is not that of a corpse, nor are her limbs corrupt—use her as you will.

CALIMACHUS: Oh Drusiana, Drusiana, how I worshipped you! What tight bonds of love entwined me, deep in my inmost heart! Yet you always ran from me. You always opposed my desires—Now it lies within my power to force you, to bruise you and injure you as much as I want.[46]

(Bonfante, 63)

Hrotsvitha interrupts this sensational rape at the last moment by causing a serpent to appear; Calimachus dies. In a subsequent scene, the resurrected Calimachus admits he sought to violate the corpse of the chaste Drusiana:

CALIMACHUS: Negare nequeo, quin patrandi causa facinoris accesserim, quia infelici languore tabescebam nec inliciti aestum amoris compescere poteram.

IOHANNES: Quae dementia, quae insania te decepit, ut castis praesumeres fragmentis alicuius iniuriam conferre dehonestatis?

(Homeyer, 9:11)

CALIMACHUS: I cannot deny that I came here to carry out a detestable crime, because a dread disease had gripped my very entrails and I could not contain the lawless storm of my passion.

ST. JOHN: What madness was it, what insanity possessed thee such, that thou couldst conceive of defiling the chaste body of this dead woman?

(Bonfante, 68)

By staging a rape scene in which the female character is lifeless, Hrotsvitha refutes the axiomatic notion that it is women who tempt men and provoke male lust. Once again, the author separates feminine attractiveness from male concupiscence and finds a narrative plot that makes the male character responsible for his own sexual behavior. Most important, rather than naturalize the passivity of women in the face of male desire, she stages it as horrifying and perverse.[47]

The brothel topos receives a singular twist in the "Passio Sanctarum

Virginum Agapis, Chioniae, et Hirenae" (erroneously referred to by critics as "Dulcitius"). It is drawn from the Roman *vita* of Saint Anastasia. Hrotsvitha boldly ignores the story of the saint to focus on her three servants, Agape, Chionia, and Irena. The beautiful young virgins hold fast to their Christian vows and refuse to make advantageous marriages with prominent Romans. Dulcitius, the randy governor, imprisons them: he plans to take advantage of their captivity to "enjoy their embraces." But the resistance of the three women is so steadfast that Dulcitius is confounded despite his power and authority.

Of Hrotsvitha's six plays, this one is most openly built around the threat of rape. As Sue-Ellen Case writes, "The stage setting reveals the passive position of the women as prisoners and sets up the alliance between desire and privilege in the role of the Governor."[48]

DULCITIUS: Ponite illas in custodiam in interiorem officinae aedem, in cuius proaulio ministrorum servantur vasa.
MILITES: Ut quid eo loci?
DULCITIUS: Quo a me saepiuscule possint visitari.

(Homeyer, 2:3)

DULCITIUS: I know. Lock them up in the pantry—there beside the kitchen, where the cooking utensils are kept.
SOLDIER: Why in there, sir?
DULCITIUS: So I can visit them alone as often as I want.

(Bonfante, 43)

There are distinct erotic and voyeuristic possibilities in a scene in which three virgins—*venustae* and *egregiae*—are locked together in one room. But Hrotsvitha exploits this rape scene for its comic potential. Dulcitius perpetrates the ravishment, but in the midst of hilarity that occurs at his own expense: he mistakes the greasy pots and pans for the virgins and feverishly rubs himself against the kitchenware. It is the powerful Roman who becomes a dazed "rape" victim in torn clothes covered with grimy soot.

In this famous scene, Hrotsvitha does more than actualize the medieval principle of *ludicra seriis miscere*.[49] She effects another key ideological reversal. It is the female characters who watch the "rape" of the pots and pans. The voyeuristic tendencies of the *vita* are deliberately parodied and redirected as the three virgins, the inscribed audience, observe the violation scene, holding their sides with laughter.[50] In this staging the female characters dominate the rapist.[51]

HIRENA: Ecce, iste stultus, mente alienatus, aestimat se nostris uti amplexibus.
AGAPES: Quid facit?
HIRENA: Nunc ollas molli fovet gremio, nunc sartagines et caccabos amplectitur, mitia libans oscula.
CHIONIA: Ridiculum.

(Homeyer, 4:2–3)

IRENA: Look at him, the fool. He's completely out of his mind! He thinks he is embracing us!
AGAPE: What is he doing now?
IRENA: Now he is fondling the pots and hugging the frying pans to his eager breast, giving them all long, sweet kisses!
CHIONIA: It's the funniest thing I have ever seen!

(Bonfante, 44)

The pleasure of voyeuristic eroticism is converted into the pleasure of laughter.

Hrotsvitha rejects the cultural axiom that women, including saintly virgins, are the cause of sexual transgression in men. As Dulcitius lasciviously presses his body against the pots and pans until he reaches satisfaction, he is in an erotic trance that has nothing to do with the virgins. God has placed him under the spell of his own erotic drives:

AGAPES: Decet, ut talis appareat corpore, qualis a diabolo possidetur in mente.

(Homeyer, 4:3)

AGAPE: It's only fitting that his body should be as black as his soul. It's clear he's possessed by the Devil, who has deranged his mind.

(Bonfante, 45)

The pots and pans are developed into an ingeniously domestic metaphor of the objectification of women.

In her radical rewriting of the life of Saint Anastasia, Hrotsvitha situates the demon of sexuality not in Eve, the female, but in the non-Christian:

MILITES: Quis hic egreditur? Daemoniacus. Vel magis ipse diabolus. Fugiamus!

(Homeyer, 5:1)

SOLDIER II: It must be someone possessed by a demon . . .
SOLDIER III: No, no, can't you see? It's the Devil himself!

(Bonfante, 45)

Hrotsvitha maintains and supports the traditional religious dogma and the didactic purposes of the *vita* in so far as she preaches that virginity and chastity are the greatest good a woman can achieve in her lifetime. What she refuses to preach, and even opposes, is the traditional Christian message about female weakness and sinfulness. In other *vitae*, the female saint, virginal though she may be, is still so "sexy" that she leads man to sin, in thought if not in deed.[52] In this way hagiographers maintain the oppressive contradiction in patristic theology: as long as a woman has a woman's body she cannot escape her sinful state. Hrotsvitha works to undo the double bind of the female *vita*, in which the virgin, however pure, is so physically attractive that it is she who causes lust to grow in the heart of man.

Hrotsvitha devises plots that display female strength, purity, and courage. She uses her stories to disassociate female characters from the patristic opprobrium of sexual transgression. In her sexual narratives the male characters are not the victims of female charms but are responsible for their own sexual behavior.

Hrotsvitha writes at the close of an era, in "the Dark Ages." Readers might expect that in such barbaric times the literary depictions of sexual violence would be a simple reflection of the brutality of that world, or an expression of society's fear faced with the historical reality of rape, a reality that could not have been much different from the situation in the preceding century, described here by Georges Duby:

> The few ninth-century texts that survive are full of cases of abduction (*rapt*). Widows, nuns, wives, daughters, whether betrothed or not, all appear as so many quarries pursued by packs of young men. . . . Lastly, there was what seems to have been the determining factor of social ritual. For was not abduction a sort of young men's game, as Jacques Rossiaud's studies show collective rape to have been in the towns of pre-Renaissance France? (Duby 1983, 38–39)

Hrotsvitha's uses of sexual violence are creative, strategic, thoughtful, funny, and even optimistic. They do not conjure up images of cowering, helpless victims. Her sexual plots are clearly in service of her celebration of women.

How does another tenth-century author, believed to be male, treat rape in a female *vita*? The tenth-century Latin *Passio Sancte Margarite* was a popular version of the life of Margaret of Antioch, found in many medieval manuscripts throughout Europe.[53] Saint Margaret was a virgin martyr believed to have died in fourth-century Antioch. Her legend probably originated in Greek in the seventh or eighth century; it came to enjoy enormous popularity in the Middle Ages. Hrotsvitha did not choose to tell her story.

Margaret was a consecrated virgin living in the city of Antioch. Olibrius, the heathen prefect, saw her tending her sheep one day as he passed: "et statim concupivit eam" (and immediately desired her greatly [54]). He declares that he will take her as either his wife or his concubine, because of her great beauty. The scene can be construed as a literary depiction of *raptus*: Olibrius sends his soldiers to seize Margaret. When the prefect learns of her devotion to Christ and hears her steadfast refusal to renounce her faith, he grows angry and decides to have her tortured.

The Latin author elects to follow one hagiographic trajectory Hrotsvitha eschews in her female saints' lives: the grisly description of the martyr's torture. Olibrius repeatedly asks Margaret to renounce Christianity. Each time she refuses, he orders the torture to continue:

> Nam impius prefectus cum clamide operiebat faciem suam, quia pro sanguinis effusione non poterat eam aspicere. (Francis, 180–82)
>
> Indeed, the heathen prefect, crying out, hides his face, because he cannot look at her profuse bleeding.

After continued beatings, Margaret is sent to prison. There she undergoes another kind of test: a hideous, fire-breathing dragon appears from the corner of her cell. Frightened, Margaret kneels and prays. The dragon then swallows her: "suspirans deglutivit eam in ventrem suum" (sighing, he swallows her into his stomach [244–45]). But Margaret makes the sign of the cross and the dragon dies, splitting in two:

> Et beata Margarita exivit de ore draconis, dolorem nullum habebat in se. (Francis, 247–49)

> And Saint Margaret comes out of the dragon's mouth, without having suffered any pain.

This startling scene is explained to the audience in the following lines, when a second devil, "sedentem ut hominen" (resembling a seated man [250]) confesses that the "devouring" was an attempted rape:

> Ego quidem misi fratrem meum Rufonem in similitudinem draconis, ut obsorberet et tolleret memoriam tuam de terra, et obrueret virginitatem tuam. (Francis, 277–80)

> I even sent my brother, Rufon, in the form of a dragon, to swallow you and destroy all memory of you on earth, and tarnish your virginity.

The saint then vanquishes this manlike devil, Beelzebub. Margaret ultimately dies a martyr's death:

> Et angeli tollentes animam eius cum virtutibus ascendere super nubes clamantes et dicentes hec: . . . Sanctus, sanctus, sanctus Dominus Deus sabaoth, pleni sunt celi et terra gloria tua, osanna in excelsis. (Francis, 496–500)

> And angels took her soul to carry her into the heavens, lamenting and saying: . . . Holy, holy, holy, Lord God of the Sabbath, heaven and earth are full of thy glory. Hosanna in the highest.

In comparing this tenth-century *vita* of a virgin martyr to the treatments of female saints seen in Hrotsvitha's texts, we note that the discourse of sexual violence presents at least three signal differences. In the Margaret story, rape is portrayed as a symbolic experience: a swallowing. This painless ravishment is curiously removed from reality.[54] Equally significant: it is no longer the central male character of the heathen seducer who is responsible for the rape. Sexual violence has been dissociated from men and attributed to dragons and devils.[55] The male "concupiscence" suggested in the first lines (*concupivit eam*) is displaced from Olibrius and projected onto a fire-breathing dragon.

Hagiographic writing continues to flourish in the twelfth century, the period of courtly discourse. Though it is no longer fashionable to refer to the twelfth century as a "renaissance," the hegemonic view of the twelfth century as a time of civilization and refinement continues to receive tacit support in many quarters. Whether or not the century is a time of enlightenment for male society, it is the nadir of female monasticism and also female sainthood.[56] The legend of Saint Margaret will undergo still other permutations in the twelfth century, a time known as a period of transformation in gender constructs.

One of the best-known Old French authors of the courtly period, Wace, translates and adapts the Latin life of Saint Margaret just examined.[57] Wace's Old French version of the virgin's *vita* is of particular interest because he is at the same time a leading innovator in the great new genre of the courtly period: Arthurian romance. How does a romance writer treat the hagiographic themes that we examined in the work of a tenth-century woman?

Wace tends to follow the Latin *vita* quite closely. Margaret is a young girl who renounces her noble birth to embrace Christianity. In an obvious example of *imitatio Christi* she humbly tends sheep. Noticing her great beauty, Olibrius decides to take possession of the "shepherdess." But at the very start of the narrative, Wace changes the Latin *concupere* to *aimer*, making a cautionary tale of heathen lust into a story of love at first sight:

Margerite vit, *si l'ama*.
Par ses chevaliers li manda
Que sa moillier de li feroit,
Se ele france feme estoit;
Et se ele ert altrui ancele,
Por ço qu'ele ert et gente et bele,
En sognantage la tendroit,
Del sien a grant plenté aroit.
quant cil la damoisele pristrent
Et li mostrerent et li distrent,
El conmença fort a crier
Et Jhesu Crist a apeler.

(Francis, 97–108 [emphasis added])

He saw Margaret; *he loved her*. Sending his knights, he ordered that he would make her his wife, if she were a free woman, and if she were the servant of another, because of her noble demeanor and beauty, he would take her in concubinage and she would have an abundance of his wealth.

When the men captured the damsel and explained her fate, she began to cry out loudly and call on Jesus Christ.

Wace's subtle transformation of the heathen villain is perceptible not only in those early lines, which introduce him as a man in love, but also in the scenes of torture. The crowds who look on, Wace's inscribed audience, plead with Margaret to yield, assuring her that Olibrius will kill her despite the pain it would cause him: "Mult se paine de ti ocire" (It would pain him greatly to kill you [206]). Thus Wace hints at a new and more complex image of the villain as a conflicted lover-torturer. Consequently, the moment at which the sight of Margaret's blood forces Olibrius to cast his gaze aside takes on a romantic denotation it did not have in the Latin version:

Olimbrius et autre gent
qui o lui erent a torment,
Quant il voient de sa char tendre
De totes pars le sanc espandre,
Lor ex et lor chieres covroient,
Car esgarder ne le pooient.

(Francis, 253–58)

When Olibrius and the other people with him at the scene of torture saw blood flow over every part of her tender flesh, they covered their eyes and their faces, for they could not bear to look.

The writer of romance here links love and torture. The relationship between desire and dominance which Hrotsvitha refused to stage becomes literal.[58]

Because Wace follows the Latin quite closely, it is important to notice the points at which he expands on his source. At the same time as Wace suggests that the heathen is torn by his love for Margaret, he amplifies the scenes of her torture.

Que l'antraille qui est ou cors
Per les plaiez pandoit defors.
Quant batue fui longuement
Et lo cors ot trestot sanglant,
Puis fui an la chartre menee.

(Francis, 273–77)

When her entrails were spilling out of her wounds, when she had been beaten at great length and her body was completely bloodied, she was taken to prison.

As in the Latin source, the climactic test of this saint comes when a hideous, fire-breathing dragon appears in her prison cell:

Li deables la goule ovri,
Tote a bien pres le transgloti,
Mais la crois qu'ele ot fait de Crist
Crut el dragon, crever le fist,
Del dragon Margerite issi
qui onques nul mal n'i senti.

(Francis, 333–38)

The devil opened his muzzle and would soon have swallowed her entirely but she made the sign of the cross of Christ and caused the dragon to die. Margaret came forth from the dragon without feeling any pain.

Both the anonymous tenth-century hagiographer and Wace present the legend of Margaret as a symbolic tale of Beauty and the Beast.[59] In the work of these two poets, sexual violence is projected onto a fire-breathing dragon. The experience of rape is stuporous and trancelike: a woman suffers no pain from sexual assault.

Mon frere t'envoié Rufon
Qui ert sanblable de dragon,
Le cors de toi asorbesist
Et ta virginité tolsist,
Mais tu l'as par la crois ocis.

(Francis, 367–71)

I sent my brother, Rufon, who resembles a dragon, to swallow your body and to deflower your virginity, but you killed him with the sign of the cross.

Wace has not only shifted the characterization of Olibrius. The female character of Margaret, too, has undergone a change: "his version places vernacular hagiography closer to romance."[60] The dynamic, soldierly heroines who confounded powerful men in Hrotsvitha's hagiographic *opera* have been transformed. Wace's choice to portray Margaret as the spouse of Christ, spurning all other lovers, allows him to bring out the romantic potential of the narrative material.[61]

It would be misleading to account for the different uses of rape as a narrative sequence in Hrotsvitha's hagiography, the *Passio Sancte Margarite*, and Wace's *Vie de Sainte Marguerite*, by any simple model of causality. Their variety is a function of many factors. The first factor considered is usually that of individual authorial choices and styles. One important factor that might explain transformations in the hagiographic representation of sexual violence is that of historical change in cultural attitudes. The tenth-century texts of Hrotsvitha and the anonymous hagiographer are conceived in a world dramatically different from the twelfth-century milieu of Wace. Yet other variants may be explained by changes in spirituality and forms of religious devotion. Furthermore, the genre of the *vita* evolves as literary styles and conventions change. The factor I have highlighted in contrasting the work of the tenth-century Hrotsvitha and the tenth-century *vita* of Saint Margaret is the difference between the agenda of a woman writer and the objectives of a male author. For a woman, there is a great deal at stake in the literary depiction of rape—painful or painless, avoidable or inevitable—and concomitant presentation of female characters—as complicitous or defiant, helpless or triumphant.

* * *

In the central hagiographic tradition, the representation of the female saint in a sexual plot acts to feminize weakness and sexual transgression and to legitimize sexual violence as a test of the saintly female. Hrotsvitha transforms that plot to subvert the hagiographic troping of rape. She depicts male violence against women as a way to represent female virtue, courage, and power. In the twelfth century, Wace characterizes Olibrius as a love-struck *raptor* and Margaret as an almost romantic heroine. The later poet's conflation of domination and love, torture and passion, can be placed in the historical context of the legal changes outlined in the Introduction. In twelfth-century canon law the reader perceives the blurring of distinctions between forced and voluntary sex. In both legal and literary texts, the violence of the male is construed as an expression of conflicted love, the stuff of which romance is made.

2. The Poetics of Rape Law: Chrétien de Troyes's Arthurian Romance

> Rape is not recommended but one will be allowed under specific conditions if the author feels it is necessary to make a point.[1]

Our close reading of female sexuality and male brutality in Wace's *Vie de Sainte Marguerite*, disclosed there gestures belonging to the power struggle behind "romantic love." Wace, we know, was also the first writer of vernacular Arthurian romance. The very name of Arthurian romance conjures up images of valor, courtliness, and gentility; we hardly associate courtly literature with sexual violence. Yet from the earliest stages of courtly romance, the character of Arthur is linked with the narration of rape. Wace recounts the liminal episode of Arthur's combat against the giant of Mont Saint-Michel.[2] Arthur learns that a giant abducted a young virgin, Helen, niece of the Duke of Hoel, and sequestered her at Mont Saint-Michel. There Helen dies while being raped by the giant:

La pucele volt porgesir,
Mes tandre fu, nel pot sofrir;
Trop fu ahugues, trop fu granz,
Trop laiz, trop gros et trop pesanz;
L'ame li fist del cors partir,
Nel pot Heloine sostenir.

(*Brut*, 2857–62)

[The giant] wants to have carnal knowledge of the virgin, but she is tender and her body cannot bear it. He is too tall and too large, too ugly, too enormous and too heavy. Her soul is driven from her body; Helen cannot hold up under his weight.

The act of avenging this rape is Arthur's first heroic exploit in France. Arthur goes immediately to fight the giant, whom he kills in singlehanded combat:

je irai, dist Artus, avant,
Si me combatrai au jaiant.

(*Brut*, 2919–20)

"I will go forth," said Arthur, "and fight the giant myself."

Arthur's name, his rule, and his knights, will henceforth be associated with the motif of the *pucelle esforciée*.

The significance of rape to romance is not often discussed.[3] Medieval romance structure depends on episodic units which recur systematically but are joined in ever-changing ways, units such as the knight's dubbing, the battle, the journey through the forest, the crossing of water, the hospitality of an unknown *châtelain*, the feast day, and many other set pieces. What has rarely been said is that rape (either attempted rape or the defeat of a rapist) constitutes one of the episodic units used in the construction of a romance. Sexual violence is built into the very premise of Arthurian romance. It is a genre that by its definition must *create* the threat of rape.

If Wace is considered the first author of Arthurian narrative in medieval France, Chrétien de Troyes is held to be its master.[4] In his romance, Chrétien deftly conflates the themes of love and force so that male domination and female submission are coded as emotionally satisfying and aesthetically pleasing. In this unprecedented conflation, sexual violations, now romanticized, can scarcely be recognized as violent acts.

A fecund paradox informs Chrétien's use of sexual violence: rape is both proscribed and moralized, banished and aestheticized, so that it can be contemplated again and again. In romance, "ravishment" seems as natural as heterosexual love. Chrétien blurs the lines between seduction and aggression. Violation can no longer be distinguished clearly. Rape becomes one of the poet's tropes. Chrétien's troping of rape leads the audience to ignore the physicality of rape and its literal consequences so that the audience will focus instead on the ideology of chivalry. Chrétien interrupts the immediacy of violence to open a locus of moral reflection on chivalric codes. This chapter seeks out a "violent" reading precisely at the point where romance appears to shift in the opposite direction. Since Chrétien tends to veer away from the literal violence of rape and embed it in romantic situations, the praxis of this chapter is to uncover the violence concealed in romantic love.

Chrétien's romances teach that rape is wrong, the act of base men. But they simultaneously aestheticize rape as a formulaic challenge: potential assaults are set up at regular narrative intervals so that knights can prove their mettle. The audience is led to ignore the literal consequences of violence against women.

The medieval poet represents sexual violence in two types of paradigmatic scenes. The motif of the *pucelle esforciée* can be used to depict simple rape, or forced coitus. *Raptus mulieris* or "ravishment" depicts the abduction of a woman; the sexual threat to her can either be made explicit or remain implicit. Both narrative types can be endowed with a range of meanings. In Chrétien's romances, rape and ravishment function in five principal ways. First, as a chivalric test, they constitute a trope for military prowess. The test can take the form of a combat with a would-be attacker, the punishment of a rapist, or the rescue of a victim: all count as testimonies to a knight's mettle. Second, as an ethical test, rape offers a moral challenge. Because Arthur's knights are charged with the protection of helpless damsels, a knight may face a difficult choice between two conflicting duties, but he must always give priority to his ethical responsibility to ladies in distress. Third, as a social marker, rape distinguishes the nobility from other classes: most of Chrétien's would-be rapists are of inferior social origin, while all female victims of assault or abduction are of noble birth. Fourth, the motif of *raptus* frequently encodes a patriotic message: a noblewoman is abducted as a test of one kingdom's strength. Through this sentimentalized adventure of kidnapping, the audience learns a lesson in political hegemony. Finally, rape or *raptus* can be troped as an aesthetic marker of and testimony to physical beauty. In a violent twist, the heroine is subjected to the threat of assault in poetic demonstration of her attractiveness.[5]

Each of the functions just evoked can of course be used with varying effects: sometimes Chrétien eroticizes these scenes, sometimes he renders them comical, and at others he uses them to didactic ends. The titillating potential of the rape scene in hagiography was discussed in Chapter 1. The meaning and form of Arthurian romance work, whether consciously or unconsciously, to justify the male listener's pleasure in the recitation of various feats, including acts of violence against the female body. In the ravishments of romance, the preliminary aesthetic pleasure allows the medieval audience a less acceptable source of pleasure: imagining a forbidden erotic scene.[6]

Chrétien's pattern in presenting rape respects the rules of literary *bienséance*.[7] The poet presents sexual violence in ways that make it complicated to interpret, both giving the audience a pleasurable cerebral challenge and avoiding any break with romance decorum. Well-known as an ironist, Chrétien sometimes uses humorous twists or ironic reversals, as in scenes of mock rape, inadvertent violation, or imaginary rape, to handle this controversial subject.[8]

Chrétien situates any actual rapes in the past tense. Once the hero arrives on the scene, rape is maintained as a constant threat but is not actually represented, to avoid creating a reaction of shock. Chrétien does not show the blood or tears of a victim. Characteristically, the description of an assault is carefully circumscribed and framed by moral considerations. Rather than linger to inspire in the audience pity for the victim of an attack, and rather than allow the audience to take too great a pleasure in the representation of an erotic scene, Chrétien consistently displaces the attention of the audience toward the male character in the sequence.[9] He thus creates sympathy for the knight and justifies the audience's interest in rape by leading it toward an intellectual analysis of moral dilemma.[10]

An overview of Chrétien's five romances reveals that he knits together ambiguities so heavily knotted they cannot always be unraveled.[11] The following examples are grouped not to give a synoptic view of each romance, but rather to illustrate the tangled complexity of the five functions and their varying effects.[12]

Rape functions as a romance set piece to display chivalric prowess, as we see clearly in *Yvain ou le Chevalier au lion*, which contains a significant reworking of Wace's prototype, Arthur's combat with the giant at Mont Saint-Michel, together with a popular hagiographic topos: the threat of prostitution. Chrétien stages the potential violation in the episode in which the giant Harpin threatens to abduct Gauvain's beautiful young cousin. The girl's father pleads with Yvain to do battle with Harpin:

ou se ge ne li voel livrer
ma fille; et quant il l'avra
as plus vix garçons qu'il savra

en sa meison, et as plus orz,
la livrera por lor deporz,

(*Yvain*, 3864–68)

And if not, I must hand my daughter over to him. I know that as soon as he has her he will turn her over to the vilest servants and the most loathsome young men in his house, so that they can take their pleasure with her.

Chrétien avoids the actual representation of this or any rape. But in this passage we recognize the poet's fascination with the language of sexual violence, whether actual or imagined. As if he feels a curious desire to linger—or to cause his listeners to linger—over the contemplation of a collective rape, Chrétien repeats the brutal terms of the threat later in the very same scene:

s'areste li jaianz, et crie . . .
. . . a sa garçonaille la livera a jaelise,
car il ne l'ainme tant ne prise
qu'an li se daingnast avillier;
de garçons avra un millier
avoec lui sovant et menu,
qui seront poeilleus et nu
si con ribaut et torche pot,
que tuit i metront lor escot.

(*Yvain*, 4107–18)

The giant stops and calls out [that] he will give [the daughter] to be taken by his lowest servants, because he himself does not love her enough to be besmirched by possessing her. She will have well over a thousand of these ruffians, over and again, and they will be lousy and naked like slime and scum, and every one will have his money's worth.

The topos of the chivalric test overlaps with the romance tendency to erotic titillation. Although the poet avoids staging the actual assault, he twice evokes the spectre of a multiple rape, as if to give his audience permission to return to the contemplation of a pleasurable but forbidden sight.

In *Yvain*, Chrétien tropes rape as a competition, a contest between the villain and the hero. The threat of rape, repeated and heightened as it is, underlines the insult to the virgin's father and glorifies the hero's bravery. The author is examining sexual violence from various male viewpoints: what dilemmas does rape create for men? In the end, Yvain defeats the giant and the daughter remains unharmed.

Like other romance authors, Chrétien also uses the threat of rape to test the hero's character and sense of duty.[13] Let us recall in *Le Chevalier au Lion*, the incident of the giant, Harpin, who has laid claim to the beautiful virgin daughter of Gauvain's relatives. The motif of the *pucelle esforciée* is used to test Yvain's moral responsibility as well as his knightly skills. The damsel's father begs Yvain to save his daughter from rape and prostitution, but Yvain makes excuses: any other knight from King Arthur's court could undertake the deed (3897–3901). The father replies that all the other knights are gone. Yvain hesitates still; he has to reach another damsel, Lunete, by noon the next day:

. . . "Biax dolz sire chiers,
je m'an metroie volentiers
en l'aventure et el peril,
se li jaianz et vostre fil
venoient demain a tel ore
que n'i face trop grant demore,
que je serai aillors que ci
demain a ore de midi"

(*Yvain*, 3937–44)

"Good noble sire," says he, "I would gladly undertake this dangerous adventure if the giant and your sons would come early enough tomorrow so that I would not have to wait too long, because I have to be elsewhere tomorrow at noon."

Chrétien continues to stretch the episode as far as he can, building tension and suspense as the audience waits to see whether the rape will occur. The next day Yvain waits until *prime*, six in the morning, then bids farewell to the terrified *pucelle*. Her frantic pleas cause him to pause once again in another lengthy deliberation:

D'angoisse a un sopir gité
que por le rëaume de Carse

ne voldroit que cele fust arse
que il avoit aseüree;

(*Yvain*, 4070–73)

He sighs with anguish. For all the kingdom of Tarsis he does not want to see [Lunete], whom he promised to protect, burned at the stake.

et d'autre part, autre destrece
le retient, la granz gentillece
mon seignor Gauvain son ami,
que par po ne li part par mi
li cuers, quant demorer ne puet.
Ne por quant encore ne se muet,
einçois demore et si atant
tant que li jaianz vient batant

(*Yvain*, 4077–84)

On the other hand, another's distress makes him stay. He thinks of the great kindness of milord Gauvain, his friend, and his heart nearly breaks at the thought of being unable to stay. In spite of everything, he does not move but remains and waits so long that the giant arrives, running rapidly.

Rape is presented as a thorny point in the question of male honor. More powerful than the sight of the maiden's anguish, the thought of his friendship with Gauvain, another knight of Arthur's court, gives Yvain pause.

Having created an atmosphere of high suspense and grave danger in which to test his hero's sense of chivalric duty, Chrétien now tests the prowess of Yvain who, with the help of his lion, defeats the giant and saves the damsel. Chrétien has devoted 540 of a total 6,808 verses to this actualization of the *pucelle esforciée* motif as test of the hero. He has economically combined the ideological function of romance, as a glorification of chivalry, with one of its didactic functions, to teach men to protect women, at the same time as he has managed to exploit its erotic potential.

Similarly, in the Lovesome Damsel sequence of the *Chevalier de la Charrette*, Lancelot is forced to choose between his commitment to the pursuit of the queen and the rescue of a lady who is being attacked before his eyes. Lancelot breaks into a lengthy interior monologue: should he or should he not risk taking on all the knights and servants present to prevent the rape?

Lancelot's pause is typical of his reaction to a number of different situations in the text:

Li chevaliers a l'uis s'areste
et dit: "Dex, que porrai ge feire?
Meüz sui por si grant afeire
con por la reïne Guenievre.
Ne doi mie avoir cuer de lievre
quant por li sui an ceste queste:
se Malvestiez son cuer me preste
et je son comandemant faz,
n'ateindrai pas ce que je chaz;
honiz sui se je ci remaing.
Molt me vient or a grant desdaing,
quant j'ai parlé del remenoir;
. . .
Ne ja Dex n'ait de moi merci,
se jel di mie por orguel,
et s'asez mialz morir ne vuel
a enor que a honte vivre."

(*Lancelot*, 1096–1107, 1112–15)

"God, what could I do? I have set out with the grand goal of pursuing queen Guenevere. I must not have the heart of a hare, since it is for her sake that I have undertaken this quest. If cowardliness controls and commands me, I will never gain that for which I strive. If I stand here I will ruin my reputation. . . . May God not have mercy on me—I do not say this out of pride—if I prefer to die honorably rather than to live shamefully."

The hero's pause is, among other things, an element in Chrétien's troping of rape. Lancelot's monologue interrupts the sense of danger and the immediacy of the violence in the scene. At the very moment in which the audience might see rape in all its horror, the interest is shifted to a moral meditation on chivalric honor. The pause also prolongs the contemplation of a female nudity: frozen in time, the naked damsel is held down on the bed as this monologue unfolds. Chrétien manages the potentially exciting but also unbearable representation of rape by transforming it into a knightly test. It is certainly not surprising that the twelfth-century poet examines rape from a male viewpoint in *Yvain* and *Lancelot*. This preoccupation with male honor effectively indicates that the texts are destined for a male or mixed audience in a male culture. It is worth noting however that the meditations on male honor simultaneously enable the audience to sustain its interest in the rape scenes.

The *Conte du Graal* offers a comic variation on a scene of sexual attack used to test the hero's character. What is new in the *Graal*, although common in other medieval genres, is Chrétien's use of humor to veil violence. The ignorant Perceval discovers a beautiful damsel alone in her tent in a meadow. In fact, however, Perceval is not so ignorant; his mother has already instructed him in the law of Arthur's land:

De pucele a mout qui la beise;
s'ele le beisier vos consant
le soreplus vos an desfant,
se lessier le volez por moi.

(*Graal*, 544–47)

He who receives a kiss from a young girl receives a great deal. If she grants you a kiss, and forbids you to take the rest, please leave her alone for my sake.

Despite the young lady's tears and pleas, Perceval pins her to the ground and, though she struggles and resists, he steals twenty kisses and a ring.

dist: "Pucele, je vos salu
si com ma mere le m'aprist. . . .
—Einz vos beiserai, par mon chief,
fet li vaslez, cui qu'il soit grief,
que ma mere le m'anseigna." . . .
Li vaslez avoit les braz forz,
si l'anbrace mout nicemant,
car il nel sot fere autremant,
mist la soz lui tote estandue,
et cele s'est mout desfandue
et deganchi quan qu'ele pot;
mes desfansse mestier n'i ot,
que li vaslez an un randon

la beisa, volsist ele ou non,
.XX. foiz, si com li contes dit

(*Graal*, 680–81, 691–93, 698–707)

[Perceval] said: "Maiden, I greet you, just like my mother taught me. . . . Before I leave I will take a kiss, by heavens," said the young boy, "whether anyone likes it or not, just like my mother taught me." . . . The young boy's arms were very powerful, and he kissed her very awkwardly, for he did not know any better, he pulled her beneath him and despite the fact that she fought back and tried as hard as she could to get away, her resistance was useless, for the boy kissed her without interruption, like it or not, twenty times, as the story tells.

Rarely has sexual assault looked more endearing.[14] The hero is excited by the damsel's sexuality, and he does not know his own strength. Since he takes nothing but kisses, it is unclear whether he transgressed his mother's law. And since Chrétien claims he takes this from *li contes*, he is not responsible for it.

Does Chrétien use sexual violence simply to inculcate chivalric ideology in the male audience, concomitantly aestheticizing this literary glance at female nudity? *Perceval* offers a good example of the moral intricacies in Chrétien's troping of rape. The story of the Demoiselle de la tente does not end with this scene. Perceval will meet her again, only to learn that his assault provoked the jealous rage of the damsel's knight, Orgueilleux de la Lande. The maiden will lead a wretched life of abject suffering because of the way Perceval forced himself upon her. Thus, after the comedy, Chrétien fleetingly suggests that the episode was not harmless for the female character. D.D.R. Owen has argued that Chrétien here shows compassion for women and what they suffer because of male violence, displaying: "a renewed interest, in his late writings, in the mental damage that sexual aggression can inflict, and not only on its immediate victims."[15] But two considerations prevent a simple reading of the story of the Tent Damsel as proof of Chrétien's sympathy for victims of sexual violence.

First, Chrétien shifts the responsibility away from the young boy and leads his audience to forgive the *niais* for several reasons: it was an innocent encounter, nothing more than a few kisses; Perceval simply misunderstood his mother's advice about women; Perceval later grieves for the pain the damsel suffers because of his ignorant behavior.[16] Chrétien will go on to focus on the maiden's knight as the true villain in the episode.

The second element that argues against interpreting this romance as one that should "earn him a place of honour among the great French *moralistes*"[17] is that Chrétien here uses one of his preferred strategies for shifting attention away from a victimized female character. The poet opens a locus for an ideological meditation: in this case he inserts a violent diatribe against female nature. The damsel's knight accuses the maiden brutally:

Fame qui sa boche abandone
le soreplus de legier done,
. . .
que fame vialt vaintre par tot
fors a cele meslee sole
qu'ele tient home par la gole
et esgratine et mort et tue,
si voldroit ele estre vaincue;
si se desfant et si li tarde.
Tent est de l'otroier coarde,
si vialt que a force li face,

(*Graal*, 3845–46, 3850–57)

A woman who offers her mouth will give the rest easily . . . for a woman wants to win in everything except in this battle alone. She takes the man by his face and scratches and bites and stuns him with her blows, yet she wants to be vanquished; she defends herself, but she cannot wait. She is too cowardly to grant it freely, and wants him to take her by force.

By placing this in the mouth of the unsympathetic Orgueilleux de la Lande, the author informs its misogyny with a double function. One of its effects is to move the audience to pity, for the audience knows the Orgueilleux is mistaken. But here, as elsewhere in *Le Conte du Graal*, Chrétien embeds misogynist discourse on the perfidy of women in such equivocal folds that the diatribes become misconstruable. Its ultimate effect is to shift attention toward the brutality of the villain and *away* from the violence of Perceval's behavior in the tent.

It is clear that Chrétien does not hesitate to raise thorny questions about male honor and power, as Owen suggests. In the final analysis, however, the poet reflects not as much on female victims as he does on the heavy moral responsibility heroes bear for their actions.

While Chrétien uses the motif of the *pucelle esforciée* frequently, he also relies on the representation of *raptus mulieris* to bring out additional elements in the representation of the hero. By representing *raptus* as a political tactic or military strategy, Chrétien shifts the reader's attention away from the female body and places it on the question of the hero's political role in a power struggle and his development as a leader. Two of Chrétien's romances are built on the narrative structure of *raptus*. *Le Chevalier de la Charrette*, the romance in which Chrétien takes up the question of courtly love more fully than in any other, turns entirely on the *raptus* of the queen. This violent ravishment opens the romance and provides a recurring theme throughout.

The latent sexual implications of *raptus* pierce through the veil of romance when Bademagu refuses to let his son Meleagant, Guenevere's abductor, touch the queen:

La reïne a boene prison
que nus de char a li n'adoise,
neïs mes filz cui molt an poise,
qui avoec lui ça l'amena:
onques hom si ne forssena
com il s'an forssene et anrage.

(*Lancelot*, 3362–67)

The queen is safely in prison. Whoever covets her body is forbidden to touch her, even my son, who brought her here, and who resents it bitterly. Never was any man as enraged as he, who is beside himself with anger.

There we glimpse the sexual violence at the heart of *raptus*.

Raptus is also one of the central motifs in *Cligès*: Fenice is "stolen" no fewer than four times. Chrétien uses the kidnapping of the heroine as a marker of the hero's evolution as a powerful leader. Initially, Alis asks the father of Fenice for her hand in marriage. The father regrets that she is already promised to the Duke of Saxony: nothing less than *raptus* could change the situation (2634–40). Alis immediately prepares to do battle in order to take Fenice from her betrothed. Cligès leads the fight against the army of the Duke of Saxony, gaining a heroic reputation and winning Fenice for his uncle Alis. Then the Duke of Saxony, angry that his bride has been abducted, prepares a military attack and succeeds in kidnapping Fenice:

De ceste chose* est liez li dus; *raptus
Cent chevaliers senez, et plus,
Avuec l'espie a envoiez;
Et cil les a si avoiez
Que la pucele en mainnent prise.

(*Cligès*, 3597–3601)

The duke is delighted to learn of this [abduction]. He sends more than one hundred seasoned knights with his spy. The spy leads them so directly that they take the maiden prisoner.

Next it is Cligès's turn to abduct Fenice, and love gives him superhuman strength to defeat the Saxon army and deliver the heroine (3654–3770). When Cligès finally learns that it is he whom Fenice loves, he proposes to *abduct* her yet again, like Paris carried off Helen:

Dame, fet il, si croi et cuit
que mialz feire ne porrïens
Que s'an Bretaingne en alïens;
La ai pansé que vos an maingne.
Or gardez qu'an vos ne remaingne!
C'onques ne fu a si grant joie
Eleinne reçeüe a Troie,
Quant Paris li ot amenee,

(*Cligès*, 5234–41)

My lady, says he, I think and believe that we could not do better than to leave for Brittany. That is where I thought I would take you away. Do not prevent me from taking you, for never was there such great joy since Helen was welcomed at Troy when Paris carried her there.

Chrétien's hero cites the classic literary *raptus*, comparing Fenice to Helen of Troy, and himself to Paris.[18]

But Fenice does not want to be carried off. She prefers a false death, after which Cligès must come and steal her from the tomb (6124–29). When Alis learns that Cligès has taken his wife, the emperor is enraged:

Et dit, se il n'en prant vengence
De la honte et de la viltence
Que li traïtes li a faite,
Qui sa fame li a fortraite,
Ja mes n'avra joie en sa vie.

(*Cligès*, 6519–23)

He says that if he does not avenge the shame and affront done to him by the traitor who abducted his wife, never again in his life will he know joy.

In *Cligès* Chrétien leads us through a tangled series of "rapts": abductions, counterabductions, false abductions. As objects of exchange, women test the strength of dukes, kings, and emperors. Chrétien spins a tale in which the heroine is torn from leader to leader, marriage to marriage, thus providing the young and untried Cligès an opportunity to win his "lettres de noblesse." The violence of the exchanges is rendered misty by the depiction of Fenice's passionate love for Cligès, her final *raptor*.[19]

The romance of *Cligès* braids a chain of heroism, *raptus*, and female beauty. It demonstrates that ravishment and irresistible female beauty are inextricably entwined. The initial *raptus* of Fenice was, from a narrative viewpoint, prepared and justified by a lengthy description of Fenice's incomparable beauty (2675–2729). Fenice's beauty also causes the young Cligès to fall in love and spurs him to prove his chivalric mettle by abducting the heroine. The reference to Helen of Troy crystallizes the romantic mystification and justification of violent abduction as a moving tribute to a woman's beauty: *raptus* is the ultimate compliment. But like the story of Helen, the romance of *Cligès* is also an expression of political hegemony, presented as an aesthetic and sentimental adventure.

Is ravishment consistently linked to the beauty topos in Chrétien's corpus? The poet has already exploited the erotic potential of rape by linking it to violent abduction in his first romance, *Erec et Enide*.[20] *Raptus* plays a key role in the central *avanture* of the text. To punish Enide for speaking her mind, Erec orders her to dress in her most magnificent finery and sets off to teach her submission and silence. In truth, he will use his wife as a kind of lightening rod: an invitation to crime. Predictably, Enide's beauty draws bandits, robbers, and the unwanted attentions of two counts, who make "romantic overtures" to Enide.

Count Galoin, the "comte vaniteux," hears of Enide's beauty even before he first meets her:

"Et avoec lui mainne une dame
tant bele c'onques nule fame
la mitié de sa biauté ot."

(*Erec et Enide*, 3237–39)

"And he leads with him a lady so beautiful that never did any woman have half of the beauty she possesses."

Upon meeting the heroine, Galoin is overpowered by his attraction to her:

Molt parolent de mainte chose,
mes li cuens onques ne repose
de regarder de l'autre part:
de la dame s'est pris esgart;
por la biauté qu'an li estoit
tot son pansé an li avoit;
tant l'esgarda com il plus pot,
tant la covi et tant li plot
que sa biautez d'amors l'esprist.

(*Erec et Enide*, 3275–83)

They speak of many things, but the count never ceases to look in the other direction, so taken is he with the sight of her. Because of the beauty in her, all his thoughts are with her. He stares at her as hard as he can; he covets her. She pleases him so much that he falls in love with her beauty.

Chrétien repeats the word *biauté* twice in this passage. Inflamed by love, the count threatens Enide in terms that are scarcely veiled:

"Ne me deigneriez amer,
dame? fet il: trop estes fiere.
Par losange ne par proiere,
ne fereiz rien que je vuelle? . . .
Certes, je vos met an covant
que, se vos mon talant ne feites,
ja i avra espees treites."

(*Erec et Enide*, 3338–41, 3346–48)

"You will not deign to love me, lady?" says he. "You are too proud. Neither by praise nor by pleading, can I get what I want? . . . I promise you that if you do not do what I want, swords will be drawn."

This attempted rape bears a double or overlapping function. Chrétien "harnesses the repeated threats or acts of sexual aggression to the motif of physical beauty, with each element reinforcing the other."[21] The attacks on Enide serve as a test of Erec's chivalric strength, enabling him to vindicate himself from the charge of uxoriousness made against him earlier in the story.

In the story of the Count of Limors, the count finds Enide weeping over the body of Erec, proclaims her a widow, and orders her to marry him immediately. When Enide refuses, the count moves from seduction to violence:

Et li cuens la fiert an la face;
ele s'escrie, et li baron
an blasment le conte an viron: . . .
"—Teizies vos an tuit! fet li cuens;
la dame est moie et je sui suens,
si ferai de li mon pleisir."

(*Erec et Enide*, 4788–90, 4799–4801)

So the count slapped her in the face. She cried out, and the barons standing near the count rebuke him. . . . "Shut up, all of you," says the count. "The lady is mine and I am hers, so I will have my pleasure of her."

Erec regains consciousness just in time to save Enide from the count's pleasure. In a burst of heroic strength, the hero splits the count's skull and rescues Enide. In this and other scenes of assault in *Erec et Enide*, Chrétien uses the recurring threat of attack as testimony both to Enide's "ravishing" beauty and to Erec's knightly prowess. Rape proves itself to be a very economical narrative device in *Erec et Enide*.

One of Chrétien's common patterns is established as early as his oldest romance: sexual violence is frequently staged but rarely successful, both out of respect for literary decorum and also to teach the male audience that patriarchy is benevolent and sexual violence is proscribed.[22] Here we touch on one of the central paradoxes of Arthurian romance. In a curious tension, the genre both forbids rape and sentimentalizes it as a weak man's response to overpowering female attractiveness.

The profound contradiction at the heart of *Erec et Enide* is never addressed: why does Erec make his wife look as "ravishing" as possible in order to expose her to assault? Chrétien's Arthurian romances use the threat of sexual violence both didactically, to teach the audience that male violence against women is wrong, and sexually, to offer the audience an opportunity to indulge in the contemplation of a highly taboo scene: forced sex. This paradox is papered over by the rules of the genre and minimized so effectively that romance scholars themselves have remained blind to it, wrapped up in the moral and aesthetic puzzles offered by the genre.[23] *Erec and Enide* shows how this blindness is created by the text. Chrétien carefully controls the malevolent attacks so that Enide is seen as sex object only fleetingly. Furthermore, Chrétien has cautiously separated and distanced Enide's potential to titillate from the scenes of sexual violence. Chrétien shows Enide's sensual attractiveness in a much earlier scene. When Erec first sees his future wife, she is dressed in (revealing) rags and tatters:

La dame s'an est hors issue
et sa fille, qui fu vestue
d'une chemise par panz lee,
delïee, blanche et ridee;
un blanc cheinse ot vestu desus,
n'avoit robe ne mains ne plus,
et tant estoit li chainses viez
que as costez estoit perciez;
povre estoit la robe dehors,
mes desoz estoit biax li cors.

(*Erec et Enide*, 401–10)

The lady of the house came out with her daughter, who was dressed in a chemise with wide tails, white and folded; beneath the gown she wore a white slip, for she had nothing else to take the place of a dress. The slip was so old that the sleeves were worn through at the elbows. This outer clothing was poor, but the body beneath it was beautiful.

This description of Enide in torn undergarments provokes, at an intellectual level, a moral reflection on the status of the feudal system in the twelfth century and the fate of impoverished petty vassals. At a preconscious level, it also affords the audience a chance to examine and enjoy, covertly and with impunity, Enide's beautiful body through the peepholes of her torn undershirt. Erec cannot take his eyes off her body:

Tot remire jusqu'a la hanche,
le manton et la gorge blanche,
flans et costez et braz et mains;

(*Erec et Enide*, 1475–77)

Staring, he admires all of her, as far as her hips: her chin and white chest, her thighs and sides, her arms and hands.

If there were any doubt about the deliberateness of this voyeurism, we have only to note that Chrétien titillates his audience in the same way a second time. When Erec brings his future bride to the royal court, he insists that she be (un)dressed in the same fashion. Erec points out the holes in the sides of her slip to the queen and the court:

Povretez li a fet user
ce blanc chainse tant que as cotes
an sont andeus les manches rotes.

(*Erec et Enide*, 1548–50)

Poverty wore this white slip so thin at the sides that both the sleeves have torn.

The audience is left to imagine the spectacle that shows through the torn sides of the thin chemise.

The subject of Enide's "sexiness" is then set aside and carefully placed in the background of this romance, while the questions of Erec's chivalric prowess and responsibility to the feudal community are foregrounded during the quest in a way that makes the audience comfortable with the heroine's attractiveness. Chrétien's skillful handling of eroticism in *Erec et Enide* is confirmed by the mainstream critical tradition which grapples earnestly with the moral issues of marriage or the equality of the married couple in this romance.

It is no coincidence that what is arguably the most titillating of all erotic scenes in Chrétien is also the most charged with ironic reversals, snarled moral questions, and intellectual challenges for the reader.[24] The test of prowess, the test of character, and the motif of female beauty are brought together in one sequence of *Le Chevalier de la Charrette*. Soon after the *raptus* of the queen we find the lengthy tale of Lancelot's relationship with the Demoiselle Amoureuse. Bathed in misty light, this sequence creates such confusion for reader and critic alike that it invites us to focus squarely and at length on the representation of rape. It is a passage in which a beautiful lady stages her own rape as a test of the hero's mettle and of her own attractiveness. Chrétien presents the scene from the viewpoint of Lancelot and lingers over the story, giving it 1,078 lines in a romance of which he wrote 6,000 lines. Such focus suggests that Chrétien wants his audience to reflect on sexual violence.[25]

After a shared meal, the Lovesome Damsel asks Lancelot to take a walk so she can go to her chambers and "get ready for him." Surprisingly enough, Lancelot agrees, leaving the audience to assume that he will be unfaithful to Guenevere. Suddenly the hero hears the lady's cries for help and races to her room. One of her knights, surrounded by her male servants, is about to rape her. Chrétien draws the gaze of his audience across her naked body:

et voit tot en mi son esgart
c'uns chevaliers l'ot anversee,
si la tenoit antraversee
sor le lit, tote descoverte; . . .
Cil voit que molt vileinemant
tenoit la dameisele cil
descoverte jusqu'au nonbril;

(*Lancelot*, 1064–67, 1080–82)

He sees there that before his very eyes a knight has pushed her on her back and holds her pinned to the bed, completely stripped. . . . [Lancelot] sees clearly that the lewd fellow holds her obscenely, stripped to her navel.

When we compare this close-up view of rape to the careful distancing of Enide's titillating nudity from the violent assaults in *Erec et Enide*, we realize how much more boldly Chrétien can exploit the potential of sexual violence to excite the audience when the female character is not the heroine.

Lancelot decides to take on the armed men. Upon witnessing the hero's valor, the lady abruptly calls off her knights, who depart obediently, leaving Lancelot to wonder at the meaning of this mock assault. And leaving the implied audience, ignorant like Lancelot until this moment, to ponder at the meaning of this episode.

The scene necessarily engenders a double "reading": in the first reading we pity the woman as victim of a brutal rape. In our second or retroactive reading we sympathize with the male character, Lancelot, who is revealed to be the victim of the lady's machinations. The damsel seems cynically calculating now that we realize she had herself stripped to the waist as she cried out "Aïe! aïe!"

What is the poetic function of this erotic scene, in which Chrétien strips his character and pins her to the bed? Is the author evoking a set of familiar clichés: women provoke rape, women enjoy rape, it is dangerous to judge rape charges because often women falsely accuse men of rape? The scene is not that simple. The mock rape problematizes the romance ethos of chivalric valor, as well as Chrétien's messages about sexual violence. After the knight's soul-searching monologue, the *avanture* proves to be an empty one. The Lovesome Damsel did not need to be saved.

Owen has argued that the sequence of the Lovesome Damsel is "amusing," a "humorous variation on the rape/abduction theme."[26] The comic elements are, in my opinion, less in evidence here than elsewhere in Chrétien's corpus. I would argue that even more than comic, the sequence is intended to be erotic. Chrétien allows the male audience to watch the spectacle of a woman being stripped and assaulted in front of a group of men, a taboo pleasure indeed in the context of courtly romance. He then papers over his rule-breaking, neutralizes the attendant guilt, or perhaps anxiety, by presenting the audience with challenging aesthetic and moral problems to solve. The aesthetic puzzle is that of the irony created by the mock-rape: we must reflect a good deal on the meaning of a rape scene in which the victim herself sets up the scene. The moral dilemma is that of a man's priorities when he must choose between his responsibility as a lover and his duties as a knight. The sight of Lancelot torn between his quest for Guenevere and his duty to protect women from rape permits the audience to enjoy both the intellectual challenge and the erotic pleasures of this sequence.[27]

* * *

It is not an arbitrary coincidence that the thorny scenes of assault in *Lancelot* and *Perceval* are built upon and bound up with the question of rape law. Chrétien has already built a story of sexual violence around a fictional law. In what is arguably his earliest literary text, the story of *Philomena*, Chrétien rewrites the Ovidian tale of Tereus and Philomena as found in the *Metamorphoses*.[28] It is worth a digression here to look at Chrétien's previous treatment of rape in order to highlight the specificity of sexual violence in his romances.

In Ovid's version, Tereus, husband of Procne, falls in love with Procne's beautiful sister, whose Latin name is Philomela. Frustrated by his burning desire for her, Tereus fantasizes about committing *raptus* and carrying her off. Eventually he takes Philomela deep into the forest and rapes her. In her fury and horror, the victim swears that she will throw aside all modesty and tell her story to everyone. To prevent this, Tereus cuts out her tongue. Mute and imprisoned, Philomela cannot reveal the wrong she has suffered:

os mutum facti caret indice. grande doloris
ingenium est, miserisque venit sollertia rebus:
stamina barbarica suspendit callida tela
purpureasque notas tilis intexuit albis,
indicium sceleris;

(Ovid, *Metamorphoses* VI, 574–78)

Speechless lips can give no token of her wrongs. But grief has sharp wits, and in trouble cunning comes. She hangs a Thracian web on her loom, and skillfully weaving purple signs on a white background, she thus tells the story of her wrongs.[29]

By sending the tapestry to Procne, Philomela manages to tell her sister the story of her rape.

Chrétien's *Philomena* maintains Ovid's aestheticization of the rape in the form of the beautiful tapestry. But the medieval poet introduces and leans heavily on a "law," one not found in the *Metamorphoses*.

Por ce, s'ele iert sa suer germaine,
N'estoit mie l'amors vilaine,
Car uns lor deus que il avoient
Selonc la loi que il tenoient
Establi qu'il feïssent tuit
Lor volante et lor deduit.
Tel loi lor avoit cil escrite
Que quanqu'il lor plest ne delite

Pooit chascuns feire sanz crime.
Itel loi tenoit paiennime.
Por ce se poïst cil deffandre,
S'il fust qui l'an vosist reprandre,
Ne ce qu'il li pleisoit a feire
Ne devoit nus a mal retreire.
Mes or leissons lor loi ester.

(*Philomena*, 219–33)

For if she had been his sister, their love would not have been guilty, because one of their gods had established, according to the law they obeyed, that they could do anything they wished or desired. This law was theirs and in writing: if it pleased or delighted him, any man could do what he wanted without committing a wrong. The pagan world obeyed this law. Therefore [Tereus] could have defended his action, if it happened that anyone wanted to make a charge against him. But because he was doing what he pleased, no one could accuse him of wrongdoing. But now let us put their law aside.

The fictional law Chrétien invents, invokes, and then "puts aside," actually deals with incestuous adultery. But the medieval poet quickly shifts our attention away from that fact. Repeating the word *loi* four times in the space of twelve verses, and dwelling on the lexicon of pleasure (*volante, deduit, plest, delite, plesoit a feire*), Chrétien allows the audience to infer that Tereus's rape of Philomena was justifiable. Chrétien appears to provide Tereus with an excuse. The point is key for our purposes here, because there is no such law in Ovid.

Chrétien follows Ovid's aestheticization of rape in the form of a beautiful tapestry. Chrétien departs from Ovid in framing the sexual relations between Teresus and Philomena as a legal question and then offering a law that might protect Tereus. Chrétien departs even further from Ovid by drawing the reader's attention away from the physical pain and emotional suffering of Philomena. He deemphasizes the grisly nature of Ovid's tale and focuses on male rights, including the right to pleasure.

The story of Gréorréas, in the *Conte du Graal*, provides another example of Chrétien's singular focus on rape laws and customs. When Gréorréas angrily steals Gauvain's horse, we learn that he does so because Gauvain once punished him for raping a virgin. The punishment was grotesquely dramatic: Gréorréas was forced to eat with dogs, his hands tied behind him, for a month. But Gauvain justifies his strange act of law enforcement:

Por quant mout bien savoies tu
qu'an la terre le roi Artu
sont puceles asseürees.
Li rois lor a trives donees,
qui les garde et qui les conduit,
ne ge ne pans ne ge ne cuit
que tu por ce mesfet me haces
ne que por ce nul mal me faces,
que gel fis por leal justise,
qui est establie et asise
par tote la terre le roi.

(*Graal*, 6872–85)

Nonetheless you were well aware that in the land of King Arthur maidens are guaranteed protection. The king, who protects and safeguards them, declared a truce on their behalf. I do not think or believe that you hate me because of your own misdeed or that you would do me harm on that account, for I [punished you] legitimately in the name of justice, as it is established and set down throughout the king's land.

The passage reminds us of the prototypical rape story in Geoffrey and Wace, linking Arthur to the surveillance of sexual assault. A truce had been declared in Arthur's kingdom: the right to violence against women was suspended. The law of Arthur seems unequivocal as it is articulated by Gauvain. But looking more closely we see how Chrétien undercuts Arthur's law. The sentence is so grotesque that it draws all attention to the plight of Gréorréas, the rapist. No mention is made of the raped virgin. The audience cannot have any response to her pain or suffering because her story is silenced.

Legal discourse in the *Graal* is coded in two tangled rape narratives: the tale of Gréorréas, just examined, and that of Guiromelant, who once attacked the wholly ambiguous character of the Male Pucelle. We learn later in the *Graal* that a knight named Guiromelant had killed her lover and forced himself on her:

Et la pucele fu m'amie,
mes ensi nel fu ele mie
qu'ele onques me deingnast amer,
n'ami ne me deingnoit clamer
n'onques ne fist point de mon buen,
car ge l'amoie mau gré suen,
qu'a un suen ami la toli
qu'ele soloit mener o li:
si l'ocis et li en menai

(*Graal*, 8301–9)

The maiden was my lover, but I was not hers, because she never deigned to love me or to call me lover or to do anything good for me, since I loved her against her will. I took her from her lover, the man whose company she kept. I killed him and led her off.

It could be said that Chrétien here offers an explanation for the odious and insufferable behavior of the Male Pucelle: she saw her lover murdered and was the victim of *raptus*. But Chrétien deflects attention away from her story, forestalls the potential response of pity, interrupts our reconsideration of the Male Pucelle, and draws our attention to a misogynist diatribe against this "she-devil" in the mouth of Guiromelant:

Ha! car i fust ele noiee,
que mout est plainne de deable,
qant ele vos dist si grant fable.
Ele vos het, nel puis neier,
si vos voloit feire neier
an l'eve hideuse et parfonde
li deables, cui Dex confonde!

(*Graal*, 8336–42)

Ha! she should have been drowned, for she is full of the devil when she tells you such a lie. She hates you, I cannot deny it, and wants to see you drown in the deep and hideous water, that devil—may God destroy her!

Guiromelant's speech reinforces the negative characterization of the female character, circumventing any reflection on her victimization. As with the story of Lancelot and the Demoiselle Amoureuse, Chrétien raises doubts as to the character of women who find themselves victims in stories of sexual violence.

When Guiromelant killed the Male Pucelle's lover and carried her off, he may have broken Arthur's law, but he was actually obeying another rape law, one also created by Chrétien de Troyes. It is the story of Lancelot and the Lovesome Damsel, a sequence as embroiled as that the story of the Male Pucelle, that gives us the key to the poetics of rape law in Chrétien's corpus. Arthur's law, as codified in the *Graal*, must be compared to the rape law in the land of Logres. In *Lancelot*, on the morning after the mock rape, the Lovesome Damsel explains the country's rape law to Lancelot:

Les costumes et les franchises
estoient tex, a cel termine,
que dameisele ne meschine,
se chevaliers la trovast sole,
ne plus qu'il se tranchast la gole
ne feïst se tote enor non,
s'estre volsist de boen renon;
et, s'il l'esforçast a toz jorz
an fust honiz an totes corz.
Mes, se ele conduit eüst
uns autres, se tant li pleüst
qu'a celui bataille an feïst
et par armes la conqueïst,
sa volenté an poïst faire
sanz honte et sanz blasme retraire.

(*Lancelot*, 1302–16)

The custom and policy at that time were as follows: any knight meeting a damsel who is alone should slit his own throat rather than fail to treat her honorably, if he cares about his reputation. For if he takes her by force, he will be shamed forever in all the courts of all lands. But if she is led by another, and if some knight desires her, is willing to take up his weapons and fight for her in battle, and conquers her, he can without shame or blame *do with her as he will.* (emphasis added)

The coding of rape in this representation of the law of Logres is breathtaking: rape itself is not a crime. "He can without shame or blame do with her as he will." Chrétien creates a facsimile of legal discourse in which rape is permissible as long as a man remembers that the rules of good sportsmanship apply. Chrétien offers the audience the contemplation of a world in which rape is an accepted male right.

The law of Logres is literary: it is romance law. This is the law of a literary genre that must create rape: in romance, women must be attacked so that men can become heroes. The hero cannot attack a woman who is alone, for that would serve no purpose in the romance economy. On the other hand, if a knight sees a ravishing lady and wants to do battle with her protector in order to "save" this beautiful damsel, that is in perfect obedience with the rules of romance.

Chrétien's ravishments are subtle and complex. A striking tension underlies his use and presentation of sexual violence. Chrétien's romances teach that rape is wrong, the act of base and undisciplined men. They teach the good knight to protect, not abuse, women. Arthurian romance evokes male aggressiveness, arouses anxieties and desires, then works to neutralize them.[30] But Arthurian romance also aestheticizes rape as a formulaic challenge: it sets up the threat of assault at regular narrative intervals so that each hero can prove his mettle by neutralizing that danger. The reader is taught to ignore the literal consequences of violent behavior and regard it as a moment of glory in the story of a knight's life.[31]

* * *

Courtly romance discovers in the representation of rape a space where the audience can enjoy the taboo pleasure of a titillating scene without transgressing romance decorum. The moral and social complexities raised by erotic moments work to deflect attention away from the pleasure of imagining violence against the female body. We must acknowledge the profound ambivalence in Chrétien's uses of literary rape. No one could read them as an actual incitation to or sanctioning of violence. But we must also acknowledge that their ultimate effect is to turn the audience away from the consequences of sexual violence, away from a reflection on the physical suffering of women, and to focus its attention on the chivalric dilemmas of male feudal culture. Far from empowering a female audience, Arthurian romance transforms rape into a romantic adventure: the heroine who is subjected to the threat of assault both enjoys the great compliment to her beauty and basks in the reflected glory of the triumphant knight who protects her.

* * *

A brief coda here will point to directions for further study and research in medieval romance. While Chrétien de Troyes cannot be considered the most typical author of twelfth-century romance, he certainly was the most influential and his texts were taken as models by subsequent generations of medieval poets. What happens to Old French romance after the work of Chrétien?[32] The literary manifestation I want to consider briefly here is a subsequent trend toward ironic, misogynistic romances, texts which alternate between the parodic and the obscene. Within this new strain of romance, the representation of male violence against women becomes more explicit, exposing what was idealized and mystified in earlier narratives, such as the Arthurian romances of Chrétien. Hue de Rotelande's *Ipomédon* is but one example of such antifeminist texts, for, as Roberta Krueger has argued, it lays bare the misogyny beneath the adoration of twelfth-century courtly love literature.[33] The romantic courtly quest is exposed as sexual and violent conquest.

As obscene and cynical as the love story is in *Ipomédon*, such a demystification of romance may have the positive (if inadvertent) effect, as Krueger hypothesizes, of enabling female listeners to reflect on the underlying presuppositions of courtly discourse in its coding of male and female: "The bluntness of Hue's antifeminist interventions and the insistence of his closing remarks invite controversy and discussion about women's place in his romance."[34]

One significant example of romance transformations in the thirteenth century offers a great deal of material for further thought. Guillaume de Lorris begins an allegorical dream vision of the "art of love" in his *Romance of the Rose*. As if to aestheticize completely the sexual drives at the heart of the romance narrative, Guillaume transforms the courtly lady into a flower: the Lover's quest becomes that of plucking the bud. Jean de Meun's celebrated continuation of Guillaume de Lorris's romance is one of the seminal texts of the thirteenth century, if not of the French Middle Ages. As John Fleming has demonstrated, the later poet parodically continues the rose quest, stripping it of aestheticization and revealing it to be wholly carnal.[35] The "seduction" of Rose, the courtly lady, is depicted blatantly as the rape of a virgin. The Lover compares his heroic efforts to deflower the rose to Hercules' assault on the cave of Cacus:

Formant m'i convint assaillir,
souvant hurter, souvant faillir.
Se bohourder m'i veïssiez,
por quoi bien garde i preïssiez,
d'Herculés vos peüst mambrer

quant il voust Cacus desmambrer:
.III. foiz a sa porte asailli,
.III. foiz hurta, .III. foiz failli,
.III. foiz s'asist en la valee,
touz las, por ravoir s'alenee,
tant ot soffert peine et travaill.
Et je, qui ci tant me travaill
que tretouz an tressu d'angoisse
quant ce paliz tantost ne froisse,
sui bien, ce cuit, autant lassez
conme Herculés, ou plus assez.

(*Le Roman de la Rose*, ed. Lecoy,[36] 21587–602)

I needed to attack with all my strength, repeatedly thrusting, repeatedly missing. If you had seen me in combat, if you had paid careful attention, you would have remembered Hercules when he wanted to dismember Cacus. Three times he assaulted the door, three times he thrusted, three times he failed, three times he sat down in the valley, quite exhausted, to catch his breath again, after suffering such difficulty and fatigue. And I, so fatigued that I was tormented and shaking all over because the barrier would not break, I am, believe me, just as exhausted as Hercules, or even more.

After seventy-five ensuing verses, which describe the tight, narrow passageway into which the Lover forces himself with repeated thrusts, the hero "plucks the bud":

Par les rains saisi le rosier,
qui plus sunt franc que nul osier;
et quant a .II. mains m'i poi joindre,
tretout soavest, san moi poindre,
le bouton pris a elloichier,
qu'anviz l'eüsse san hoichier,
Toutes an fis par estovoir
les branches croller et mouvoir,
san ja mul des rains depecier,
car n'i vouloie riens blecier;
et si m'an convint il a force
entamer un po de l'escorce,

qu'autrement avoir ne savoie
ce don si grant desir avoie.
A la parfin, tant vos an di,
un po de greine i espandi,
quant j'oi le bouton elloichi.
Ce fu quant dedanz l'oi toichié
por les fueilletes reverchier,
car je vouloie tout cerchier
jusques au fonz du boutonet,
si con moi samble que bon et.

(*Rose*, Lecoy, 21675–96)

I took the rosebush by its branches, more noble than those of any willow, and when I could reach it with two hands, quite gently, without pricking myself, I started to pull at it because I wanted to have it without shaking it badly. By necessity I had to bend and break the branches, without doing damage to the sides, for I did not want to wound it in any way. I had no choice but to use force to break off a little bark. I knew no other way to have this gift that I desired so greatly.

In the end, let me tell you, I spilled a bit of seed on the ground, once I had shaken the bud. It happened when I reached deep inside, folding back the little leaves completely: I wanted to feel everything, right to the depths of the little bud. That was the way that felt good to me.

Jean de Meun's "happy ending" turns a cynical eye on courtly love. As Leslie Cahoon persuasively demonstrated, Jean ruthlessly exposes the genteel hypocrisies of romance and boldly asserts the violence at the heart of male seduction and courtly love.[37] What Krueger writes of Hue de Rotelande's obscene closing passage holds true for Jean's final rape scene:

> His impudent epilogue, which follows close on the heels of a sentimental conclusion, forces us to see that the tensions between men and women within the text extend to cultural tensions beyond the text. We are left with serious questions about how male sexual domination and contempt for women lie so close beneath the surface of the happy ending.[38]

Are we to read Jean de Meun's calculated and detailed rape scene as erotic material intended to titillate a male audience in the way that Chrétien's Lovesome Damsel sequence does? Or should it be viewed, as Fleming contends, as a mocking lesson on the medieval sin of *luxuria*, in which the Lover is transformed into the quintessential Lecher?[39] Cahoon shows that this satirical attack on the courtly lover undercuts the romance message that love is powerful and constructive, to generate a new interpretation: that sexual seduction is cruel and courtly love hypocritical.[40] In a chapter on *Le Roman de la rose*, Georges Duby disagrees that Jean de Meun can be considered antifeminist at all.[41] The point on which all these critics concur, and which deserves further exploration, is that Jean's rape of the rose constitutes, if not a mordant commentary on, at least the logical extension of, the repressed violence in the romance of courtly love.

3. Replaying Rape: Feudal Law on Trial in *Le Roman de Renart*

The archeology of feudal rape law discloses itself in a group of twelfth- and thirteenth-century Old French texts entitled *Le Roman de Renart*, a cycle of narratives in which the characters are humanized animals.[1] The genre draws its sources from universal folklore. In the French medieval avatar, the hero is the trickster fox Renart. Composed between approximately 1171 and 1250, the collection is made up of elements, of varying length and homogeneity, called "branches." A great number of poets participated in the cycle, but we know nothing of them and most of the branches are anonymous. It is assumed the different authors were literate clerics. The genre enjoyed immediate success, a fact attested to by the considerable number of manuscripts, translations into other medieval vernaculars, and also the abundance of iconographic references to Renart in medieval art. The material was initially addressed to a chivalric audience, but was soon aimed at and heard by a broader, general public. Some branches are epic, staged in feudal courts, some parody romance and other popular literary genres, some are situated in the animal world. All are marked by the one permanent feature of the genre—its constant irony.

One group of the *Renart* texts is about the formulation, the authority, and the application of rape law in society. The authors of Branches VIIa, VIIb, I, and VIII display a detailed knowledge of French feudal law, apparent in their construction of legal discourse, their elaborate representation of the feudal judiciary in trial scenes, and their insistence upon posing sexual conflicts in judicial terms. Far from condensing their legal erudition to spare their audience, these poets foreground and highlight the legal procedure of the day, confident that their listeners take great interest in feudal law and are perfectly capable of assimilating its technical points. Indeed, law and legal learning held an important place in the value system of the noble elite in feudal society.[2]

Practitioners of the comparative study of law and literature today have discussed various ways in which the literary text relates itself to law, none of which can begin to account for the complex interweaving of literary and legal models in *Le Roman de Renart*. Legal discourse in the *Renart* is not a metaphor of something else, of another preoccupation or theme.[3] Nor can these *récits* be scrutinized for impassioned human voices, protesting the harsh impartial reason of medieval law.[4] These branches of *Le Roman de Renart* can be read as a set of social texts, to be juxtaposed to another, closely related set of social texts, the legal documents of the same period.[5] The *Renart*'s depiction of trial procedures, oaths, ordeals, trial by combat, and royal pardon, reveals that the preoccupations of the legal and social communities overlap.

A dialectical reading of literature, history, and law is certainly not without precedent among medievalists. There is a methodological tautology inherent in medieval studies, whether we read poetic works in light of secondary sources or study feudal history in light of contemporaneous literary texts. Textual interpretations have for centuries been conceived dialectically, based on historical accounts themselves based on the objects of inquiry. The hermeneutic power of this paradox is double. It plunges us into the medieval way of conceptualizing, which established no epistemological distinction between factual and fictional texts. Second, it teaches us there is no "source," there is no original object or fact that can be retrieved and that is the Middle Ages. There is only the study of the ways in which discourse is constituted and comes to construct relations of power in society. We cannot produce records of historical fact, but only analyze texts, whether legal, literary, religious, or scientific, as they work to produce representations of "reality."

R. Howard Bloch's *Medieval French Literature and Law* illuminates the singular exchange between literary and legal texts in the French Middle Ages:[6] "Based upon formula, gesture, and ritual, the procedures of the feudal court resembled more than superficially the literary performance. Both fulfilled in different ways a common purpose—the affirmation of an acknowledged set of shared beliefs and aspirations through the articulation of a collective history."[7] As Bloch demonstrates, the languages of poems and of legal documentary material are strikingly similar. Their narrative structures draw on shared paradigms. Legal documents are written with conventional literary forms; and literary texts like the *Renart* that focus on legal issues are as documentary in nature as the vernacular *coutumiers*, or collections of customary law.[8] An earlier example of such a reading practice in legal history is Yvonne Bongert's rich tome, *Recherches sur les cours laïques du Xe au XIIIe siècle*, a legal examination that draws with great profit on texts of medieval literature and underscores their detailed representation of legal procedure as prescribed in customaries, charters, statutes, and other records.[9]

The goal of this chapter is to examine the ways in which legal and literary languages subvert cultural models in *Le Roman de Renart*. I hasten to add that their relationship to medieval society is not always subversive, however, as Bongert and other scholars have documented correctly. The images of the feudal court and the courtroom speeches offer an accurate mimesis of twelfth-century royal justice and litigation procedure. Branches VIIa, VIIb, I, and VIII often reproduce exactly legal practices such as summons, ordeals, juries, rules of evidence and procedure. They make clear reference to actual twelfth-century controversies over rape law, sexual crime, and the influence of canon law on royal jurisprudence. But the principal relation of the *Renart* trial scenes to medieval legal philosophy and procedure is one of subversion. The *Renart* stories undermine the feudal principle of immanent justice, which grounds centuries of legal thought, institutions, and practices. Immanent justice is the ideological basis of trials, oaths, and ordeals in the secular medieval court. In the feudal legal system, innocence or guilt is deduced from visible evidence. The innocent party will win the combat or remain unscathed in trial by fire. God makes the truth seen and tangible.[10]

The authors of the *Renart* trial scenes demonstrate, with comic accuracy, the fallibility of oaths, the superstitious nature of ordeals, the dishonesty of the secular judiciary, and the impotence of feudal law enforcement. The characters who take the role of judges are so filled with personal prejudices that their partisan willfulness makes a mockery of divine justice. The jurors on the council of peers are motivated by spite, fear, family ties, and greed. Visibly, they do not seek to follow God's leading. Oaths are so easily manipulated that they prove nothing if not the cleverness of liars. Trial by combat is shown to be an arbitrary matter of physical strength and simple luck. Furthermore, the "divine" outcome of such combats can be quickly overruled by royal whim. Finally, the central character of the trickster hero reveals, with hilarious regularity, the impotence of the royal court to enforce its rulings or make itself respected.

The legal notion of immanent justice and the judicial practices that support that principle are not the simple or sole objects of subversion in the

Renart rape trials. They seek also to undermine a powerful cultural discourse, that of *fin 'amors*, and one of the literary models that disseminates that discourse, courtly romance. The character of Hersent and the story of her rape by the hero open a space for a cynical parody that strips courtly discourse of its idealizing pretensions and scathingly mocks the feminizing ethos of romance. The teeth of medieval misogyny are bared in and through the discussion of Hersent's rape and the successive trials of Renart the rapist. The depiction of outrageous and joyous indifference to women challenges any literal-minded acceptance of the courtly "celebration" of the feminine. The transformation of Hersent's love affair with the hero into a story of rape demystifies the reigning literary ethos of courtly romances.

The *Renart* poets take advantage of literary parody to reveal the absurdities of feudal law and exploit legal language as an opportunity to parody the reigning models of the feudal literary hegemony. The effect of the ceaseless irony in these animal stories is to lay bare the repressive potential, aesthetic as well as moral, of literary and legal norms. *Le Roman de Renart* offers a subversive thesis which may seem strangely modern to the twentieth-century reader: legal discourse is an exercise in power, changing the way people live; literary discourse constructs ideology and shapes the way people view one another and institutions, a subtler exercise in power. Furthermore, the *Renart* reveals the two discourses are not dichotomous: legal concepts also frame views of relationships, purvey ideology, and shape moral aspirations.[11] The organic interweaving of the two offers a medieval version of the unity of discourse. The authors' repeated choice of a subject as controversial as rape law reveals the deliberate nature of this subversion.

* * *

To foreground the specificity of legalism in *Le Roman de Renart*, let us first examine its most immediate textual model. Branches VIIa, VIIb, I, and VIII (Roques's edition) relate Renart's rape of a married woman, his summons, trial, escape, retrial, sentencing, and eventual pardon. The initial plot, the sexual assault, is directly inspired by an almost identical story in a slightly older twelfth-century Latin text, the satirical *Ysengrimus*, signed by one Magister Nivardus.[12]

The *Ysengrimus* is monastic satire built on a series of beast fables drawn from medieval folklore and the Latin stories of Aesop.[13] It relates the conflicts between its hero, Ysengrimus the wolf; the villain, a fox named Renardus; and various members of the animal kingdom. It is composed of seven books, which total 6,576 lines, and is dated in the 1150s. It was probably composed in northern France or Flemish Belgium for performance by monks within conventual walls.

Liber V contains three narrative sequences: the tonsure of Ysengrimus by Renardus; the rape of Ysengrimus's wife by Renardus; the wolf's conversion to monastic life. The rape story (lines 705–820) is relatively brief, as the following summary shows:

> Renardus arrives in the wolf lair where he finds Ysengrimus' little cubs gathered around their mother, who is confined to bed. Renardus defecates on the little ones and runs away. Enraged, the ailing mother tries to persuade the fox to come back. She intends to take revenge. With saccharine blandishments she coaxes him back, then hides behind the door in order to punish him. But when Renardus throws mud and sticks at her, the wife loses all patience and makes the mistake of chasing after the fox. Delighted, he leads her to his den. The small fox enters easily, but the she-wolf is too large and becomes wedged in the entry, unable to move in or out. Renardus exits by another hole, circles back to his enemy's wife, and gleefully violates his captive from behind, joking:
>
> "Alter," ait, "faceret, si non ego; rectius ergo
> Hoc ego, quam furtim quis peregrinus, agam."
>
> "Someone else," he said, "Would do this, if I didn't; it's better therefore that I should do it than some passer-by on the sly."[14]

The Latin version is doubtless archaic because it remains isolated in the poem and does not affect later episodes or events, as Léopold Sudre demonstrated in his nineteenth-century study of the *Renart*'s sources in folklore.[15] The female wolf character bears no name and does not play a large role. Her characterization is simple: she wants to protect her children. Only in the later, interpolated verses, 818.1 to 818.18, do we find the suggestion that the she-wolf "warmed to the game." If it is correct, as many have assumed, that *Ysengrimus* was composed for entertainment within the monastery, a performance in which the monks played the roles of the animals, this sexual assault from behind may have functioned as an in-house satire of homosexual practices.

The authors of the French *Roman de Renart* use that brief episode to quite different ends. It is greatly expanded and generates three more narratives devoted to a detailed representation of legal practices in secular courts. More interesting still, the expansion incorporates an exposition of various attitudes toward male sexual violence against women.

Branches VIIa and VIIb, the oldest of the French branches, are dated between 1170 and 1177 and are signed by Pierre de Saint-Cloud, of whom we know nothing other than his name.[16] Branch VIIa is cast in the world of the beast fable, not the feudal world of epic. Gustave Cohen opined that "La plus belle branche et la plus caractéristique est la deuxième qui tourne autour du viol de la louve par Renart en présence de ses louveteaux."[17] Whatever the critic may mean by "beautiful," the narrative function of rape in Branch VIIa remains similar to its function in the Latin text; it is neither a testimony to the power of female beauty nor a vehicle to prove male prowess, but an act of violent humiliation.

Maintaining the fundamental element of humiliation, the French poet deviates from the path traced by Master Nivard in essential ways. For one thing, Pierre de Saint-Cloud develops the characterization of the female victim by interpolating a prior act of adultery, making Hersent complicitous with Renart. For another, Pierre transforms the question of sexual violence into a legal issue.

The French author begins his version by doubling the *Ysengrimus* story of the fox's visit to the she-wolf, adding a previous encounter between Renart and his enemy's wife. By introducing this new scene, Pierre will reorient this and several other branches. The female character, now endowed with a name and personality, is no longer a cipher of the maternal: she becomes a bold woman of sexual appetite who is not only a willing partner in her sexual relations with the fox but actually initiates them.

Hersant saut sus, lieve son chiez,
si le rapele de rechief
et açaine a son graille doit

(Roques, VIIa, 5743–45)

Hersent lifts her head and leaps up. She calls Renart to her side and beckons him with her skinny finger.

Pierre portrays Renart as the reluctant lover who finally relents to Hersent's sexual appetite:

Hersant a la cuisse haucie,
a qui plaissoit mout son ator.

(Roques, VIIa, 5792–93)

Hersent, thoroughly pleased with the situation, has her thigh lifted in readiness.

The two characters commit adultery with mutual satisfaction and zest.

At this point in the branch, Pierre de Saint-Cloud conflates his rewriting of the *Ysengrimus* with that of another literary model. Pierre here begins his cynical parody of Béroul's romance of Tristan and Iseut, composed c. 1160,[18] by adding this episode, which is without precedent in Nivard's *Ysengrimus*. This cynical scene of adultery between Hersent and Renart invites a comparison with courtly romance. Both the "Romance of Tristan" and the "Romance of Renart" make a mockery of immanent justice and show the fallibility of the feudal legal system.[19] In Béroul's *Roman de Tristan*, Iseut, the married woman, is guilty of adultery, but her husband—who is the king—believes her to be innocent. She will be exonerated. The very different result of the "courtly love" affair between Renart and Hersent will be seen in the subsequent episode, when Hersent's courtly lover rapes her. Hersent will be an innocent victim, but her husband—and the king—believe her to be guilty. Iseut's word is sufficient: she need only take an oath, which the audience knows to be cunning and false, to be cleared. Hersent's word is not sufficient in the eyes of the court: she must offer to undergo the ordeal of cold water to clear herself, even though the audience knows she is innocent. The romance, as cynical as it is, maintains the myth of courtly love while Pierre de Saint-Cloud undermines it by presenting Renart's "uncontrollable love" as rape.

Many critics have stated that Pierre echoes the Tristan and Iseut story, but none has noticed the brilliant economy of this move. By turning to Béroul's text, Pierre accomplishes three important goals. First, he embarks on his parody of courtly romance. Next, the interpolation of the romance allows him to introduce the theme of adultery. Finally, the parody of adulterous courtly love shapes (and perhaps explains) the rewriting of *Ysengrimus* as a legal drama. The construction of Hersent's carnal delight authorizes a substantial *glissement* in the story: what was, in the Latin satire, the question of an innocent victim's rape will be shifted to a debate on the role of the female in the crime of adultery.[20] Pierre de Saint-Cloud can now frame sexual behavior as a *legal* matter.

When Isengrin returns home, his indignant cubs inform him that he has been cuckolded. Hersent immediately defends herself, offering to swear a legal and binding oath that she did not commit adultery:

que, s'om me laissoit esconduire
par sairement et par joïse,
jel feroie par tel devise
c'om me feïst ardoir ou pandre.

(Roques, VIIb, 5872–75)

If I were allowed to defend myself by oath or by ordeal, I would do it even if I were to be burned or hanged.

Georges Duby has documented the faithfulness with which Old French texts such as the *Roman de Tristan* and the *Renart* obey actual legal procedures. The details of the literary text

> show to what extent such infractions of the marriage laws were viewed as matters of secular justice and did not fall within the jurisdiction of the Church. . . . It was for the members of the household involved to observe the effect of the red-hot iron and to hear the wife swear her innocence, taking God as her witness and laying her hand on the Gospels or some holy relic. Certainly it was not a matter for the husband to decide on his own. He had to heed counsel.[21]

As Duby's remarks suggest, Pierre's text may subvert the literary discourse of courtly romance but is not yet subversive with respect to feudal law, which it faithfully portrays.

At this point Pierre de Saint-Cloud returns to the Latin model. In the next scene, the couple comes upon the fox in the woods and gives chase. Pursued by Hersent, the small fox easily enters his *chastiaus*, or lair; Hersent tries to follow, but she is still so round from her recent pregnancy that she gets stuck. Delighted, Renart sees his opportunity to "faire de lui son plaissir" (5940). Unlike Chrétien de Troyes, Pierre de Saint-Cloud does not veil or romanticize the assault but makes it unambiguous that this assault is wholly unlike the lovers' previous tryst:

Il n'est ileuc qui la resqeue,
mais que seulement de sa queue,
que ele estraint si vers les rains,
que des .II. pertuis daerains
n'en pert .I. defors ne dedanz.

(VIIa, 5945–49)

There is nothing that can rescue her, except for her tail, which she squeezes so tightly between her legs that it hides the two holes in her behind.

The poet makes it clear that Hersent does not want to be violated and struggles to protect herself as best she can.

Et Renart prist la qeue as danz
et li reverse sor la crope
et les .II. pertuis li destoupe,
puis si saut sus, liez et joianz,
si li fait tot, ses iauz veanz,
ou bien li poist, ou il li plaise.

(5950–55)

But Renart grabs her tail with his teeth to pull it up over her and uncover the two holes. Then he jumps on her, gay and happy, and does it to her whether she likes it or not.

Hersent is in no doubt as to the nature of Renart's action: "Renart, c'est force et force soit" (Renart, if this is rape then you'll have to rape me [5958]). As if to make certain the audience has understood that there is no complicity on the part of Hersent, the poet has Renart redouble his efforts:

Sire Renart tel li redone
que toute la fouse en estone.

(5959–60)

Sir Renart gives it to her again, so hard that the whole earth resounds with the noise.

The humiliation of the female character was already italicized in the Latin text by the wife's degrading position: she is trapped in a hole and subjected to a sodomistic entry from behind. The French poet underscores still more heavily the humiliation of rape. Insult is added to injury when Isengrin appears to witness his wife's shame. As if such a multiplication of degradations were not sufficient, Pierre invents a new, scatological insult. While Isengrin strives mightily to free his wife from the hole, she loses control of her bodily functions: "Isangrin voit qu'ele se voide" (Isengrin sees her soil herself [6047]).[22] The wolf frees his wife and then turns his rage on her:

"Hä! fai il, pute orde vivre,
pute serpant, pute coleuvre,
bien ai veüe toute l'euvre;
bien me sot Renart acupir:
je le vi sor voz rains croupir,
ne vos en poez escondire."

(VIIa, 6069–75)

"Ha!" says he, "whoring piece of living filth, whoring snake, whoring serpent, I saw the whole job; Renart really knew how to cuckold me! I saw him humped over your back. You can do nothing to excuse yourself."

The irony of this colorful diatribe lies in the audience's knowledge that Hersent is falsely accused.

Definitively altering the character of the Latin *Ysengrimus*, Pierre opens a generous opportunity for the scrutiny of feudal law and the examination of rape as a legal question. Although Hersent does tell the truth about her innocence, her earlier willingness to perjure herself when guilty colors this declaration:

"A la cort Noble le lïon
tient l'en les plaiz et les oiences
de mortés guerres et de tences;
la nos alons de lui clamer:
bien tost le porroit amander,"

(VIIb, 6088–92)

"At the court of Noble the lion trials and assizes are held in cases of wars and disputes. That is where we should go to bring a complaint. He could rectify the situation very quickly."

Even the truth, coming from the wolf's wife, no longer sounds like the truth. Branch VIIa ends as the married couple decide to take their case to court.

As in Arthurian romance, so too in the *Renart*: rape affords the characters their *lettres de noblesse*. In a cynical twist, Pierre shows that rape may humiliate females but it makes male animals into noblemen. Branch VIIb (Martin Va), by the same author and dated c. 1174–77, is known as "La Cour de Noble." It is the first of the French branches in which the animals leave the rural space of the beast fable and enter the feudal kingdom of mock-epic. In other words, as a result of the rape episode, these animals metamorphose into knights, proudly strutting about the royal court.

In its initial passages, Branch VIIb matches the historical information we possess of a feudal king's assembly.[23] As king, Noble is judge at his court. Isengrin comes forward to make his accusation, which he frames astutely:

Renart est cil qui toz max same,
car il m'a honi de ma fame;
Renart ne doute marïage,
ne loiautez ne conparage.

(VIIb, 6137–40)

Renart is he who sows all evil, for he shamed me by dishonoring my wife. Renart does not respect marriage or loyalty or family relations.

Isengrin's argument is that the rape was a crime against the king's peace, the husband, and patriarchy.

Pierre de Saint-Cloud further problematizes his portrait of the wife, complicating the nameless and marginal mother-wolf in the Latin version. Hersent is not romanticized as a helpless victim, nor is she painted cynically as a vindictive liar. Acting as her husband's witness, she prudently begins her testimony with the history of her past relations with Renart. Knowing that in a rape trial the sexual history of the victim is always in question, Hersent's intelligent strategy is to prevent any insinuation of her complicity in the attack:

—Voire voir, sire, ce dist ele:
des le jor que je fui pucele,
m'ama Renart et porsüi;
mais je li ai toujorz fouï,
n'ainz ne voil mon cuer aploier
a riens qu'il me seüst proier.

(VIIb, 6147–52)

"True, true, sir," she said. "Since the day I became a maiden, Renart loved and pursued me. But I always ran from him. I did not allow my heart to be swayed by anything he promised me."

The audience has a conflicted reaction to Hersent's testimony: having witnessed her lusty seduction of the fox during his initial visit, we know she is capable of lying. But we also know she tells the truth about the rape:

serree me vit ou pertuis,
si sailli fors par un autre uis,
par derriers vint, si me honi
tant con li jeus li abeli.

(VIIb, 6159–62)

He saw me squeezed in the narrow space and jumped out of his den by another hole. He came up behind me and dishonored me, enjoying the fun as long as he liked.

Pierre portrays a rape victim who believes that the only way she will receive justice in a court of law is by telling half-truths. In a moment of legal philosophizing unusual for the twelfth-century, Hersent adds that her husband's grief and rage are great indeed, but "Je sui cele qui en ai honte" (It is I who bear the shame of this [6165]).

Turning to the character of the king, rightful judge, Pierre begins to undermine his mimesis of actual feudal practice. The lion's first action as judge is to interrogate the victim: "si conmance un poi a sourire" (then he begins to smile a little [6201]). His questions show undisguised cynicism and suspicion: Are you certain you never loved Renart (6209)? Why were you so foolish as to let him enter your house alone, if you were not his lover (6212–13)? How can you expect us to believe that he actually raped you in front of your husband (6222–24)?

Isengrin, official constable of Noble's court, is a character who knows his feudal law well: the role of the judge in a secular court is that of mediator, not decision-maker. It is the council of peers that will take charge of the actual sentencing.[24]

"Sire, fait il, vos ne devez,
se vos lest, moi ne lui desfandre.
Ainz devez plainement entendre
a sa clamor, que que nus die,
tant c'on l'ament ou l'esconduie;"

(VIIb, 6226–30)

"Sire," says he, "you should not, if it please you, take sides with me or with him. You should just listen to Hersent's complaint, regardless of what anyone says, and decide whether to retain or dismiss the case."

Noble hopes to solve the problem between his vassals quickly by projecting blame onto the female character, scapegoating the woman for feudal conflicts and the inadequacies of the legal apparatus.[25] As the scene progresses, the king shows increasing reluctance to pronounce any judgment at all. Pierre shakes the audience's faith in divine justice by portraying a judge eager not to mediate but rather to avoid taking any action in a conflict between two powerful barons, Renart and Isengrin.

Next, Pierre takes on the hypocrisy of courtly love discourse. In verses 6201–24, the king gave the lie to the courtly idealization of women by being openly contemptuous of the alleged rape victim. A few verses later, like a good romance reader, the king interprets forced sex as an expression of passion; he does not want to see anyone mistreated in his court simply because they are accused of love (6237–40):

"Ce, fait il, que Renart l'amot
l'escuse auques de son pechié,
c'il par amors vos a trichié."

(VIIb, 6248–50)

"The fact," said he, "that Renart loved her excuses him somewhat from his sin, because he cheated you out of love."

Duby redefines this use of "love" in his analysis of *Le Roman de Renart*:

> The people who laughed at these tales were on the side of the rapists, who embodied the power of aggressive virility. For there is no doubt about it: what these works called "love," whether in Latin or in various dialects of the vernacular, was quite simply desire, the desire of men, and men's sexual exploits. This is true even of the tales of courtly love. Their theme was violent, sudden "love," which, like a flame, once kindled was irresistible.[26]

In the case of Pierre de Saint-Cloud, his juxtaposition of rape and "love" is a deliberate part of his literary parody as well as his undermining of feudal justice.

Feudal law, oral, unfixed, traditional, finds itself in a state of crisis as the nature of feudalism itself begins to change dramatically in the twelfth century. Secular courts are turning to the example of canon law, which has retained a written tradition for centuries, and which has a strict and highly codified procedure.[27] The role played during the trial by the Italian camel reveals Pierre's grasp not only of international law but also of the legal situation in the mid-twelfth century. As was the practice in real medieval court sessions, the king turns to an eminent guest, the papal legate and "jurist of great authority" (6263), Chameau. Like a true canon lawyer, Chameau claims to hold the institution of marriage in high regard. But Pierre's comic use of legal langauge in his portrait of the camel undercuts the legal position of the ecclesiastic dignity:

"Qare, mesire, me audite.
Nos trobat en decret escrite
legem expresse plublicate
de matrimoine vïolate."

(VIIb, 6269–72)

"Hear ye, signore, leesten to me. We finded written in zee Decretum
these law, she plublicly expresses against violating of matrimonkey."

The esteemed canon lawyer goes on at great length about the seriousness of Renart's crime, but he does so in unintelligible foreign jargon that hints pointedly at his stupidity.

The twelfth century saw an important revival of the study of Roman law in northern Italy and France. Roman law traditionally punished rape by death and confiscation of property. Pierre, perhaps mockingly, assigns the camel the wrong position: this churchman's proposed sentence conforms to Roman, not canon, law.

Primes le doiz examinar,
et s'il ne se posse espurgarrr,
grever le puez si con te plasche,
que mout a grant chose mesfache.
Hec est en la moie sentanche;
s'estar no vel en amendanche,
de si que parmaine comune
universe soue pecune,
de lapidir la corpe ou arde
de l'aversier de la renarde.

(VIIb, 6273–82)

First you must question zee accused and if he cannot defend for himself you must sentence him as you will, for he has committed a very gravious crime. Ecco my sentence: if he does not will to pay damages, let his fortune be confiscated and let him to be stoned or to burn, this she-devil Renarte.

The *Renart* poet deliberately uses the animal frame to set up a public forum on rape; he devises the courtroom setting and invokes the controversially severe Roman law to survey existing attitudes toward sexual violence. The length of the ensuing debate and its central position in this branch indicate that both Pierre and his medieval audience were interested in the question of rape law and were aware of the controversy surrounding rape's punishment. Unlike Chrétien de Troyes, the author of Branch VIIb presents assault not as a romantic compliment but as a disruptive offense, tearing at the fabric of the social community.

The trial scene undermines the idea of immanent justice by showing the effect that the judge's subjectivity has on the court. Noble tries once again to pose the question of sexual violence as a personal matter of passion, to be seen from the viewpoint of the rapist:

si jugiez de ceste clamor,
se cil qui est sorpris d'amor
doit estre de ce ancorpez,
se ses conpoinz est acoupez.

(VIIb, 6313–16)

Go judge this accusation and decide whether he who is under the influence of love must be punished if the other partner is implicated.

Pierre—who never misses an opportunity to ironize—does not entirely suppress the romance version of rape. King Noble is there to represent that school of thought.

Brichemer, the seneschal, begins the instruction. He invokes correct legal procedure, inflecting it to obey the king's wishes: the plaintiff must provide a witness. Furthermore, a wife cannot be trusted as a witness; Hersent's testimony must be dismissed because she will gladly lie on behalf of her husband (6332–50). Pierre here illustrates one of the differences James Brundage identifies between secular and canon law in the twelfth century:

> Gratian had little to say about specific procedures in sex cases. He opposed the use of ordeals in ecclesiastical courts and . . . preferred that Church courts rely upon proof through the testimony of witnesses and he included in his work several canons relating to the evaluation of their evidence. . . . Although he believed that women were inherently incapable of exercising jurisdiction, Gratian was willing to allow them to testify, particularly in adultery cases.[28]

Soon the jurors abandon their quibbling over the trustworthiness of Hersent's testimony to express their outrage on a more pressing legal point. Plateau provokes a significant change in the deliberation when he informs the council that Renart also stands accused of theft: Renart stole from Isengrin's provisions (6387–6400). Reminded of this, the jurors suddenly take the affair more seriously. The animals are indignant: Renart has bilked almost all of them of food. Indeed, as later chapters will show, theft is an extremely grave crime in feudal law and court records agree that it is punished more severely than sexual assault.[29]

During the rape trials, the character of Brun, the bear, moves to center stage and functions, like Noble, as a focalizer in the legal debate. With the exception of Chameau, the papal legate, Brun is the only member of the court to regard rape as a serious offense. Like the canon lawyer, Brun is in favor of a stricter provision for sentencing:

Por ice seroit avenant
que Renart fust pris maintenant,
si li lïast on mains et piez,
puis fuist gitez trestoz lïes
en la chartre ou en la joole,
puis n'i eüst autre parole
que de fuster ou d'escoillier,
des qu'il esforce autrui moillier.

(VIIb, 6633–40)

For this reason it would be appropriate to arrest Renart now, to tie his hands and feet, to have him thrown in jail or prison, and without further ado to whip or castrate him, because he raped another's wife.

Literary critics have frowned upon this passage as an example of Brun's personal vindictiveness. But Brun's speech accurately reflects twelfth-century legal principles. Feudal law, from the time of the Carolingians, subscribed to the *lex talionis*; that is, in any crime the offending member should be severed.[30] The call for castration is legally correct.

Brun stands out not only as the best informed peer but also as the advocate of a legally innovative position. In Pierre's survey of opinions on sexual violence, Brun's position is striking to the modern reader because he examines rape from the viewpoint of the victim, rather than the rapist:

d'esforcier fame n'i a el,
ne se c'estoit fame jael;
on en doit fort justise pandre,
que autre foiz n'i ost atandre;
et qu'est donc d'une fame espouse
qui dolantre en est et hontouse
de ce que ses mariz le sot?

(VIIb, 6641–47)

There is no other way to punish the rape of a woman, even if it is a woman of ill repute. We must enforce a severe judgment, so that Renart does not dare attempt it again. And why would we be more indulgent when it is a married woman, who suffers and feels shame because her husband knows what happened?

Brun's notion that the punishment should not be less for raping a dishonest woman or a nonvirgin is a legal idea not yet current in the twelfth century but one that will become law later in the Middle Ages.[31] Pierre de Saint-Cloud is not always playing around in his legal debates: his mockery of the current legal system is inspired by or at least open to serious thoughts of reform.

The seriousness never lasts, however, and that is one of the permanent features of trickster literature. When Pierre describes the most recent developments in canonistic thought on rape prosecution, he places those ideas in the crooked and grimacing mouth of the caustic ape. Cointereau, the court cynic, counters Brun's impassioned plea by spouting the position of Gratian, the influential canonist who revised rape law in the first part of the twelfth century:[32]

Por Dieu, se Renart a mesfait,
de pecheor misericorde.

(VIIb, 6658–59)

For the love of God, if Renart has done wrong, let us have mercy on the sinner.

Pierre makes a mockery of Gratian's call for brotherly love by assigning it to the jeering ape.

Anxious to placate the king, Brichemer, "conme bons rectorïens," dutifully summarizes the proceedings for Noble:

"Sire, fait il, nos estïens
alez le jugement enquerre,
selonc la guise de la terre."

(VIIb, 6704–6)

"Sire," said he, "we have acted in accordance with the customs of the land in this matter."

Brichemer reassures Noble that Isengrin must find another witness because Hersent's testimony has been dismissed. Renart is to appear the next day to swear an oath. Roonel, a dog, will preside. Whatever Roonel decides will bind both parties (6713–40). Again, Pierre describes actual feudal procedure: the role of the judge is essentially conciliatory; as mediator, he tries to find a solution to which both parties will freely agree in order to avoid further conflict.[33] But in respecting this procedure, Brichemer uses the technicalities of feudal law to carry out the king's obvious wish that the court take no action against Renart. Furthermore there is heavy irony as the role of judge is handed from a lion to a dog.

The poet portrays the feudal court as a place in which it is easy to put the question of rape aside. No audience could mistake Noble's delight upon being relieved of his responsibility as judge:

Li lïons respont en rïent:
"Ja, par les sainz de Belleant,
ne fuse si liez por .C. livres
con de ce que j'en sui delivres."

(VIIb, 6741–44)

The lion answered joyfully: "By all the saints in Bethlehem, if someone gave me one hundred pounds I would never have been as happy as I am to be rid of this case."

This is one of the passages that led John Flinn, an important *Renart* scholar, to conclude that Noble is a specific satire of Louis VII.[34] But the lion's reluctance to take on the role of judge accurately represents a commonplace historical reality, as we have seen: it was very difficult, in early medieval France, to persuade any powerful person to judge disputes, so unpopular was the responsibility.[35] By painting the king's uncontained and undignified glee, Pierre de Saint-Cloud suggests that the feudal judiciary system, far from being an instrument of immanent justice, is a farce. Noble tries from the outset to sabotage the procedure, first by placing the blame on the victim, then by foisting responsibility on others. Were it not for the stubborn persistence of one peer, Brun, the rape case could have been summarily dismissed.

Pierre de Saint-Cloud has reproduced the legal language and the trial procedures of a feudal court with such attention to legal detail that Flinn refers repeatedly to Pierre's profound respect for the legal system of his day.[36] Such an interpretation can scarcely account for the implications of the subsequent passage in Branch VIIb, which reveals neither admiration nor respect for feudal law. The irreverent poet undermines his mimesis of the legal system when he abruptly shifts back to the beast-fable world, ridiculing the medieval practice, still current in twelfth-century France, of taking oaths on saints' relics. On the day Renart comes to court, the council scene dissolves in comic bathos. Roonel, the canine judge, is easily bribed by Isengrin and invents a harebrained scheme: the dog will roll over and play dead; the other animals will force Renart to swear by the dead dog's tooth; then Roonel will leap to life and catch the traitor. The branch ends predictably enough as the fox escapes in his inimitable fashion and returns to his castle, mocking exultantly.

The seriousness of the rape trial is converted into laughter. The final irony in trickster literature is that its subversiveness never fully articulates any reform. Ultimately the trickster overturns anything that may initially appear to resemble a moral program. It is the law of the genre, the ideology of the form, that the trickster text will always remain finally amoral. Pierre's cynical closure is appropriate both to the ideology of trickster literature and to the episodic nature of the *Renart* stories.[37] Nonetheless, the modern reader cannot fail to notice the number of important ideas that Pierre managed to raise along the way.

Pierre de Saint-Cloud altered Nivard's tale of rape in important ways. The French poet problematized his model by turning the wife into an adulterous liar: he doubled the Latin scene of sexual transgression by interpolating an adultery trial scene from the "courtly" Tristan and Iseut story. But in Pierre's text that sexual transgression is not mystified as an expression of desire. It serves to develop the character of the she-wolf from that of an anonymous mother into a more complex, conflicted, intelligent, and imperfect wife, falsely accused of lying. Equally important, the French author presented rape as a political, social, and *legal* matter. He undertook a discursive investigation of the varying attitudes toward sexual violence in the legal community: an expression of overwhelming love; an inevitable and predictable fact of life; an error to be forgiven in the spirit of Christian love; a serious harm to social institutions; a criminal offense that damages all women. Most important, Pierre subverted the notion of immanent justice by showing the many foibles of the feudal legal system, its jurors, judges, and rules of evidence, weaknesses that could only impede a display of God's will.

For all the antifeminism in the images of Hersent's concupiscence and subsequent humiliation, in the cynicism of Renart's joyful immorality, and in the contemptuous impatience of the king, this openly misogynist examination of sexual violence is in many ways less repressive than Chrétien de Troyes's aestheticized ravishments. First of all, literary and legal languages play off one another not in order to moralize rape as a male test or romanticize it as a compliment to female beauty, but to show that the inadequacies of feudal law open a generous space for the legal protection of the rapist and the silencing of the most appropriate witness: the victim. Secondly, as Roberta Krueger has argued in the context of romance, the egregious nature of this literary misogyny cannot have escaped the notice of medieval listeners. Its controversial cynicism must have invited the audience to consider women's place in courtly love, as well as in feudal courts.[38] Pierre's depiction of a failed rape trial sows the seeds for the audience's reflection on sexual violence.

* * *

Pierre de Saint-Cloud did not miss the mark when he banked on his audience's taste for legal controversy. In 1179, approximately four years after Pierre ends Renart's trial in comic chaos, an anonymous poet composed what would become perhaps the most popular *Renart* branch in the French Middle Ages, Branch I, "Le jugement de Renart."[39] It is the account of Renart's second trial for rape, and as such it raises many questions. Why does this later writer continue Pierre's story, rather than choose fresh material? Why stage yet another rape trial, foregrounding once more the question of medieval law? And why does this second trial narrative become so popular, despite its repetitive character?

The author of Branch I, fully aware of Pierre's success, is eager to avail himself of the strategy: he, too, poses rape as a legal matter and uses Noble's court as a dramatic forum on the topic of sexual violence. The continuator begins by explicitly invoking the authority of Pierre de Saint-Cloud, in an ironic *auctoritas*. He criticizes Pierre for abandoning the best part of the story:

Perroz . . .
laissa le mieuz de sa matiere
quant il entroblia les plaiz
et le jugement qui fu faiz,
en la cort Noble le lion,
de la grant fornicacion

que Renart fist, qui toz max cove,
envers dame Hersent la love.

(I, 1:3–10)

Pierrot . . . abandoned the best of his material when he neglected to continue the trial and the judgment that took place in the court of Noble the lion, for the great fornication committed by Renart—in whom all evil smoulders—against Hersent the she-wolf.

At the same time, this author begins his version with a notable shift in emphasis. The opening lines refer to the rape as *fornicacion*, which in the medieval taxonomy of sexual sins falls under the heading of adultery, not *raptus*. It is no coincidence that in medieval penitentials there is no category for rape per se, but it is classified as a form of adultery.[40] The *glissement* in Branch I is subtle but definite: the issue of sexual assault is recolored and squarely presented as a question of adultery.[41]

As in Branch VIIb, Isengrin steps forward at Noble's court and cries for justice. But even in the husband's language a change manifests itself:

et dist au roi: "Biax tres douz sire,
faites me droit de l'*avoutire*
que Renart fist a m'espousee,
dame Hersant, qu'ot enserree
a Maupertuis, son fort repere,
qant il a force li vost faire.
A force li fist il li rous!"

(I, 29–35 [emphasis added])

Isengrin said to the king: "Esteemed and noble sire, let me have justice in the *adultery* that Renart committed with my wife, lady Hersent, who was stuck in Maupertuis, his fortress, when he wanted to rape her. He raped her, that redhead!"

This poet employs a new term, *avoutire*, the Old French word for adultery. In fact, in verse 40, Renart is accused of *avoutire* a second time.

Following Pierre's lead, the anonymous poet "holds court" to survey the opinions of the legal and social community. The king is assigned the same role: eager to minimize the seriousness of rape, Noble advises Isengrin not to embarrass himself by exposing the matter in front of everyone: it is a very small thing and does not deserve such grief and rage (I, 45–52). Brun, still positioned at the head of the legal avant-garde, exhorts Noble to carry out his responsibility and to ensure justice and protection to all his people (53–78). Bruyant scoffs at Brun's seriousness; since everyone knows that Renart is incorrigible, Isengrin should simply take matters into his own hands, rather than make such a nuisance at court (79–102). Grimbert, ever the yes-man, sides with the king: if Renart did it for *love*, what is the harm? Insengrin takes this much too seriously. The fault is all with Hersent; she is not an honorable woman (103–31).

Like the earlier texts, Branch I represents Hersent as a complex and somewhat contradictory character. Hersent finds herself, as in Branch VIIb, on trial and accused. She blushes and feels ashamed; her pulse races; she is overly dramatic:

"Sire Grinbert, je n'en puis mais:
. . .
j'en feroie bien un jouïse
en eve chaude ou en feu chat,
mais esconduire riens ne vaut,
lasse, chaistive, mal ostrue!
que je n'en serai ja creüe."

(I, 135, 140–44)

"Sir Grimbert, I can not bear this any more: . . . I would be more than willing to undergo the ordeal by hot water or trial by hot iron, but my denial would be worthless, unhappy me! pitiful woman! unfortunate one! because I would never be believed."

In medieval jurisprudence, both plaintiff and defendant can be asked to undergo ordeals: the burden of proof is shared. All the ordeals mentioned in this branch were in use in the mid-twelfth century. The trial by cold water consisted of plunging the accused, usually a woman, into a vat of freezing water: "And in the ordeal of cold water whoever, after the invocation of God, who is the Truth, seeks to hide the truth by a lie, cannot be submerged in the waters above which the voice of the Lord God has thundered."[42] In other words, if she sank, she was innocent; if she floated to the surface, she was guilty.

The ordeal of the glowing iron consisted in heating an iron until it was red hot; the plaintiff or the accused then took the iron in hand and attempted to tell the sworn truth: "Afterwards let (the iron) be placed on a frame, and let no one speak except to pray diligently to God, the Father Omnipotent, to deign to manifest His truth in the matter."[43] An unscathed hand was the proof of innocence.

It was not uncommon, according to medieval records, for plaintiffs and defendants to propose to take oaths, only to rethink their bravery at the last moment and retract the offer.[44] Hersent has already volunteered more than once to undergo a *judicium*. Here she appears to lose heart and claims that such an ordeal would be pointless because no one would believe her. Pierre's cynicism betrays reservations about the supposedly sacred character of ordeals and their inherent justice. Indeed, most forms of ordeal gradually fell out of practice after the twelfth century, even though the feudal courts preferred them to duels.[45]

Following Pierre's lead, the author of Branch I extends the parody of Béroul's *Roman de Tristan*. When Iseut is accused of adultery, she is not required to undergo an ordeal, but composes an oath of her own in which she declares that no man has been between her thighs except the king and the leper (Tristan disguised as a leper) who carried her across the ford. As E. Jane Burns demonstrates in her study of Béroul's text:

> This recasting of the standard legal oath is in blatant violation of the judicial code which requires that trial by ordeal and oath be conducted according to precise verbal formulas. In feudal jurisprudence, the slightest alteration of the verbal text could automatically render the proceedings invalid. But within the structural composition of Béroul's romance, the twisted truth is *de rigueur*, a necessary tool in protecting the lovers from unjust punishment.[46]

Like Iseut, the character she parodies, Hersent renders her plea of innocence with an oath she herself invents and which bears a double sexual meaning:

Mes, par les sainz que l'en aeure
ne se Damedieu me sequeure,
onques Renart de moi ne fist
que de sa mere ne feïst.

(I, 145–48)

By the saints we all worship, may God save me if I lie, never did Renart do to me anything he did not do to his mother.

At the same time as she attempts to vindicate her reputation, Hersent succeeds in insulting Renart with a slur that retains its power to offend even in the twentieth century. Such an obscene travesty of an actual legal procedure functions both to make a mockery of feudal law and to unveil the lie at the heart of courtly love. The deceitfulness that was cast in a romantic light in Béroul's romance is demystified as Hersent's obscene cunning.

Branch I continues to replicate the format of Branch VIIb. The poet circles the council of peers to present a variety of opinions. The members are of a mind to arrest Renart by force (233–43). Noble, however, ever fearful of alienating a formidable baron and eager to shift blame on a powerless individual, objects strenuously. The king wants Hersent, the plaintiff, to undergo the ordeal (244–55). When her husband demurs, Noble angrily informs Isengrin that there will be no more discussion of this conflict with Renart and that anyone who breaks the king's peace will be dealt with harshly (270–82). Isengrin has lost "his" case. Renart will go untried and unpunished, in the name of peace.

During the twelfth century the medieval judiciary strives to suppress private wars between vassals and encourages them to have recourse to the court system. Hersent and Isengrin are the literary construct of one attempt to adhere to the new feudal law, to desist from private warfare and individual revenge, and to bring political conflict into a court, to be solved in a way that will satisfy both parties. It is the king who is represented as inadequate to the new legal philosophy. He fails to honor Hersent and Isengrin's adherence to legal reform, fails to promote legal reform, and seems to yearn for earlier days, when vassals took the law into their own hands.

All would be lost for Isengrin and Hersent, heroes of the new law, were it not for the arrival of a dead chicken. The author of Branch I, eager to exploit his narrative framework, spins the trial into motion again with new impetus. Lady Coupée, Renart's latest victim, is at that moment wheeled before the court on a funeral bier, accompanied by the dirges of her fowl friends (295–351). This new crime functions just as did Plateau's mention of theft in Branch VIIa: rape was not serious enough to warrant the king's justice, but murder is. It is the sorrow of Chantecler the cock, whose manhood is injured, that moves the patriarch to feeling:

Je ferai ja Renart mander
qant cist cors sera anterrez,
si que vos a voz iaux verrez
com grant vangance en sera prisse.

(I, 388–91)

When this corpse has been buried, I will command Renart to come, so that you can see with your own eyes what great vengeance will be exacted for this.

In faithful accordance with actual practice, Renart is entitled to receive three summons to court.[47] First, Noble sends Brun to arrest the fox, invoking once again "l'*avotire* et de l'orgoil, de la traïson qu'il a faite" (the *adultery*, the overweening pride, the treason that Renart committed [410–11; emphasis added]). Renart tricks the bear with honey (492–720). Badly wounded, Brun returns to Noble's court where he faints. The king's sympathy for Chantecler now turns to rage at the prospect of losing a vassal:

"Bruns, dist li rois, Renart t'a mort,
ne cuit qu'autre merci en aies;
mes par la mort et par les plaies
je en ferai si grant vangence
q'on en parlera jusqu'an France.
. . .
dites moi au rous de pute aire
que il viengne a cort por droit faire
en ma sale devant la gent;
si n'i aport or ne argent
ne parole por lui desfandre,
fors la hart a sa geule pandre."

(I, 740–44, 747–52)

"Brun," said the king, "Renart has done you in. Do not believe that I will have mercy on him again. In the wounds and death he will suffer, I will take such great vengeance that even as far as France people will talk of it. . . . Tell the redhead of ignoble birth that I say he must come to court so that justice be done in my hall before the people. Let him bring neither gold nor money nor words to defend himself, nothing but a noose to hang about his neck."

The second messenger is Tibert, the frightened cat, whom Renart also tricks with a promise of food (752–934). Then Noble sends a written letter, his seal affixed, with the third messenger, Grimbert. The written summons appears to convey greater force. When Renart opens the letter and reads that he is sentenced to hang, his fear is great and he confesses a litany of sins to Grimbert:

Sire, gié esté entechiez
de Hersent, la fame Isangrin;
mais ore vos di en la fin
que ele est a droit mescreüe,
que voirement l'ai ge foutue.

(I, 1048–52)

Sire, I was infatuated with Hersent, the wife of Isengrin. But I will tell you the whole story: she is rightly suspected, because I really did fuck her.

When Renart finally confesses, it is to adultery, not rape. He vigorously adds that Hersent is guilty, too. And when the fox appears in court the next day, he shrewdly changes *foutue* to *amee*, whitewashing his crime in a romantic turn that is sure to appeal to the king. It is no longer adultery, but the crime of love:

D'Isangrin ne sai ge qui dire:
ce ne puis ge pas esconduire
que je n'aie sa fame amee,
mes puis que ne s'en est clamee
et puis qu'i n'i ot braies traites
ne huis brisiez, ne portes fraites,
s'ele m'a chier et ele m'ame,
cil fous jalous de coi se claime?

(I, 1283–90)

As for Isengrin, I do not know what to say. I cannot deny that I loved his wife, but since she never complained, and since I did not pull off her knickers or break into her house or push down her door, if I was dear to her and she loved me, what is this jealous fool complaining about?

The council of peers assembles. Renart is blindfolded and led to the gallows, but his desperate pleas for mercy finally move the king, who agrees to let Renart make a pilgrimage. No sooner is the fox released then—cursing and insulting Noble—he wipes his arse with his pilgrim cloak and throws it at the council members. As in Branch VIIb, the text ends when Renart escapes to his castle.

The trial scenes in Branches VIIb and I of *Le Roman de Renart* scrutinize the medieval hesitation in cases involving the sexual violation of a married woman: is it rape or adultery? It was assumed that a wife, knowledgeable about sex and men, could only be complicitous in her own rape. The authors undermine this ideological assumption by depicting a wife who, despite her zestful taste for sexual activities, resisted Renart as best she could and was not at all complicitous in his assault.

At the same time as they scrutinize secular medieval law, highlight its inherent contradictions, and illustrate its failings, the authors of Branches VIIb and I parody medieval romance. Both poets subvert Béroul's version of the Tristan and Iseut story by highlighting the ambiguity of those characters, and the discourse of courtly love.

Despite the moments of broad obscenity, scathing misogyny, and grotesque bathos, neither Pierre de Saint-Cloud nor his continuator falls into a simplistic stance. These branches of *Le Roman de Renart* examine a range of medieval attitudes toward sexual violence and actually point out the ways in which the feudal legal system supports cultural indifference to male violence against women.

* * *

In 1190, approximately fifteen years after Pierre de Saint-Cloud wrote the first trial and ten years after the composition of the second *jugement*, another continuator takes up the case of Hersent's rape one last time. Branch VIII, "Le Duel judiciaire," returns to Noble's court where we hear the king renarrate Renart's countless sins. The events are by now highly familiar; the medieval audience has heard them repeated but apparently without diminished pleasure.

The author of Branch VIII continues to exploit the trial format. Renart offers to undergo an ordeal or combat to prove that all the charges are lies. Jealous of his wife's honor, Isengrin is still intent on proving that the fox raped Hersent:

Dist Isengrin: "Certes, Renart,
jel moterroi de moie part
que vos a force l'asaillites,
en con trover pas ne faillites;
voienz mes iauz, vousist ou non,
li batites vos le crepon.
. . .
ce ne porrïez vos desfandre
ne vos en veïsse descendre
et voz braies sus remonter;
ne m'est honte del raconter."

(VIII, 7842–48, 7853–56)

Isengrin said: "Renart, in truth, I will for my part show that you attacked and raped her, and did not fail to find her cunt; before my very eyes, against my will, you rode her rump. . . . You can not defend yourself against the fact that I saw you get off her and pull up your breeches. It is no shame for me to tell."

Renart exhorts Isengrin to stop embarrassing himself by saying such indecent things about Hersent in public, but the impassioned husband will not be still (7859–8068).

In faithful mimesis of medieval practice, a trial by combat, the *Judicium Dei* or *jugement de Dieu*, is arranged.[48] Each combatant lays down his security and names four guarantors. The duel deserves our full and final attention because it culminates the intertextual saga of Hersent's rape and shows how the anonymous author of the 1190 branch rewrites the work of his predecessors. On the day of the duel, Hersent prays for her husband, and this is what she asks of God:

Hersant prie por son saingnor
que Diex li face tele honor
que ja de la bataille n'isse
et que Renart vaintre le puisse,
qui mout souëf li fist la chose
en la tesniere ou iert enclose.

(VIII, 8191–96 [emphasis added])

Hersent prays for her lord, that God might so honor him *that he not come out of the combat alive and that Renart defeat him, Renart who did it to her so sweetly when she was wedged in the burrow.*

After thousands of verses debating the question of Hersent's violation, the second continuator undoes the complexities of Branches VIIa, VIIb, and I in order to reveal the "truth": Hersent enjoyed being raped.

In the thick of the fighting, the faithful Isengrin finally yields to public opinion:

[Isengrin] dist: "Foux est qui met s'entente
en fame n'en riens qu'ele die:
poi est de fames qui voir die,
par fame est plus noise que pais,
ja la moie ne querrai mais.
Fame fait haïr pere et mere,
fame fait tuer son conpere,
par fame sont ocis .M. home,
fame est de toz max la some,
fox est qui trop i met s'entente."

(VIII, 8522–31)

[Isengrin] said: "He who places his thoughts in a woman or in anything she says is mad: few are the women who tell the truth. Women are responsible for more discord than peace. Never again will I seek out mine. Women make you hate father and mother; women make you kill your friend; because of women a thousand men are slain; women are the sum of all evil. Whoever fixes his thoughts on them is mad."

In this misogynist diatribe against women, the language usually reserved for Renart is now shifted to womankind: "de toz max la some." The discourse is unlike the studied ambiguities in the representation of the feminine in earlier branches. If we look at this shift in chronological terms, we notice that its date, 1190, corresponds to the approximate date of Chrétien de Troyes's *Conte du Graal*, the one romance in which Chrétien inserts diatribes that are overtly degrading to women. It is possible that Chrétien and the author of Branch VIII are both responding to a historical shift in attitudes toward women, an early example of the backlash against the courtly positioning of the feminine that will break out more virulently in the thirteenth and fourteenth centuries.[49]

Thus the controversy closes. Isengrin will eventually win the duel, but Noble will grant Renart a royal pardon regardless. It would appear that the anonymous poet of Branch VIII could not endorse or sustain the multiple ambiguities of the earlier trials, in which the difficult questions of Hersent's motivations, Renart's violence, the king's indifference, and the court's inadequacies were tossed into the air. Like skilled jugglers, the authors of Branches VIIa, VIIb, and I kept the many pins in constant play. It is as if this movement, this open-ended uncertainty, were too much for the author of Branch VIII, who allowed the juggling pins to drop, and brought in a final verdict against the victim. The miracle of the earlier branches is their brash willingness to portray outrageous contempt for women, to entertain the complexity of social attitudes toward sexual violence, and to scrutinize the existing legal apparatus for judging rape.

We have stressed the ways in which *Le Roman de Renart* undermines the literary discourse of courtly romance and the legal principle of immanent justice. The *Renart* is not always subversive, however. Its relationship to the legal system of the day is in many passages mimetic; it faithfully reproduces actual medieval practices. While these images are not subversive, they are profoundly cynical and pessimistic. The *Renart* appears to trace the disintegration of the feudal court system. In the earliest trial, Branch VIIb depicts an attempt at legal adjudication. But the judge himself thwarts correct procedure, and the court falls back on the practice of swearing on saints' relics. In the second trial, Branch I reveals the failure of adjudication. The court has recourse to oaths and even threatens the old-fashioned ordeal. In the third trial, the courtroom itself has vanished: the king resorts to the violence of a duel on the field of combat. Concomitantly, Branch VIII ends with the scapegoating of the female plaintiff, implying that her dishonesty is the cause of this conflict. The audience watches images of the feudal law system degenerate from branch to branch. *Le Roman de Renart* documents the slow disintegration of feudal practices, as an oral tradition collapses under the increasing predominance of the written. This literary text uses the legal question of rape as a vehicle to convey the conflicts tearing at the tenuous judicial and political order in feudal society.

* * *

In conclusion, lest the modern reader imagine that *Le Roman de Renart* can be made to disclose a well-hidden medieval strain of protofeminism, I want to bring to the center the question that lingers in the margins of this chapter. The female reader cannot fail to notice that Hersent's raped body is the text on which this legal debate, however subversive or thought-provoking, is inscribed. The violated female body stands patiently before the court, in branch after branch, as the vehicle for a male study of feudal jurisprudence. As in Chrétien's romances, sexual violence is construed as a problem for men. Rape is only part of a larger dilemma: that of maintaining order and strength in the chaotic feudal world.

4. The Game of Rape: Sexual Violence and Social Class in the Pastourelle

> How can we account for persistent associations of masculinity with power, for the higher value placed on manhood than on womanhood, . . . without some attention to *symbolic systems*, that is to the ways societies represent gender, use it to articulate the rules of social relationships, or construct the meaning of experience.
>
> —Joan W. Scott, "Gender: A Useful Category of Historical Analysis," 1063

Just as the trial scenes in *Le Roman de Renart* create an imaginary place in which rape can become comic, so too does the medieval pastourelle constitute a discursive space in which one can laugh at the spectacle of rape. The pastourelle further resembles the branches of the *Renart* discussed in the previous chapter in that its levity does not preclude a degree of seriousness. The pastourelle uses the representation of sexual violence as a symbolic system which functions as a locus of political thought, inscribing its reflection on law, power, and social class on the body of the female character. The pastourelle tropes rape as the inevitable encounter between the members of two different social milieus.

The existence of an indigenous pastoral poetry in the French Middle Ages is in itself hardly surprising, especially since the poetry of Virgil was known, translated, and studied in medieval schools.[1] This new pastoral genre, a lyric form called the *pastourelle* (*pastoure* is the Old French term for "shepherdess") appeared in the European twelfth century.[2] The songs were first composed in the Provençal language of southern France, then flourished in Old French in northern France.[3]

The medieval pastourelle displays predictable differences from the paradigm established in Virgil's *Eclogues*: the love celebrated is heterosexual, never homosexual; the poet-narrator takes on not the voice of the rustic shepherd but that of the knight. The genre presents several possible variants. The "classical" type tells of a knight's encounter with a young shepherdess in a secluded rural setting. The text uses both narrative and dialogue to relate how the knight attempts to seduce the country girl (whether with words of love, promises of marriage, gifts of clothing or jewels). This type usually ends with the departure of the knight, of his own accord or at the insistence of the shepherdess, who sends him on his way. Sometimes the seduction scene is interrupted by the arrival of one or more shepherds, who rescue the female character by turning their violence against the poet-observer. In the tableau type, or *bergerie*, shepherds and shepherdesses play bucolic games and sing songs, as the knight simply observes their rustic celebrations. In one variant of this type, the knight witnesses a quarrel between the shepherd and shepherdess. In another, the knight converses alone with the shepherd.

One medieval innovation is radically discontinuous with the pastoral tradition. In a variant of the classical "encounter" type, the songs become lyric variations on the themes of gender, power, and sexual violence. This type repeatedly narrates the same event: a knight is riding down the road when he sees a comely shepherdess alone in a meadow. The bucolic mode is interrupted by the spectre of a potential act of violence that is anomalous in the context of the pastoral tradition: rape. In approximately 18 percent of the extant Old French pastourelles (thirty-eight of the one hundred and sixty texts included in my count), the shepherdess is raped by the medieval knight.[4]

In two centuries of literary criticism, the sanguine representation of sexual violence in these songs has eluded analysis. In W.T.H. Jackson's classic 1954 article on satire in the pastourelle, he wrote of the "love passages" in which the knight "consorts with the members of a despised class to gratify sensual desires."[5] Gaston Paris hurried by the category of pastourelles in which the knight "a raison de la bergère," reasoning that they are merely "le récit d'une bonne fortune sans conséquence et qui ne laisse pas de souvenir."[6]

In the pastourelle, fictional seduction and rape are staged as a struggle between the powerful (the male knight) and the powerless (the female peasant), in order to give expression to conflict between social classes. As Joan Scott has written of texts in general, "concepts of power, though they may build on gender, are not always literally about gender itself."[7]

Our survey of contemporary pastourelle criticism reveals that the most effective rationalization or "naturalization" of rape in the genre lies in its representation as a function of social class. The pastourelle genre mediates class conflict by displacing it onto a sexual axis where its violence can be directed at the figure of the woman.

The pastourelle presents itself as a dialogue between representatives of two different worlds. The stock characters discuss this social polarization and debate the wisdom of class structures. Such stylized dialogue has convinced most critics that the principal or real subject of the pastourelle is social politics and that the genre is a form of social satire or political allegory. The construction of gender can then be viewed as a mere cipher in a comic allegory of medieval society. Such readings enable the critic-reader to ignore the sexual violence that motivates the rape sequences.

In this conflation of class and sexual violence, the pastourelles do not depart from, but participate fully in, the prevailing discourse of their day. Andreas Capellanus, author of a highly problematic text on the subject of gender, social class, language, and seduction, proferred this *mode d'emploi* for the man who desires a peasant woman, in his twelfth-century *De Arte Honeste Amandi*: "And if you should, by some chance, fall in love with such [peasant] women, be careful to puff them up with lots of praise and then, when you find a convenient place, do not hesitate to take what you seek and to embrace them by force" (1:11, "The Love of Peasants"). Much critical ink has flowed in disputes regarding the degree of irony in that passage. Putting aside the thorny question of André's intention, it is worth noting that when, in the thirteenth century, Drouart La Vache translates André's text into French, Drouart takes the opportunity to expand on the passage in question:

> Et, s'ainsi avient qu'il te preigne / Talent d'amer fame vilaine, / Se tu pues a bon point venir, / Tu ne te dois mie tenie, / Ains dois acomplir ton plaisir / Tantost, sanz querre autre loisir, / Et a ton pooir t'en efforce . . . Car c'est maniere de vilaine / Qui s'amour ne vieut otroier, / Tant la sache .I. hom biau proier, / Et que plus biau la proiera, / Plus vilaine la trouvera. / Si l'estuet .I. peu forcoier.[8] (vv. 4519–33)

> And if it should happen that a desire seizes you to love a peasant woman, and if you can go all the way, you should not control yourself. On the contrary, you should take your pleasure on the spot, without seeking further permission, and force yourself on her to the best of your ability. . . . For this is the custom of peasant women, who never do want to grant their love. Despite a man's skill in eloquent pleading with her,

> the more elegantly he pleads, the more churlish he will find her. Therefore he will have to use a little force.

The pastourelle is, for the medieval poet, this "convenient place"—the convenient discursive space to use a little force. When eloquence fails, there is another language which the peasant woman understands:

Mult longuement l'alai proiant,
que riens n'i conquis;
estroitement tout en riant
par les flans la pris:
sus l'erbe la souvinai,
mult en fu en grand esmai,
si haut a crie
'bele douce mere de,
gardez moi ma chastee.'
Tant i luitai que j'achevai
trestout mon desir;

(Bartsch, 3:42, 28–38)

I went on pleading with her for a long time, but got nowhere; laughing all the while, I took her tightly by the hips: I pushed her back on the grass; she was in great terror, and began to cry out: "Dear sweet Mother of God, protect my chastity." I struggled until I accomplished everything I wanted to do.

In this literary genre, the poet need not hesitate to indulge himself or his audience with complaisant images of sexual violence.

The discourse on social class in the pastourelle functions partially as a veil. If this were social satire, as Jackson argued, the shepherdess could be represented as unattractive, for instance.[9] The peasant figure could smell of the pigsty. The courtly knight might then turn from her in disgust. But the pastourelle neither favors nor criticizes one social class more than another. The verbal tug-of-war between characters resembles the never-ending fights between Punch and Judy. There will always be another episode.

The pastourelle does not function only to mystify the unpleasant realities of medieval class tensions. It also has a positive power to construct. Gender is not a mere empty field in which power is articulated, as Joan

Scott has shown: "Significations of gender and power construct one another."[10] This literary genre produces gendered subject-positions and symbolically legitimizes the relations of power that join them. While the pastourelle may seek to explore and reflect upon class conflict, it also codifies and maintains another reality, sexual experience, through its representations of male violence against women.

The social conflict between the female peasant and the male knight ultimately works to maintain the sexual politics represented in the pastourelle. The textual representations of a debate over social class have successfully convinced medievalists that the genre illustrates a sincere medieval belief in divinely instituted social hierarchy.[11] It is then but a small step for the contemporary reader to enjoy the depiction of an attack on a female body, concluding that it is the semiotic representation of medieval politics.

In the conflict between the knight and the shepherdess, to borrow another phrase from Scott, " 'man' and 'woman' are at once empty and overflowing categories."[12] They are empty to the extent that they have no fixed meaning in the real, they do not stand for real men and women, but they are overflowing because they are filled with suppressed definitions that do function in the real. The overly simplistic categorization of these fictional rapes as mere allegories of social class, empty of sexual meaning, is belied by the texts themselves, which show that their construction of gender overflows with meaning for medieval culture.

A survey of the pastourelles of the *Chansonnier de Montpellier* offers a first clue to the importance of gender and sexuality in this literary genre. In three of these songs the shepherdess is raped not by the knight, but by the shepherd, her social counterpart:

Il l'embrasa,
sour l'erbe la jeta,
si la baisa,
et li fist sans delai
le geu d'amors . . .

(Rivière, Mp LXXIV, 12–16)

He took her in his arms, threw her on the grass, and kissed her. Without waiting he did the game of love to her.

The terms used to describe Marion's rape by her social equal are similar to those used in the "classical" pastourelle:

Desous soi la ploie
et trois fois la besa;
desceint li sa corroie,
et puis dit li a:
"J'abaterai la croie
du peliçon Maroie."

(Rivière, Mp LXXXVIII, 10–14)

He pulls her beneath himself and kisses her three times. He undoes her strap and then says to her: "I will take the white color out of Marion's fur."

(The editor translates verses 13 and 14 as sexual: "je la culbuterai par terre pour lui enlever son pucelage" [I will knock her over on the ground to take her virginity].) The interchangeability of the roles of the knight and the shepherd shows that the rhetoric of social class displaces the other central issue: gender.

One modern critic actively minimizes the sexual significance of the pastourelle rape scenes. William D. Paden fears that if we study the sexual violence in the genre we will have to stop reading it, and "in so doing we would risk losing a rich genre that contains poems of violence but even more poems of delightful *jouissance*."[13] Inveighing against a tendency to "confuse fact and fiction, literature and life,"[14] Paden proposes a reading of the medieval pastourelle based on Freud's *Jokes and Their Relation to the Unconscious*: "A more promising model for the rape poems might be the dirty joke. . . . Freud sees the dirty joke as 'directed to a particular person, by whom one is sexually excited.' "[15] Curiously, Freud's point seems to escape Paden. Any rigorous boundaries between literature and life are dissolved entirely in Freud's paradigm; the text (the dirty joke), according to Freud himself, *constitutes* an act of sexual aggression performed by the teller on behalf of one listener and at the expense of another (the woman).[16] Following Freud's theory, the rape scenes of the pastourelle would be an act of sexual aggression on the part of the medieval poet who, again in the Freudian view, would like to "rape" the female listener on behalf of the male audience.

Properly understood, Freud's model does indeed have a potential application to the study of eroticism in the medieval pastourelle. Freud believed that in jokes as in literature a fantasy lies at the basis of the text. The fantasy is often unacceptable. Literary form is the "fore-pleasure" that allows the fantasy to escape censorship:

> The writer softens the character of his egoistic day-dreams by altering and disguising it, and he bribes us by the offer of a purely formal—that is aesthetic—yield of pleasure in the presentation of his phantasies. We give the name of an *incentive bonus*, or a *fore-pleasure*, to a yield of pleasure such as this, which is offered to us so as to make possible the release of still greater pleasure arising from deeper psychical sources.[17]

The strict formal patterns of the pastourelle permit and authorize both author and audience to enjoy a deep and forbidden pleasure: that of contemplating the unacceptable fantasy of rape in an acceptable way.[18]

Sexual violence serves many functions in the pastourelle, but none has been so overlooked as the erotic pleasure it offers the male audience. Rape is aestheticized in a way that both manages and encourages the erotic satisfaction of the listener.[19] The pastourelle aestheticizes assault as a sociosexual game and therefore a source of pleasure for the playful, resilient, and plastic female character, thus enabling rape to become a source of pleasure for the male listener and critic as well. The shepherdess bounces back pertly after an attack: unhurt, dry-eyed, cheerful, and refreshed.

The pastourelle makes the brutal spectacle of rape bearable by first sketching its violence and then aestheticizing the brutality by quickly inserting ludic or euphoric verses:

Quant je vi ke por proier
ne por prometre juel
ne la poroie plaixier,
k'en feisse mon avel,
jetai lai en mi l'erboie;
ne cuit pais k'elle ait grant joie,
ains sospire,
ces poins tort, ces chavols tire
et quiert son eschaipement,

(Bartsch, 2:17, 34–42)

When I saw that neither by my pleas nor my promises of jewels could I please her, whatever my whims, I threw her down on the grass; she did not imagine she was to have great pleasure, but sighed, clenched her fists, tore her hair, and tried to escape.

Just as the text reaches the point at which the harshness of that evocation could disturb the listener or the point at which it may inspire sympathy for the female character, it veers off and aestheticizes the violence.[20] In a slapstick ending, the panting shepherdess thanks the knight and asks him to return.

A departir me dist 'sire,
per si reveneis sovent;

(45–46)

As I was leaving she said to me, "Sire, come back this way often."

In no fewer than twelve pastourelles does this same technique appear: a scene of forcible rape is interrupted by coos of female pleasure or followed by the victim's thanks and request for more of the same.[21]

Quant j'ai veu ke par mon biau proier
ne me porai de li muels acointier,
tout maintenant le getai sor l'erbier
en mi leu de la praelle,
si li levai la gonelle,
et apres la fourreure
contremont vers la senture,
et elle s'escrie
"Robin, aue,
cor pran ta massue!"

(Bartsch, 3:48, 31–40)

When I saw that with all my eloquent pleas I could not get to know her better, I immediately threw her on the grass in the middle of the meadow. I lifted her dress and then the fur lining way above her belt. She cried out, "Robin, help! Take up your club!"

But the listener is not allowed to stop and contemplate the negative implications of the violation. The effect of the verses that follow is to render the rape scene ambiguous:

je li proie ke soit coie.
dont s'acoise, noise ne fist plus:
si menaimes nos solas
sor l'erbete et sor les glas
bras a bras.
Riant juant somes andui assis
les le boisson ki iert vers et foillis.

(Bartsch, 3:48, 41–47)

I begged her to be quiet. At that she calmed down, and made no more noise: we went on taking solace on the grass amidst the branches, in one another's arms. Laughing, playing, we sat down together next to the bushes, green and leafy.

When the poet superimposes this new image of the couple, laughing and enjoying sex, the reader is allowed to reinterpret the preceding verses. How reassuring to realize that the shepherdess only pretended to resist rape in order to salve her conscience.

One song, "L'autrier par un matinet" (The Other Day in the Early Morning), represents an assault on a virgin, who at first moans with pain at being deflowered:

En sovinant li baisai
sa bouchete et son vis cler.
quant l'autre ju conmencai,
si s'est prise a dementer:
"ai mi lasse, que ferai?
je sai bien que je morrai."
mais por li reconforter
li dis "douce creature,
endures les dous maus d'amer:
plus joenete de vos les endure."

(Bartsch, 3:35, 40–49)

Laying her down I kissed her little mouth and bright face. When I started the other game, she began to grieve: "Unhappy me, what will I do? I am certain I will die." To comfort her I said, "Sweet creature, you must suffer the sweet pain of loving: younger girls than you have suffered it."

That representation of pain is immediately circumvented, however, by euphoric verses which show the female character transported with delight on a second go-round:

Lors a itant la laissai
un petitet reposer,
et a joer conmencai
por li le mieus deporter.
et quant en point la trovai,
une autre fois fait li ai;
mais ainc ne li vi plorer
ains me dist 'biaus amis dos,
tote la joie que j'ai me vient de vos.'

(Bartsch, 3:35, 50–59)

So I let her rest a little bit, and then recommenced my playing in order to amuse her better. When I found she was ready, I did it to her one more time. This time I no longer saw her cry, but heard her say to me: "Good, gentle friend, all the joy I have comes to me from you."

Paden's analysis unwittingly demonstrates Freud's point that form is fore-pleasure. Paden argues that in many songs "the woman appears to be happy" and concludes that the existence of such happy poems "precludes a view of the whole genre as a 'celebration of rape.' "[22] Such is the interpretation created and authorized by the pastourelle. Even the shepherdess herself is made to call rape a game:

"sire, g'iere marrie
quant vos venistes ci.
or ai lo cuer joli,
vostre geus m'a garie."

(Bartsch, 2:13, 62–65)

"Sire, I was broken-hearted when you first arrived here. Now my heart is happy; your love-play has cured me."

The pastourelles often depict Robin, a recurring name for the shepherd and *ami* of Marion, as indifferent to the pain of the shepherdess; Robin assumes that she succumbed for the sheer pleasure of being unfaithful:

Maintenant sens demore
corui a cele sore;
ele crie et si plore,
dist "Robins trop demore!"
fis en ma volente
tant ke j'oi a plante
de li en petit d'ore.

(Bartsch, 2:14, 61–67)

Without waiting any longer, I got on her; she cried out and wept, saying "Robin, you're staying away too long!" I did what I wanted with her until I had had plenty of her in a short time.

Robins sens demorance
vint en grant esmaiance;
. . .
puis dist 'conchies sui,
si fail a covenance:
tu as fait autre ami.
quant ma foi te plevi,
bien deceus m'enfance.'

(71–72, 76–80)

Without further ado, Robin came running in great dismay . . . then said, "I have been dishonored, you have failed your promise: you have taken another lover. I plighted my troth, and you have deceived my youthfulness."

Thus far I have examined only the texts in which assault occurs, and it may be objected that those texts constitute a small percentage of the corpus: approximately 18 percent of the extant Old French pastourelles. Should the majority be viewed as the narrative norm and the rape texts dismissed as exceptions to the spirit of the genre?

The appearance of the stock character of Marion in much of the corpus suggests that we should not be guided by numbers alone when interpreting the pastourelles as a corpus. The character of the shepherdess is shaped intertextually; the songs in which she is *not* attacked offer a hermeneutic key to understanding the acceptability of rape throughout the corpus.

Songs in which the shepherdess eagerly agrees to have sex with the knight prepare and justify the sexual violence in the others.

The shepherdess character sometimes actualizes the literary type of the faithful lover, true to Robin (or to the Virgin).[23] In many pastourelles she manages to chase the knight away. Most often, however, the pastourelle presents the shepherdess as easily seduced by the knight. The shepherdess may be seduced by talk of love: the knight swears he has never seen anyone so lovely and will die if he cannot touch her.[24] In her brown burlap cloak, Marion can be cajoled with gifts of clothing and promises of jewels.[25] She can be had by hints of marriage.[26] She can be swept away by the promise that the knight will take her to his splendid castle where she will no longer tend sheep in the cold winter storms. Marion is, in some songs, eager to sleep with the knight in order to take revenge on Robin, who is dallying with someone else. Or she wants to make love simply because her mother told her she must not. In other words, the majority of the pastourelles create a familiar intertextual profile that legitimizes a view of the shepherdess as an unreliable character—greedy, ambitious, deceitful, or unfaithful. The audience is familiar with the genre and its stock characters, so that its reaction to the rape of the shepherdess is filtered through this intertextual characterization. In fact, the circumvention of rape in the majority of the texts suggests to the audience that Marion is a plucky wench, not helpless victim. The corpus functions intertextually to create a familiar female character and the corresponding implication that Marion precipitates, and enjoys, the game of rape.

In the pastourelle, sexual violence is made tolerable by its formal aestheticization through devices such as plot, character, and refrain. That aestheticization is frequently facilitated by the use of humor in the erotic representation. Just as, in the eighteenth century, Voltaire rendered rape slapstick in *Candide*, writing that Cunegonde was raped "autant qu'on peut l'être"; so, too, does the pastourelle make the spectacle of assault tolerable through comic mediation, as it makes the audience complicitous by soliciting its laughter.[27] The humor distracts us from the brutality figured in these little songs. No need to investigate the meaning of rape itself: it is only part of the joke.

The comic techniques of the pastourelle are varied. The characters are sometimes given burlesque names: a knight is dubbed Putepoinne (Bartsch, 2:52), a peasant is called Englebert de Haickecort (Bartsch, 2:36). The shepherdesses occasionally sing ludicrous songs as they watch their sheep. One young shepherdess sits in the middle of the road, singing the following refrain over and over:

Les mameletes me poignent,
  je ferai novel ami.

(Bartsch, 2:50, 7–8, 15–16, 23–24, 31–32, 39–40)

My little breasts are tingling; I'm going to meet a new lover.

In any literary genre, parody can be seen as a useful test of key features. The pastourelle canon parodies itself in Bartsch, 2:75, a comic text from which much can be learned about the medieval perception of the genre's meaning. The reversal of the elements in the parodic structure indicates the hierarchy of the narrative events. The parody shows a shepherdess who rapes the knight.

Lors me prist a embracier
et molt m'aloit estraignant,
qu'ele mi vouloit bezier,
mes je m'aloie eschivant.
voirement
de moi fist tout son talent
et me descouvri
et me foula et ledi
plus que je ne di.

(Bartsch, 2:75, 37–45)

Then she began embracing me and was holding me very tightly, for she wanted to kiss me, but I was trying to get away. In truth, she had her way with me, stripped me naked, trampled and abused me, more than I can say.

What better indication that sexuality and power were perceived by medieval poets and listeners as the genre's key subject?[28]

Aestheticization and humor are linked in yet another way in the pastourelle. Comic mediation functions in concert with the formal, lyric structure.[29] The pastourelle is a musical performance. The minstrel or jongleur sings and mimes the piece before the audience. The musical scores that remain extant indicate that the pastourelles were song-and-dance numbers with quick and lively melodies, no matter what the narrative content. The prescriptions of a medieval theoretician, Guillaume Molinier, afford a glimpse of what the pastourelle music was expected to sound like:

> La pastourelle exige toujours un chant nouveau, agréable, et gai. Il ne doit pas être aussi lent que celui du vers ou de la chanson; au contraire, il doit être un peu sautant et vif.[30]
>
> The pastourelle genre always requires a song that is new, agreeable, and gay. It should not be as slow as that of poetry or of the *canso*; on the contrary it should be a bit skipping and lively.

A lighthearted effect is achieved also by a lyrico-dramatic strategy, one more example of Freud's fore-pleasure of form: the use of the musical refrain.[31] The texts that depict rape frequently assign the stanzaic refrain to the character of the shepherdess, thereby showing the female voice to be as jovial or nonchalant after the representation of rape as it was at the start of the song. In the refrain of Bartsch, 2:32, "L'autre jour mi chivachai" (The Other Day I Was Riding), the shepherdess's recurring line, "ai! ai! ai!," is at first a cry of sadness, then after another stanza a cry of pain, and finally after the knight has forced himself on her a cry of orgasmic ecstasy: *ai! ai! ai!* Thus the audience is allowed both to laugh and to imagine that rape is a pleasurable game.

When the knight first espies the peasant she often sings a happy bit of nonsense verse: Tu-re-lu-re-li, tu-re-lu-re-lay. In the pastourelles with unchanging refrains, the shepherdess is forced to sing the same tune even when the knight has torn off her skirt and raped her: Tu-re-lu-re-li, tu-re-lu-re-lay. The following verses are from the final stanza of a five-stanza pastourelle:

La pastourelle enbraissai
ki est blanche et tendre,
desor l'erbe la getai,
ne s'en pout deffendre:
lou jeu d'amors sens atendre
li fix per delit,
et elle a chanteir se prist
. . .
"se j'avoie ameit trois jors,

je diroie a tous:
bones sont amors."

(Bartsch, 2:8, 45–55)

I kissed the shepherdess, so white and tender, and threw her on the grass, she could do nothing to defend herself; without waiting I played the game of love on her, and she began to sing: [Refrain] "If I had loved for three days, I would tell everyone how good love is."

If critics have long remained blind to the rapes of the pastourelle, it is because the genre's obsessive repetition of the moment in which violence makes difference into subordination has been made comical so that the audience can comfortably experience *jouissance* at the spectacle of rape.

A further look at the female character of the shepherdess reveals that the pastourelle constitutes a textual arena in which yet another conflict is played out: these songs are the locus of a literary debate over the construction of gender. In most of the pastourelles, as Joan Ferrante has pointed out, Marion speaks not like a shepherdess but more like the medieval idea of a courtly lady dressed in a shepherdess' costume.[32] She is as quick and witty as the knight, with whom she engages in word play and parodic casuistry:

Pastorelle, trop es dure
. . .
si me lessiez prendre proie en vo pasture.

'Chevalier, se dex vos voie,
puis que prendre volez proie,
en plus haut leu la pernez que ne seroie;
petit gaaigneriez et g'i perdroie.'

(Bartsch, 2:61, 25, 28–32)

"Shepherdess, you are too hard, . . . Let me take my prey in your pasture." "Knight, as God loves you, since you want to take prey, let it be in a higher place than mine; or you would gain little, and I would lose much."

Marion debates skillfully on topics such as honor, true love, fidelity, and social class.[33] Although she is portrayed as socially inferior, the language assigned her is far from rude. An audience could scarcely pity a character who constructs herself in such eloquent terms:

'Sire, or pais, je vos em pri,
n'ai pas le cuer si failli;
que j'aim miex povre deserte
sous la foille od mon ami
que dame en chambre coverte:
si n'ait on cure de mi.'

(Bartsch, 3:1, 43–48)

"Sire, hold your peace, I beg you, my heart is not so cowardly; for I prefer to be in a poor clearing in the woods with my love, than a lady in high-ceilinged chambers: for here one has no cares."

The debate over gender is intimately tied to a literary debate over genre and audience. The pastourelle was long classified as a "noncourtly" genre. Yet it was composed by the authors of courtly lyric, very often French noblemen, and performed before the same public as that genre.[34] Recent studies of troubadour lyric reveal that its construction of gender, in which the aristocratic *domna* is represented as enjoying sexual freedom and dominion over her lover, and the troubadours' depiction of a society that promoted aesthetic and social refinement and a feminized code of conduct, never existed in history, but were merely a fictive creation of medieval hegemony—a military and feudal hegemony that had little interest in the lives of women.[35]

The troubadour poets deny the powerful *domna* a voice. But they grant the powerless "shepherdess" a full range of expression. It would seem that the cost of having a voice is high. It does not prevent the shepherdess from being thrown onto the ground and violated, in an assault that is rehearsed time and again. Although she is endowed with a powerful wit and can reason long and well against her opponent, Marion is the creation of the poet who can force her to the ground as easily as he can loose her tongue.

The pastourelle both conceals and reveals two very different ways of figuring gender in the Middle Ages. For medieval poets the powerful muse of courtly lyric is manageable only as the speechless *domna*. In the pastourelle, where the female is given a voice, she can be disempowered in yet another way. In a drama set far from the court, yet played before the court audience, the poet finds a convenient discursive place in which to challenge the courtly discourse of female power and to reconstruct the age-old performance of male force and female subjugation.[36]

* * *

The pastourelle's troping of rape enables the male listener to enjoy a kind of pleasurable voyeurism usually forbidden him. I wonder whether it does not also enable an audience to reflect on the gray areas of male responsibility and power in the rules of sexual seduction as articulated in medieval law. We have seen that one symbolic codification of gender can constitute a fertile discursive field in which the outlines of other social relationships are articulated. If we place the pastourelle in the legal context of thirteenth-century France, we discover yet another way of reading its construction of opposition and gender.

The same century that saw the birth and popularity of the Old French pastourelle witnessed a judicial struggle with the legal notion of seduction. In the pastourelle we recognize the rehearsal of a cultural question debated among thirteenth-century jurists: when do arts and blandishment constitute illegal form of force in sexual seduction?[37] In staging this debate in literature, between a worldly knight and a rustic girl, aristocratic poets and their audiences display (as did the poets and audiences of *Le Roman de Renart*) the general preoccupation of medieval French culture with the legal codification of sexual violence.

In modern law, "seduction" is not always treated as a criminal offense. Susan Estrich shows how this fact

> ensures broad male freedom to "seduce" women who felt themselves to be powerless, vulnerable, and afraid. It effectively guarantees men freedom to intimidate women and exploit their weakness and passivity. . . . And it makes clear that the responsibility and blame for such seductions should be placed squarely on the woman.[38]

It can be argued that medieval canon law was in this regard more subtle than many twentieth-century penal codes, for canon law wrestles with the difficult notion of force and degrees of force in the definition of sexual violence. As Brundage points out,

> Extremely few societies allow men to overpower and ravish women without let or hindrance. But it takes keener insight and a more acute sensitivity to the notion that women should have an independent choice

of sexual partners for a society to outlaw the wilier practices of the seducer.[39]

In his twelfth-century *Decretum*, Gratian made a new distinction between using physical force to have coitus with a woman and using promises to seduce her into sexual intercourse.[40] He himself was most interested in defining the former. But in the thirteenth century, canon lawyers feel the need to address the question of sexual corruption achieved by flattery or false promises.[41] According to Cardinal Hostiensis, in his thirteenth-century *Lectura*, seduction is an illegal offense because it makes a mockery of the victim's free choice through the use of deception.[42] The statutes against seduction show that medieval jurists were capable of nice distinctions in the intersection of power and sexuality. Clearly, thirteenth-century France understood that power and powerlessness are not gender-neutral.

5. The Complicity of Law and Literature

Old French literature and medieval law offer conflicting images of sexual behavior. We can meaningfully contrast constructions of sexual practices in literature to other cultural representations, such as those that describe and define criminal sexuality. This chapter will examine two nonliterary manifestations of the discursive practice of rape: the texts of medieval law, both canon and civil, which reveal the judicial norm, and the records of medieval courts of church and state, which record judiciary practice.

Medieval rape law is complex and often contradictory. More than two legal systems coexisted in the later Middle Ages: ecclesiastical, on the one hand, and the civil or criminal law of royal, feudal, regional, and municipal courts.[1] Laws regulating rape, like other crimes, sometimes conceal (or reveal) power struggles between church and state.

The Introduction has traced the ways in which church courts and jurists struggled to impose ecclesiastical law, especially in matters of marriage and sexual behavior. The laws on *raptus* strove to settle the question of marriage between an abductor and his victim. The watershed in canon law occurred with the work of Gratian in the 1140s, which synthesized many of the inconsistencies in previous church law. Gratian established the independence of canon from state law, emphasizing that in ecclesiastical law the appropriate remedy for *raptus* is excommunication.

The Church's policy on *raptus* was deliberately lenient compared to civil law on rape: "Although he expressed no opinion as to whether the death penalty was justified in ordinary rape cases, Gratian maintained that if the abductor and his victim took refuge in a church, the perpetrator must be granted immunity from capital punishment."[2] Even though Gratian understood that a wide gap between legal theory and practice existed, and that the Church's juridical machinery for enforcing the laws was ineffective, he left the development of an apparatus for arraignment and punishment to his successors.[3]

Secular law on rape was fairly consistent throughout medieval Europe, although each country maintained its own procedures. The civil records of England in the later Middle Ages have received greater attention than those of most European states. John M. Carter's study of the widely varying punishments in thirteenth-century England shows that English society struggled to find an equitable solution for rape.[4] In the age of Glanvill (c. 1170–1230), rape was theoretically a felony, punishable by death; but convictions were extremely rare. In the age of Bracton (c. 1230–75), the rape of virgins was considered a felony, punishable by death or blinding. The Statute of Westminster I in 1275 downgraded rape to a trespass, punishable by imprisonment. The great turning point in English rape law came in 1285 when, in the Statute of Westminster II, Edward I tried to stop the growing rate of rape by declaring that all convicted rapists be punished by death or dismemberment.[5] As Barbara Hanawalt has shown, this significant legal change took at least sixty-five more years to be implemented.[6]

In recent work on sex crimes in thirteenth- and fourteenth-century Italy, Guido Ruggiero has found that rape was there treated as an extension of the customary victimization of women, that is, as a fact of life that was accepted and not considered particularly troubling in fourteenth-century Venice. Penalties were minimal. Although cases involving minors, the elderly, or incest were taken seriously, cases involving girls of marriageable age, married women, widows, or lower-class women received only token punishment.[7]

In Germany, secular law from the thirteenth through the fifteenth centuries provided the death penalty for rape.[8] The forms capital punishment took were burial alive or decapitation; but records reveal that sentences were often lessened to blinding, inprisonment, or marriage to the victim.[9] In addition, rape victims were held strictly responsible for fulfilling certain legal requirements in order to bring an accusation—first, screams and resistance, then producing witnesses or else character witnesses.[10]

Throughout the Middle Ages, northern France continued in the legal tradition of imperial Rome: rape, referred to as *fame esforcier*, by which was understood forcible coitus, was punishable by death. Philippe de Beaumanoir, a major thirteenth-century expert on customary law in northern France, states in the *Coutumes de Beauvaisis* that the punishment for rape is the same as that reserved for the most serious crimes, such as murder and treason, namely, to be dragged through the streets and hanged.[11]

One must ask whether legal texts have a privileged status as factual, that is, whether or not they represent the true practices and attitudes of society.

Medieval court records, both ecclesiastical and state, are revealing in this regard. The court act books were intended neither as a complete narrative account nor as a stenographic transcript of actual proceedings, but more like a judge's notes. Notaries limited their records to legally significant facts.[12] Nonetheless the *acta* provide valuable information about the application of law during this period. Furthermore, the language used to construct rape in the courtroom reveals much about cultural attitudes toward men and women, violence and punishment.

The *Registre de l'Officialité de Cerisy*, from the Abbey of Cerisy in Normandy, covers visits dating from 1314 to 1457 and is the earliest written evidence from rape trials in France.[13] It contains the records of regular visits that examined the behavior of the community and constitutes a dramatic representation of life in four fourteenth-century towns (Cerisy, Littry, Deux-Jumeaux, and Saint Laurent-sur-mer) from the time of the plague to the English occupation of the Hundred Years' War.

The judiciary practices of civil courts are documented in the *Registre Criminel de la Justice de Saint-Martin-des-Champs à Paris* (1332–1357), the court *acta* of a wealthy seignorial court, independent of the jurisdiction of the provost of Paris at Châtelet.[14] Saint-Martin was a Benedictine community that derived enormous wealth from its property and rents in the neighborhood. It had one of the few seignorial courts to survive and prosper until the time of Louis XIV. The community hired secular judges, called *maires* (mayors) to man its court and administer justice in its jurisdiction. The secular judges applied criminal law.

What were the discontinuities between legal theory and practice at that time? The *Registre de l'Officialité de Cerisy* does not begin until 1314, but as it is the oldest extant document recording rape trials in France, it remains a precious index to the medieval understanding of and response to rape in the hamlets of Cerisy (200 households), Littry (150 households), Deux-Jumeaux (40 households), and Saint Laurent-sur-mer (29 households) in a difficult and extremely turbulent period. Here is a picture of poverty, broken family structures, deeply rooted clerical corruption, quotidian sexual violence, incest, and social instability. The abbot's court was noticeably lax in sentencing—whether out of indifference or sheer impotence to enforce canon law it is impossible to determine. The jurors in any given sitting frequently included men convicted of criminal behavior in earlier sessions. The clergy themselves were repeatedly arraigned for crimes and recidivism.

The local churches of the area, the symbolic spiritual centers of these communities, were themselves in shambles. On May 16, 1332, during the visit to Deux-Jumeaux, the Cerisy court deplored a chronic situation: "Primo defectus est in ecclesia quia in eadem pluit et tantus ventus descendit quod luminaria ardere non possunt" (First there is a defect in the church because it rains in the said church and so much wind blows through it that the candles are not able to burn) (Dupont 385). The roof was so badly damaged that rainfall disrupted services, and the wind extinguished the candles, making it impossible for the priest to conduct Mass. The roof of Littry church suffered indignities of another sort: in 1410, Father Jean Bequet, local priest, was fined for playing tennis on top of Saint-Germain de Littry. He is typical of many in the register in that he was a recidivist: in 1413 he was arrested again for playing tennis, this time on top of Littry monastery.[15] The spiritual state of the clergy is one of the most startling lessons of the court records. Local priests and rectors are frequently cited for infractions far graver than illicit tennis: keeping concubines despite repeated fines, having children, seducing the wives and especially the widows of the parish, chronic drunkenness, and brawling.

From 1314 to 1399, an 85-year period, records of twelve rape and attempted rape cases can be found.[16] The figure is low, partly because in the Middle Ages, as at present, many rapes went unreported and also because only virgins or high-status rape victims actually had their day in court.[17]

In ten of the twelve trials the accused rapists were churchmen. Frequently the accused appear to be young clerics: their age is not given but their fathers step forward to pay their fines for them. The presence of the fathers and their willingness to pay for their sons' crime also suggest that these collective rapes may have been a sexual rite of passage, fairly well accepted in the community.[18] Since the medieval Church was more clement than the state in its dealings with rapists, it is not surprising to discover the leniency with which Church courts treated their own clergymen in rape cases.

In 1314 Jean l'Arquier, cleric, was arrested for leading a group of four clerics in a series of violent crimes against the community, including the rape of Jeanne, wife of Roger Cuquarry (entry 3). The July 5th provision for sentencing pronounced that Jean would be held in jail until he could prove his innocence. Five months later, on December 11, 1314, the court, satisfied of Jean's remorse, released him to his brother, Renaut, who promised to be responsible for the fine of 15 pounds.[19] The severity of the fine was probably due to the great number of charges on which Jean was arrested.

On August 12, 1314, four clerics—Colin de Neuilly, Raoul Roger, Jean Onfrey, and Henri Goie, alias le Panetier—were convicted of the collective rape of a widow, la Gogueree de Littry (entries 6, 7). Colin was fined 25 sous. The scribe records that because Colin is poor, his father, Pierre, paid the fine. Raoul was fined 25 pounds, paid by Raoul's father, Richard Roger, who is noted as stating that he does not want his son to be in debt. Richard Roger also paid the 25-pound fine of Jean Onfrey. Thus sexual assault appears to have been well integrated in the institution of the family in fourteenth-century Normandy and to have been held less shameful than financial debt.

Barbara Hanawalt has argued that rapists were rarely convicted in England because in the medieval legal mentality, crimes against persons were less serious than crimes against property.[20] While the Cerisy register is too incomplete to establish any systematic table of fines and its figures are too small to guarantee statistical accuracy, it does allow us a comparison of fines levied in the same year for sexual and nonsexual crimes against persons of clerical privilege. Jean de Altovillari, rector of Littry church, was fined ten pounds for frequenting taverns (entry 9h). Guillaume de Tomeris, rector and master of Littry school, was fined 100 sous for flogging a student, Philippe Malherbe (entry 18b). The student was fined ten pounds for retaliating in kind. A comparison of all fines levied in 1314 indicates that the Church exacts lesser punishments for rape than for other forms of misconduct, including crimes against persons.

In 1399, Geoffroi and Pierre, known as "Les Guillours," clerics and first cousins, were held for the collective rape of Katherine, wife of Guillaume Goubert (entry 3731). The fine was 15 pounds. As in the 1314 trial, the fathers of the young men stepped forward to pay their fine. These two fathers were themselves brothers, a fact that raises questions about the role of sexual violence in the family structure. The fine was steep for a rape charge, probably because the Guillours were recidivists known for terrorizing these hamlets. By way of comparison, we can note that in the same year, Jeanne, wife of Yvon Anglici, cleric, and Philippote, wife of Geoffroy de Cantely, cleric, were fined ten pounds for insulting one another (entry 374).

These collective rapes seem to have been youthful sprees. Patterns in the record indicate, however, that when young clerics eventually became priests and rectors, they continued to practice sexual abuse and thus constituted the second largest group of rapists brought to trial in the Cerisy court. This finding corresponds to the figures that Hanawalt and Carter have established for the clergy in thirteenth- and fourteenth-century England, where clerics constituted the largest group to stand trial for rape in the secular courts.[21] The power and prestige of their office may have led them to commit sexual abuses with a certain regularity.[22] The judges and jurors of Cerisy appear to have been complicitous in this misconduct, as the following example illustrates. On September 20, 1339, Richard Quesnel, rector of the church of Saint Marcoule, broke into the house of Mathilde la Chanteresse, and, with the aid of an accomplice, raped her daughter (entry 205). The court's pronouncement is breathtaking: "super quibus omnibus debemus conscientiam nostram informare" (Concerning which men we must examine our conscience). Sentence: none.[23] Indeed, later in the very same day, Mathilde la Chanteresse was charged with keeping a house of prostitution.[24]

In the Cerisy court, women were punished harshly for illicit sexual behavior and often received heavier fines than their male attackers.[25] A striking but not atypical example is the 1391 sentencing of Bertin Quenet for breaking into the home of Alicia, the widow of Jean Hoquet, with an accomplice, and raping her (entry 363k). Quenet was fined five sous, one of the lightest fines meted out in 1391, despite the fact, established by the court, that the men used violence to break into the widow's home. Alicia herself was fined fifteen sous, three times more, for *allowing* the two men to have carnal knowledge of her (entry 363l).

The *Registre de Cerisy* suggests that the crime of rape was already marked by the characteristics it bears today: indictment and prosecution are heavily affected by the character and status of the victim, the rapist is seldom prosecuted, and the penalties are lighter than those for other crimes of violence or crimes against property. While excommunication may sound draconian to the twentieth-century reader, it was, in fourteenth-century Cerisy, as temporary as it was difficult to enforce. Each year's record of visits begins with lengthy lists of those excommunciated in the three little towns: 85 in Cerisy in 1339, for example, 49 in Littry in 1339, a total of 33 in 1391, a total of 28 in 1405.[26] Fellow clerics and priests were commonly excommunicated by the local rector.

Canon law was well known to be more lenient than civil law with regard to rape. Although the punishment provided by law was excommunication, the Cerisy records reveal that the fines levied were rare and light: "de 5 à 10 sous en général, pas plus que pour un soufflet ou une injure" (from five to ten sous in general, no more than for slapping or insulting someone).[27]

The judiciary practices of civil court are documented in a fourteenth-century (1332–1357) record of trials held in a seignorial court situated in the area of Paris known today as the Marais, the *Registre Criminel de la Justice de Saint-Martin-des-Champs à Paris*. Just as the Cerisy register belies commonplace modern assumptions about the enlightened attitudes underlying the canon law of the medieval Church, so the Saint-Martin-des-Champs record reveals a striking contradiction between the judicial code and judiciary practice in the days of chivalry.

The Saint-Martin record is more complete and systematic than the Cerisy register. Written in the vernacular rather than the impoverished Latin of the Church scribes, it reveals that life in Paris was marked by preoccupations different from those of rural Normandy. The Cerisy church court's overwhelming concern appears to be with questions of marriage and sexuality, and with attempts at controlling the behavior of the clergy. The Cerisy register includes endless lists naming those husbands fornicating with others' wives, or those priests who have children by concubines. The focus of the Saint-Martin court, on the other hand, is on urban crime and violence. Although clergymen are frequently arrested in Saint-Martin, they plead benefit of clergy and are handed over to the Church courts of Paris.

Recorded rapes are scarce: in over 25 years only six cases are listed. In French as in English civil courts, few rape cases were tried and most ended either in acquittal or in some settlement, probably marriage or fine (settlements are not recorded in the register).[28] Despite the paucity of figures, the available data are revealing. In the six trials, one rapist receives the death penalty; two disappear; three are absolved for a variety of reasons.[29]

The first recorded rape case is as sensational as it is affecting. On July 13, 1333, Jacqueline la Cyrière was accused of luring a ten-year-old girl, Jeannette Bille-heuse, into her home to do housework. There Jacqueline helped a Lombard (Italian) soldier to rape the child. The court ordered not one but two sworn matrons to examine the ten-year-old. Their testimony is chilling: the child was deflowered, wounded, tortured, and cruelly mutilated. Jacqueline la Cyrière's sentence, to be burned at the stake, indicates that the seignorial court took her complicitous act of procurement with the utmost seriousness. There is no mention of the Lombard soldier, however. It is possible that he could not be found. But in a remarkably similar case tried in the Paris court of Châtelet in 1389, the wrath of the court focused entirely on the female accomplice while the male rapist was ignored. Katherine du Roquier was sentenced to death for procurement of her eighteen-year-old sister-in-law. In this instance, the rapist was one Jean Braque, "chevalier, maître des eaux et forêts en Normandie, maître d'hôtel et chambellan du roi, conseiller et gouverneur des finances de Valentine, . . . seigneur de Saint-Maurice sur l'Averon." Braque was not even arrested; his career continued to ascend after Katherine was burned alive.[30]

The second rape case in the Saint-Martin records again involves the rape of minors and suggests that this was a matter taken more seriously by the seignorial court than were assaults on adult women, especially wives or widows. On January 21, 1337, Jean Agnes, tailor, was accused of deflowering two twelve-year-old girls, Perrete de Lusarche, and Perrete la Souplice, both apprentices in a relative's care. The tailor was dragged through the streets and hanged, in strict accordance with the law. Jean Agnes is the only man, in this record, to have received the death penalty for rape. Here, as in the indictment of Jacqueline la Cyrière, the court's sentencing was probably a response to the victims' age and also to the fact that the two girls were both from the provinces, lived with Henri Agnes, and were therefore "property" placed in the care of Jean's family.

In a more typical provision for sentencing, on February 23, 1338, Guillaume Damours, mason, was accused of raping his chambermaid, Eudelot la Picarde. The judge ordered Eudolet to produce witnesses; to place the burden of proof on the victim in this way was standard procedure in secular medieval law. Eudelot protested that there were no witnesses. When the court reconvened, she failed to appear and Guillaume Damours was absolved.[31]

On April 20, 1338, Jehannin Fouet was accused (with a certain Noel Lasnier) of beating, striking, abusing, and raping Guillemete Dubois. Because Fouet failed to appear for sentencing, the case was dropped.

The next case is remarkable by all accounts. On September 29, 1342, Jehan Pinart was taken into custody, accused of the rape of Jehannete, daughter of Pierre Legage. The court ordered a sworn matron to examine the girl. Although this matron, Emmeline la Duchesse (a familiar name in the 25-year register), reported that Jeannette had been deflowered and raped in the past week to ten days, Pinart was absolved. The court offered no comment. Even the laconic Louis Tanon, who edited and published these records in 1877, could not resist exclaiming:

> Cette affaire est remarquable en ce que l'accusé est absous malgré la précision des faits dénoncés contre lui et le rapport de la matrone jurée qui semblait confirmer la dénonciation. (Tanon, 188, n. 2)

> This affair is remarkable in that the accused is absolved despite the exactness of the facts presented against him and the report of the sworn matron which seemed to confirm the accusation.

In the last Saint-Martin case, the accused, Angelot Burde of Lombardy, was in custody of the Paris court when, on March 10, 1340, he was brought from Châtelet prison and tried for the deflowering of Ennesot la Brissete.

Following a medical examination, Emmeline la Duchesse testified that Ennesot was healthy and intact. Based on la Duchesse's testimony, the accusation was judged slanderous; Ennesot la Brissete could then be fined for damages.[32]

Did Ennesot lie? Other explanations come to mind. One of the peculiarities of the medieval definition of rape is that coitus had to be completed for the crime to exist. Any form of sexual contact or abuse that did not lead to deflowerment did not constitute a felony, as in the case of Ennesot. Female assault victims in France, like those in England, may have suffered from primitive gynecological investigations.[33] The Saint-Martin records do not give Ennesot's age, but England offers the chilling example of a rapist who was not convicted because he was unable to deflower his seven-year-old victim.[34]

The Saint-Martin court, whose stringent rape law required punishments much harsher than the standard excommunication or fines of the Church court at Cerisy, seems to have been reluctant to prosecute. The burden of proof was placed on the victim, who had to demonstrate that she had resisted the attack sufficiently and with due form. Furthermore, if any slur could be made on her character, or if she failed to follow correct legal procedure at any point, the case would be dismissed.

A study of other crimes, for which there are more plentiful records, reveals no such reluctance on the part of the Saint-Martin court to prosecute female criminals. From 1332 to 1338, 18 of the 203 men brought (on any charge) before the court received the death penalty (1.97 percent); 10 of the 39 women brought before the court received a death sentence (7.7 percent). The figures available from the Saint-Martin register, limited though they are, suggest that women, who commit far fewer crimes, received the death penalty three times more frequently than men in this court. This is partly because, then as now, women tend to commit crimes of property rather than crimes of violence, and the taboo against theft, larceny, and burglary (the crimes women commit most) was strong. Medieval society was far more tolerant of violence than of theft.

Not only in number but in form as well do criminal sentences reveal uneven treatment of men and women. Punishments for nonsexual crimes by women were barbaric: the death penalty for women was not hanging, which was ruled out as an offense to their female modesty, but burial alive (for lesser offenses) or burning at the stake (for grave offenses).[35] We recall that in 1338 Guillaume Damours was absolved of raping Eudelot la Picarde because there were no witnesses. In August 1340, Perrete Cotelle was buried alive for stealing "57 mailles blanches de 8 deniers"; in December 1340, Phelipote la Monine was buried alive for stealing nine ounces of silk, and Perrete d'Avenant was buried alive for stealing a dress and a purse. In September 1342, Jehan Pinart was inexplicably absolved of rape, perhaps out of Christian charity or perhaps through an out-of-court settlement. In that very same month Ameline la Soufletiere was buried alive for the theft of a man's purple cloak.[36]

The Saint-Martin register indicates that medieval French law was interpreted to support a long-standing tradition of indifference to male violation of a woman's sexuality and legal personality.[37] Conversely, the Saint-Martin court punished women consistently and to the full extent of the law. Slow to protect and quick to punish, this society as revealed in the register devalued female life. What Hanawalt finds in fourteenth-century England is equally true of Saint-Martin: "There seemed to be a strong sentiment that men should not even be indicted for rape unless the victim was a virgin and even then the low incidence of indictment indicates that *opinion was not strong about punishing rapists*" (emphasis added).[38] Women were both sexual and legal victims of male-defined crimes tried by men. Susan Estrich's conclusions about twentieth-century America resonate with significance for our study of these medieval courts: in medieval as in modern law, we discover a system that claims to celebrate female chastity, but affords men broad sexual access to women and is unwilling to protect them.[39]

Who were the men trying and recording these cases? According to Hanawalt, "Lawmakers, jurors, or poets . . . accurately described the techniques of committing crimes. Indeed, probably quite a large proportion of the population, including lawmakers and enforcers, had participated personally in criminal acts."[40] Natalie Zemon Davis has studied the fictional or literary qualities of legal records to examine the ways in which authors give narrative shape to the events of a crime.[41] The language and composition of legal texts, as well as their contents, deserve analysis. Specifically, one must examine the "fictive elements" in historical documents.

Notaries were trained to limit their notes to testimony that went to the issues of reliability and credibility and to disregard anything else said or done in the courtroom. The *acta* form a kind of specialized literary genre, with strict and well-defined general conventions. But individual notaries interpreted those rules differently. The medieval courtroom records examined here are fictional to the extent that they are the compositions of individuals who could decide what statements would be summarized, what language would be used to summarize them, and which phrases would note legally significant points. The court records bear witness to the discursive practices of notaries in fourteenth-century France and therefore require interpretation.

Scrupulous attention to rape rhetoric in Venetian court records demonstrates that, in the early fourteenth century especially, the language used to report rape in Venetian records is "curiously distant and antiseptic." Ruggiero argues that such laconic reportage made minimal penalties easier to impose: "A close physical description of what individual rapes entailed might well have added considerable weight to the . . . penalties."[42]

The ecclesiastic record of Cerisy also reveals a curiously technical and cursory tone in its description of rape trials. Perhaps this is because the court notaries struggle with the constraints of a Latin they master very poorly. But the vividness of entries describing violent fights and tavern brawls suggests that the court recorder could shine in flashes of poetry and drama when the case involved a depiction of violence more to his taste (entries 394k, r).

The first quality the reader notices in the Cerisy rape entries is that of clinical distance. In the collective rape by the Guillour cousins, the clerk antiseptically notes: "Unus in presencia alterius carnaliter cognovisse, et hoc perpetrando unus alterum scienter adjuvit" (They knew her carnally, each in the presence of the other, and in this way each helped the other perform better [entry 373l]). In 1391, the recorder eschews any terms referring to the violence of an assault by two men (*raptus*, "ravishment," or *violenter*, "violently") and sparely notes that Bertin Quenet:

> infra domum relicte Johannis Hoquet de nocte intrasse contra voluntatem ejus et jacuisse cum ipsa, et Johannes Guellin secum. (363k)

> went into the house of Jean Hoquet's widow at night and lay with her against her will, and the same for Jean Guellin.

Again, the scribe avoids any term connoting force and chooses the more neutral *iacere* ("to lie with").

The second salient quality in the rape entries is a vagueness so consistent that it eventually raises the suspicion that the resulting ambiguity is deliberate. One example is the frequent use of the verb *volere* (the vulgar Latin form of *velle*, "to want to"):

> "volebat dictus Ricardus filiam dicte Matilidis suponere vi et violentia et quod debuit frangere domum dicte Matilidis." (205)
>
> The said Richard wanted the daughter of the said Mathilda to submit to him by force and violence and for that reason had to break into the house of the said Mathilda.

Father Richard Quesnel went as far as to employ an accomplice to break into the girl's home, but the presence of "volebat" casts doubt on the seriousness of the attack.

In 1369 Pierre Ediene was accused of raping a widow. The woman's testimony is recorded most succinctly: "conqueritur quod Petrus Ediene voluit ipsam rapere" (she complained that Pierre Ediene wanted to rape her [entry 235b]). Entry 235d repeats that Ediene simply "volebat coire cum quadam vidua" (wanted to have sex with the said widow). Ediene was excommunicated. He would reappear, however, six years later in 1375, accused of murder in a dramatic case recorded with flair (entry 309).

The tendency to minimize descriptions of sexual violence was equally pronounced in the fifteenth-century entries. In 1413, an attack by Pierre le Prevost, cleric, is described in vague terms. He violently entered the home of Guillaume le Guillour and attacked Guillaume's sister, Agnes, with his knife, wounding her several times "quod predicta Agnes voluntati sue consentire nolebat" (because the aforesaid Agnes would not agree to do his will). The scribe coyly avoids saying what it was that Agnes refused to consent to with this man who broke into her home and stabbed her repeatedly. The cleric is fined five sous, a paltry sum when we consider that in the same year Yvon Anglici was fined five sous for throwing a loaf of bread at Pierre Siart's head (entry 394 l).

The rape entries in the Cerisy records are characterized by laconism and an ambiguous vagueness. These stylistic features probably result from a complex of factors, including judicial, linguistic, material, geographic, and psychosocial ones. One further consideration is illuminating. In 1373, Etienne Bernart, rector of Littry church, listed as *notarius curie nostre*, "our court notary," was arrested and fined for the rape of Guillemete de Costentino (entries 235a, 292).[43] That the court recorder at Cerisy proves to be an accused rapist may well be a coincidence, but the coincidence is highly suggestive in light of Carter's finding that 39 percent of rapists in his English documents are identified as clerics.[44] Those who have the power to read and write, those "lawmakers, jurors, or poets" referred to by

Hanawalt, do indeed seem to have participated personally in many acts of sexual violence.[45]

The actual words or expressions used by the witnesses were recorded infrequently by the notaries. Only one exception to that practice, and to the common rule of stylistic vagueness, can be found in the Cerisy register. It deserves mention because it is strikingly similar in tone to the entries of the Saint-Martin register. An entry from 1369 states two men were fined for the seduction and possible rape of a minor (entries 245a, 245b). Etienne de Molendino and Guillaume le Deen, priest of Littry, were accused of seducing a young girl. The church scribe uncharacteristically records the words of the witnesses. The mother of the girl testified that Etienne de Molendino, sitting by the fire, took her daughter in his arms and seduced her with the following words: "Mea pulcra netis, ego dabo tibi / unam tunicam burelli mei" (My lovely little child, I will give you one of my burlap gowns).

These blandishments echo distinctly those of the knight in the thirteenth-century pastourelles.[46]

"Douce bergerete,
soiies m'amiete,
je vos donrai de brunete
cote trainant." . . .
Tot maintenant l'acolai,

(Bartsch, 3:23, 17–20, 45)

"Sweet little shepherdhess, be my little love, I will give you a long cloak of brunete[47] that sweeps the ground." . . . And without further ado I kissed her.

In the same entry, Jean Alain testifies that he heard Molendino's accomplice, Guillaume the priest, use similarly lyrical words of seduction, while sitting by the fire: "Pulcra neptis, oscula me, et ego dabo tibi / unam tunicam burelli mei quando factum fuerit" (Lovely child, kiss me, and I will give you one of my burlap gowns when it is done). It is as if the priest were humming scraps of a contemporary song, or the court scribe were remembering a fashionable pastourelle:

"bele, vostre amor demant. . . .
por ce vos proi et apel

que vos faciez mon voloir,
et je vos donrai mantel
de brunete taint en noir . . ."

(Bartsch, 2:64, 18, 40–43)

"Beauty, I am asking for your love . . . that is why I ask and beg that you do as I say, and I will give you a cloak of brunete."

A style has been referenced; it is the pastourelle lyric. Perhaps this genre represents a linguistic paradigm for attitudes toward sexual violence. (Sentence for Molendino and le Deen: none noted.) Certainly these discursive structures existed prior to the event. The subsequent court records represent what Davis views as "possible story lines determined by the constraints of the law and approaches to narrative learned in past listening to and telling of stories or derived from other cultural constructions."[48]

The notion of preexisting discursive structures is further reinforced by an observation in Hanawalt's work on rape. Despite the undeniable linguistic distance that separates her documents from the Old French pastourelle, Hanawalt notices similarities between her English records and a thirteenth-century Old French text: not a pastourelle, but a *parody* of the medieval pastourelle, Adam de la Halle's *Jeu de Robin et de Marion*: "The medieval play *Robin and Marion* centers around the attempted abduction of Marion and is indicative of both the techniques of the rapist (who seems to have read Andreas Capellanus) and the resistance of the victim."[49]

Court notaries practiced their writerly craft just as deliberately as did the authors of the pastourelles. In reading through the trials of the *Registre de Saint-Martin*, one finds a tendency opposite to that of the Cerisy churchmen. In contrast to the bland records of Cerisy, the rape trials of Saint-Martin seem to embody the professional scribes' greatest literary efforts.[50] Many of the rape accounts in civil records show unusual attention to narrative development, to the reproduction of direct discourse and to detail used for chilling effect. The scribes used the narrative codes available to them as a discursive model.

In the *Registre de Saint-Martin*, Ymbelot Roussel, the court recorder, has entered most trials in an economical fashion: three to six sentences summarize the prisoner's arrest, the charges, the testimony, and the sentencing. In entries for rape trials, however, the character of the writing is transformed: the record goes on for one, two, or three pages, in a kind of writerly *jouissance*. The scribe plays with direct discourse, and details of the crime are described in a literary way. There is an obvious pride taken in this work. In fact, in two separate cases Roussel signs his name to the records with a flourish: autograph and paraph. When Philippote la Monine is sentenced to execution for theft in 1340, he takes the unusual step of writing: "procès fait par Robert Neveu, notre maire, *et je Y. Roussel*." When Perrete Cotelle is also sentenced to death for theft in 1340, we read: "Procès en a esté fait par moy, *Y. Roussel*."

In the 1333 trial of Jacqueline la Cyrière, the court clerk recorded in fascinated detail the gestures, conversations, and movements involved (Tanon 40–43). With a theatrical flourish the record documents how Jacqueline set her trap for the child who was sitting on the stoop of her father's house.[51]

> la vint ladicte Jacqueline, qui la prinst par la main et lui dist: "Vien si, me soufle mon feu, et laveras mes escuelles." (Tanon 187–88)

> There came the said Jacqueline, who took [the girl] by the hand and said to her, "Come along with me, tend my fire and wash my dishes."

In a narrative marked by drama and detail, the scribe vividly relates how Jacqueline and the soldier forced the child to drink a "vile green potion" intended to render her mute, and threatened her life if ever she told what had happened.

The record of Jehan Pinart's deflowering of a thirteen-year-old girl is composed with a suspenseful pause in the narration. The narrative described how Pinart dragged her into his room and threw her on his bed. She screamed so loudly that he stuffed his cape in her mouth. She struggled with such strength that he could not completely violate her on the bed. He dragged her to another room, and pulled her onto a table in the hope of gaining better traction. Here the poet-scribe pauses:

> et là, sys ycelle table, la corrompty et despucela tout oultre. (Tanon 187)

> And there, on that very table, he corrupted her and deflowered her through and through.

As striking as the rhetorical flourishes of the Saint-Martin records are the ways in which they, like the description of the crime of Father Guillaume le Deen and his friend, seem to rework the language of medieval song. The Saint-Martin records focus on the same elements found in pastourelle rapes: the rapist's effort to pull the woman to the ground; the victim's cries for help; the name of the garments that are pulled away; the rapist's attempts to silence the victim; the force necessary to violate the victim.[52]

In the trial of Jacqueline la Cyrière, accomplice to rape, the scribe focused on the physical force required of the impatient Italian soldier:

> et la geta sur un lit, et s'efforça de gesir aveques lui, et entra entre ses jambes. Et pour ce que il seul ne pot faire son vouloir, et que elle croiot trop fort, ladicte Jaccqueline vint . . . et adonques ledit Lombart la geta jus, et entre entre ses jambes, et hurta contre sa nature, et s'efforça de entrer en lui. (Tanon 41–42)

> he threw her on a bed, and forced her to lie with him, and entered between her legs. And because he could not do his will alone, and because she cried out very loudly, the said Jacqueline came. . . . thereupon the said Lombard threw her down, and entered between her legs, and hurled himself against her private parts, and forced himself into her.

That construction is not unlike that of the thirteenth-century pastourelle, "Chevachai mon chief enclin" (I went riding, my head bowed), which offers the same configuration of narrative details.

Ne vo plux a li tencier,
ains l'ai sor l'erbe getee;
maix as jambes desploier
lai fut grande la criee.
haute crie goule beee

(Bartsch, 2:4, 49–53)

I did not want to quarrel with her anymore, so I threw her on the grass. But when I tried to pull her legs apart, oh what a cry she let out. At the top of her lungs she cried aloud.

From the trial of Jehannin Agnes, one finds the following account of the gestures of the rapist as he brutalized a twelve-year-old girl:

> là, en un selier, fist entrer, oultre son gré et par force, ladicte Perrete la Souplice, et la jeta à terre, et avala ses braies, et se mist sus lui, et s'efforça

> contre sa nature tant comme il pot, et pour ce que elle crioit, il la bati et feri, et la laissa; (Tanon 88)

> There in a cellar he forced her to go, against her will and by force, the said Perrete la Souplice. He threw her to the ground, and pulled down her underwear, and got on top of her, and forced himself against her private parts as hard as he could. And because she cried out, he beat her, struck her, and left her there.

A perusal of the Saint-Martin records reveals that thirteenth-century songs present a ready paradigm for a clerical reference. Examples abound; for instance, "En mai la rosee que nest la flor" (In May, at dawn, when the flower springs forth):

quant vi que proiere ne m'i vaut noient,
couchai la a terre tout maintenant,
levai li le chainse,
si vi la char si blanche
tant fui je plus ardant;
fis li la folie . . .

(Bartsch 2:62, 25–30)

When I saw that my prayers were worthless, I laid her down on the ground right away, lifted her shirt, and saw her flesh so white that I burned all the more. I did the trick to her.

Or perhaps a song such as "Quant pre reverdoient, que chantent oisel" (When meadows grow green again, when birds sing) offered the preexisting linguistic materials with which the court scribe constructed his own text.

Quant par ma proiere n'i poi avenir,
par les flans l'ai prinse, si la fis chair,
levai la pelice,
la blanche chemise:
a mult bele guise
mon jeu li apris.

(Bartsch, 2:76, 37–45)

When I did not succeed by my pleading, I took her by the thighs and pushed her down. I lifted her coat, then her white shirt. With my nicest manners, I taught her my game.

We have already noted the poetic efforts of the scribe in the case of Jehannete, the thirteen-year-old who fought Jehan Pinart so fiercely. The text goes on:

> la prist par la main et la mena en sa chambre, et la geta sus son lit, et se efforça de la despuceller; et que ce que elle crioit harou, lui avoit mis son chapperon sus sa bouche, afin que l'en ne l'oïst crier. (Tanon 187)

> He took her by the hand and led her into his room, and threw her on his bed, and tried to take her virginity. And because she called for help, he put his hood in her mouth, so that no one would hear her scream.

Consider, in comparison, the Old French pastourelle entitled "Quant voi la flor nouvele" (When I see a fresh flower), in which a thirteen-year-old shepherdess resists her attacker angrily:

Pris la par la main nue,
mis la seur l'erbe drue;
ele s'escrie et jure
que de mon geu n'a cure.
"ostez vostre lecheure,
dex la puist honir;
car tant m'est asprete et dure
ne la puis soufrir." . . .

(Bartsch, 2:67, 33–40)

I took her by her bare hand, put her on the green grass. She cried out and swore that she did not care for my game. "Leave your lechery. May God put it to shame, so harsh and rough is it that I cannot bear it."

After the rape in "When I see a fresh flower," the girl gets on her feet and cries out that she is thirteen years old (v. 53).

The Saint-Martin records reveal a poetic troping of rape reminiscent of that of the pastourelles. It is not surprising that clerks would draw on the pastourelle form, which both obeys and establishes the medieval conception of rape. By drawing on songs that poetically inscribe rape, the courtroom chroniclers take pleasure in the literariness of their own texts.

In the Cerisy church records, on the contrary, rape is minimized almost to the point that its violent character is dismissed through clinical and distant summary. In the secular Saint-Martin register, the texts work to make images of violence against women tolerable not by minimizing them but by troping them poetically. Here medieval law follows medieval literature, even so closely as to echo it, in the construction of discursive strategies that make linguistic paradigms of male violence against women acceptable to the learned legal audience and perhaps even pleasurable for the scribe.

* * *

The *Introduction* to this book has summarized the current theoretical debate on the ontological status of literary rape, considered by some pure fiction, a pure imaginative sign. Other critics have argued that it is related in some way, whether psychological, symbolic, or ideological, to the reality of sexual behaviors in society. Yet others view it as a reification of gender structures and power struggles. To what extent can the critic posit a direct connection between a literary figuring of the act, the way society invests the act with meaning, and the act itself?

The findings of this chapter cannot give a complete answer to such a vexed question, but they do answer it in part. My study of legal writing shows that figures of discourse "move": they travel from field to field, are re-couped, re-employed, and re-invested.[53] Linguistic paradigms first identified in fictional texts reappear in legal documents, reconverted but equally functional and bearing an equal affective charge. Poetry, song, story, all can offer men and women the words to circumscribe or describe and perhaps institutionalize experiences that are difficult to comprehend, whether painful or pleasurable. As he writes or speaks, a judge or notary can draw not only on models of legal language but also on other linguistic models, lyric or narrative. To this extent it is possible and even necessary to acknowledge that there is a direct relation between literary discourse and the world of deeds. Poetic figures, narrative paradigms, and literary topoi can all be reworked in another discursive sphere. When translated into a discursive domain such as the legal document or the courtroom session, they directly affect the way deeds are perceived, controlled, authorized, or penalized. Such linguistic fragments then function to change the past or shape the future. They become the tools of judgment and power.

Conclusion

The preceding chapters form a cultural archeology in which we can reposition the idealization of the feminine that emerges from French medieval courtly literature. When we contextualize the construction of the feminine in courtly love discourse among other contemporary discourses, their complicity in naturalizing what seems to have been the common practice of violence against women is revealed.

This book has attempted to dislodge two persistent myths about men, women, and sexual discourse in medieval France. The first is the notion that women enjoyed unparalleled sexual power and freedom in the days of courtly love. The second is the converse belief that rape was commonplace in the Middle Ages because society was so barbaric that men "did not know any better."

The first myth holds that courtly love literature reflects historical reality. Joan Kelly's landmark article "Did Women Have a Renaissance?" is an example of research inflected by this idealistic view of the Middle Ages as a time in which women enjoyed great sexual freedom: "Medieval courtly love, closely bound to the dominant values of feudalism and the church, allowed in a special way for the expression of sexual love by women."[1]

The myth of a medieval society virtually ruled by women who enjoyed sexual parity with men is almost as misleading as the myth of ignorant sexual barbarism. While Kelly's impressive accomplishments in her study, the findings concerning women in the Renaissance, remain as valid as they are precious to us, they are nevertheless grounded in a limited reading of medieval culture. Kelly cites literary texts almost exclusively. Furthermore, from the wide range of medieval literary genres, she metonymically takes two parts for the whole: courtly romance and troubadour lyric. Moreover, Kelly regards literature as reliably mimetic. Adultery, for example, is represented as tolerable; Kelly thus assumes that men tolerated it in women. By reading a wider variety of discourses, such as court records, we discover the striking medieval practice of punishing wives severely for adulterous practices that are widely tolerated among husbands. Furthermore, as the records of Cerisy showed, even female rape victims are fined and punished for their "involvement" in sexual assault.[2]

According to the second perception, the criminality of sexual violence was invisible to people in the Middle Ages. The modern notion of the *droit du seigneur*—a lord's right to deflower the bride of his peasant on their wedding night—typifies this myth of the acceptability of rape in medieval society. The texts studied in this book reveal that nothing could be further from the truth. Medieval discourse suggests that men were not only aware of the criminality of rape, they were also keenly conscious of its importance as a legal and social issue. As early as the tenth century, Hincmar of Reims cried out against the abusive practice and toleration of sexual violence.[3] The great jurists of the twelfth century struggled to redefine rape and focused on the heated issue of just punishment as well as the difficult question of compensating the victim.[4] In the thirteenth century, canonists were so attuned to the subtler forms of sexual abuse that they attempted to create laws against fraudulent seduction.[5]

It may be objected that the legal community, well-educated and trained to wrestle with ethical considerations, cannot be taken as an index of general societal attitudes. Does the literature of medieval France, created within and for a much broader audience, contradict these findings? On the contrary, it displays the same preoccupation with sexual violence as do legal texts. Medieval poets seem highly cognizant of the complexities of discussing sexual violence. Their representations of rape are neither simplistic, undifferentiated, nor thoughtless. Not only does medieval literature wrestle with the broad social implications of sexual violence, but it frequently formulates this cultural preoccupation in legal terms. *Le Roman de Renart* offers the clearest example of the interest of poets and audiences in the defining and treatment of rape.

As late as 1405, Christine de Pizan places rape law on the platform of her reform campaign in the *Book of the City of Ladies*. Christine wants to take the authors of courtly discourse at their word and to turn their talk of reverence, respect, and devotion into real social practice. Christine seizes upon the courtly doctrine of the importance of women and politicizes it. In one passage, Christine's baffled persona discusses myths about sexual violence with Lady Rectitude:

> "Si m'anuye et m'esgriesve de ce que hommes dient tant que femmes se veullent efforcier et qu'il ne leur desplait mie, quoyque elles escondissent

> de bouche, d'estre par hommes efforciees. . . ." Responce: "Ne doubtes pas, amie chiere, que ce n'est mie plaisir aux dames chastes et de belle vie estre efforciees, ains leur est douleur sur toutes autres. Et que ce soit vray, l'ont demonstré plusieurs d'elles par vray exemple, si comme de Lucresce. . . . Et a cause de cel oultraige fait a Lucresce, comme dient aucuns, vint la loy que homme mourroit pour prendre femme a force; laquelle loy est couvenable, juste, et sainte." (*Le Livre de la cité des dames*, 195, 195a)

> "I am therefore troubled and grieved when men argue that many women want to be raped and that it does not bother them at all to be raped by men even when they verbally protest. . . ." She answered, "Rest assured, dear friend, chaste ladies who live honestly take absolutely no pleasure in being raped. Indeed, rape is the greatest possible sorrow for them. Many upright women have demonstrated that this is true with their own credible examples, just like Lucretia. . . . Because of this outrage perpetrated on Lucretia, so some claim, a law was enacted whereby a man would be executed for raping a woman, a law which is fitting, just and holy."[6]

Christine's dialogue, which alludes to secular law in her day, suggests that even at the end of the Middle Ages, sexual violence continued to be viewed as a legal and political question. Rape remained an issue of considerable weight throughout medieval history.[7] Far from being blind to the criminality of sexual violence, French medieval writers spent a great deal of time imagining its representation and scrutinizing its moral and sexual contours.

* * *

Medieval texts disclose a keen awareness of the harm of rape, especially for feudal society as a whole. In point of fact, rape is a highly politicized issue in the European Middle Ages. While twentieth-century America is torn apart by the political issue of abortion, sexual violence does not figure in any modern campaign platform. How can we account for what appears to be a greater concern about rape in the Middle Ages? The answer may lie in a rather grim paradox. In a feudal society in which women were the virtual property of men, fathers (real and spiritual) and husbands debated with urgency the thorny questions tied to rape: proof, punishment, and reparation. It is possible to speculate with Sylvana Tomaselli that in the twentieth century, when women have begun to win a degree of political and social autonomy, when women are no longer the legal chattel of men, we are now left to our own devices in the face of everyday sexual violence.[8] Whether medieval texts can say anything that might empower women and men today, the readers of this book will decide for themselves.[9]

Notes

Introduction

1. For an overview of the debate over Richardson's *Clarissa*, see Sue Warrick Doederlein, "Clarissa in the Hands of the Critics," *Eighteenth Century Studies* 16 (Summer 1983):401–14. Key texts in the *Clarissa* dispute are the following: William Beatty Warner, "Reading Rape: Marxist-Feminist Figurations of the Literal," *Diacritics* 13 (Winter 1983): 28; Terry Eagleton, *The Rape of Clarissa: Writing, Sexuality, and Class Struggle in Samuel Richardson* (Minneapolis: University of Minnesota Press, 1982), 14; Nancy K. Miller, *The Heroine's Text: Readings in the French and English Novel, 1722–1782* (New York: Columbia University Press, 1980), xii, 95; Terry Castle, *Clarissa's Ciphers: Meaning and Disruption in Richardson's "Clarissa"* (Ithaca: Cornell University Press, 1982), 28, 116. For studies of sexual violence in Latin literature, see Patricia Kleindienst Joplin, "The Voice of the Shuttle Is Ours," *Stanford Literature Review* 1 1984: 25–53, and also Leo C. Curran, "Rape and Rape Victims in the *Metamorphoses*," *Arethusa* 11 (1978):213–41. On rape in Shakespeare see Catharine R. Stimpson, "Shakespeare and the Soil of Rape," in *The Woman's Part: Feminist Criticism of Shakespeare*, ed. Carolyn Ruth Smith Lenz, Gayle Greene, and Carol Thomas Neely (Urbana: University of Illinois Press, 1980), whose feminist analysis can be contrasted to that of Joel Fineman, "Shakespeare's *Will*: The Temporality of Rape," in *Representations* 20 (1987):25–76. Lynn Higgins and Brenda Silver have edited a collection of articles on literature of various periods, entitled *Rape and Representation* (Columbia University Press, forthcoming).

2. The complexity of meanings latent in depictions of rape, whether in the plastic arts, philosophy, science, or literature, is commented on by Sylvana Tomaselli in the Introduction to the volume she has edited with Roy Porter, *Rape: An Historical and Social Enquiry* (Oxford: Basil Blackwell, 1986), 2.

3. Annette Kolodny, "Dancing Through the Minefield: Some Observations on the Theory, Practice, and Politics of a Feminist Literary Criticism," in *The New Feminist Criticism: Essays on Women, Literature and Theory*, ed. Elaine Showalter (New York: Pantheon, 1985), 147.

4. Tomaselli gives this point a much broader application in her Introduction, noting that classical and premodern cultures discuss rape most openly and actively (Tomaselli and Porter, 2).

5. Tomaselli and Porter, 10.

6. Tillie Olsen, *Silences* (London: Virago, 1980), 239–40.

7. Hélène Cixous, "Le rire de la méduse," *L'Arc* 61 (1975):49; "The Laugh of the Medusa," trans. Suzanne Horer and Jeanne Socquet, in *New French Feminisms*, ed. Elaine Marks and Isabelle de Courtivron (New York: Schocken Books, 1981), 257.

8. In the following etymological study, I have drawn on several standard reference works: Frédéric Godefroy, *Dictionnaire de l'ancienne langue française* (Paris: 1889; rpt. New York: Kraus, 1961); Paul Robert, *Le Grand Robert de la langue française* (Paris: Le Robert, 1985); Adolf Tobler and Erhard Lommatzsch, *Altfranzösisches Wörterbuch* (Wiesbaden: Franz Steiner, 1954); and Walther von Wartburg, *Französisches Etymologisches Wörterbuch* (Basel: R. G. Zbinden, 1961). All English translations are mine unless otherwise indicated. Asterisks indicate reconstructions of terms from popular Latin.

9. Philippe de Beaumanoir, *Coutumes de Beauvaisis*, ed. A. Salmon (Paris: Picard, 1899), 30:7.

10. See Tobler-Lommatzsch, 3:1045–46.

11. Thirteenth-century text quoted in Tobler-Lommatzsch, 8:353.

12. Pierre Payer, *Sex and the Penitentials: The Development of a Sexual Code, 550–1150* (Toronto: University of Toronto Press, 1984), 117.

13. James Brundage, "Rape and Seduction in the Medieval Canon Law," in *Sexual Practices and the Medieval Church*, ed. Vern Bullough and James Brundage (Buffalo: Prometheus Books, 1982), 146. See also Brundage's invaluable discussion of rape in his *Law, Sex, and Christian Society in Medieval Europe* (Chicago: University of Chicago Press, 1987), 47–48, 209–10, 249–50.

14. Brundage 1982, 142.

15. Suzanne Fonay Wemple, *Women in Frankish Society: Marriage and the Cloister, 500 to 900* (Philadelphia: University of Pennsylvania Press, 1985), 33.

16. Georges Duby, *The Knight, the Lady and the Priest: The Making of Modern Marriage in Medieval France*, trans. Barbara Bray (New York: Pantheon, 1983), 40–43. Christian Gellinek has demonstrated that medieval German poetry, schematic and formulaic, should not be discounted as a source of information about the legal history of *Friedelehe* ("marriage by consent") before and after the twelfth-century canon law reforms. See Christian Gellinek, "Marriage by Consent in Literary Sources of Medieval Germany," *Studia Gratiana* 12 (1967):555–79.

17. Duby, 65.

18. Wemple, 41.

19. Wemple, 82.

20. Hincmar of Reims, *De coercendis raptu viduarum, puellarum et sanctimonialium*, C. 4, in *Patrologie Latina*, ed. J. P. Migne, 221 vols. (Paris: Garnier, 1844–64), 125:1019-20.

21. Duby, 32–33, 34.

22. *Decretum Magistri Gratiani*, in *Corpus Iuris Canonici*, ed. Emil Friedberg, 2 vols. (Leipzig, 1879–81; rpt. Graz, 1955): 1288–89.

23. Brundage 1982, 144.

24. On the difference between "minor excommunication," the penalty of exclusion from the sacraments, and major excommunication, complete social exclusion, see Elisabeth Vodola, *Excommunication in the Middle Ages* (Berkeley and Los Angeles: University of California Press, 1986), 36.

25. Pierre Lemercier, "Une curiosité judiciaire au moyen âge: la grâce par mariage subsequent," *Revue historique de droit français et etranger*, 4th ser., 33 (1955):464–74.

26. Brundage 1982, 148. Sue Sheridan Walker shows that ravishment pleas in medieval England are not "cloaks" for consensual matches, but rather for guardians securing wards: "a staged 'ravishment' would have involved an unnecessarily high price for a runaway love affair" ("Common Law Juries and Feudal Marriage Customs in Medieval England: The Pleas of Ravishment," *University of Illinois Law Review* 3 [1984]:711). Barbara Hanawalt also disputes the notion that medieval English women used the accusation of rape to marry the man of their choice: "We know far too little about medieval marriage practices to assume that this was common enough to influence criminal statistics" (*Crime and Conflict in English Communities 1300–1348* [Cambridge: Harvard University Press, 1979], 107–8 and n. 303). Hanawalt seems to contradict herself later in the same book, however: "The medieval rape cases show that some were victim-precipitated or at least accomplished with the victim's consent. Some rapes were ruses to enter into marriage. Other victims were merely seeking pleasure" (153). It is worth noting that subsequent critics cite the statement on p. 153 rather than the earlier one, even though Hanawalt gives no evidence to support the second statement.

Guido Ruggiero disputes the theory of victim-precipitated rape put forth by historians who argue that this option to marry the rapist was to the advantage of women, who may well have profited from it: "The easy conclusion in such cases would be that [the woman] used the accusation of rape to secure a husband. Actually, however, fornication prosecution resulted in marriage much more frequently than did rape. . . . For many women with limited dowry potential, rape, which robbed them of their virginity and tainted their sexual status in the eyes of their contemporaries, may have meant that their chances of marriage declined considerably. With great pressure to marry and limited possibilities, there may have been a certain dark logic in accepting the attacker as husband" (*The Boundaries of Eros: Sex Crime and Sexuality in Renaissance Venice* [Oxford: Oxford University Press, 1985], 98–99). Modern German historians also tend to present a sanguine picture of *Friedelehe*, a kind of common law or quasi marriage established by mutual consent, as a happy solution for women. See, for example, Wemple, 34.

27. Simon Kalifa, "Singularités matrimoniales chez les anciens Germains: le rapt et le droit de la femme à disposer d'elle-même" (*Revue historique de droit français et étranger* 4th ser., 48 (1970):199–225).

28. Duby, 38.

29. Kalifa, 221–24. For many years Georges Duby has made a very similar argument about the genuine objectives behind the medieval church's "enlightened" treatment of women. His most recent statement of this is found in *Mâle Moyen Age: De l'amour et autres essais* (Paris: Flammarion, 1988), *passim*. Historians of marriage in the sixteenth through the eighteenth centuries have come to similar conclusions about the history of the Church's involvement with marriage. See Jules Basdevant, *Les Rapports de l'église et de l'état dans la législation du mariage du Concile de Trente au Code Civil* (Paris: Société du Recueil général des lois et des arrêts et du Journal du Palais, 1900), as well as Ernest Bertin, *Les Mariages dans l'ancienne société française* (Paris, 1879; rpt. Geneva: Slatkine Reprints, 1975), and Gabriel Lepointe, *Droit romain et ancien droit français: Régimes matrimoniaux, libéralités, successions* (Paris:

Editions Montchrestien, 1958). I am grateful to Joan DeJean for making this point clear to me.

30. Duby 1983, 35.

31. Payer, 117.

32. Hanawalt, 4.

33. I borrow the words from Nancy K. Miller's work on the eighteenth-century novel in *The Heroine's Text: Readings in the French and English Novel, 1722–1782* (New York: Columbia University Press, 1980), ix.

34. Patricia Kleindienst Joplin's article on the cultural meanings of rape and female silence makes this point in a broader way: "Woolf's metaphor for muteness, the Manx cat, presses the ambiguities in Freud's and Milton's fictions which, like the myth of (the rape of) Philomela, conceal and reveal at once. For all posit an original moment in which an act of violence (the transgression of a boundary, the violation of a taboo) explains how difference became hierarchy, why women were forbidden to speak" ("The Voice of the Shuttle Is Ours," *Stanford Literature Review* 1 [1984]:29–30).

35. Joan W. Scott elucidates this point: "[Normative] concepts are expressed in religious, educational, scientific, legal, and political doctrines and typically take the form of a fixed binary opposition, categorically and unequivocally asserting the meaning of male and female, masculine and feminine. In fact, these normative statements depend on the refusal or repression of alternative possibilities, and, sometimes, overt contests about them take place. . . . The position that emerges as dominant, however, is stated as the only possible one. Subsequent history is written as if these normative positions were the product of social consensus rather than of conflict" ("Gender: A Useful Category of Historical Analysis," *American Historical Review* 91 [December 1986]:1067–68).

36. John F. Benton, "Clio and Venus: An Historical View of Medieval Love," in *The Meaning of Courtly Love*, ed. F. X. Newman (Albany: SUNY Press, 1968), 19–42; Georges Duby, "Les jeunes dans la société aristocratique dans la France du nord-ouest au douzième siècle," *Annales* 19 (1964), rpt. in *Hommes et structures du Moyen Age* (The Hague: Mouton, 1973).

37. See Renate Bridenthal and Claudia Koonz, eds., *Becoming Visible: Women in European History* (Boston: Houghton Mifflin, 1977); E. Jane Burns and Roberta L. Krueger, eds., *Courtly Ideology and Woman's Place in Medieval French Literature, Romance Notes*, 25:iii (1985), Penny Schine Gold, *The Lady and the Virgin: Image, Attitude and Experience in Twelfth-Century France* (Chicago: University of Chicago Press, 1985); Patricia H. Labalme, ed., *Beyond Their Sex: Learned Women of the European Past* (New York: New York University Press, 1980).

38. Georges Duby, "A propos de l'amour que l'on dit courtois," in *Mâle Moyen Age*, 74–82.

39. Scott, 1074.

40. For an excellent discussion of feminist theories as practiced by medieval scholars, see Sheila Fisher and Janet E. Halley, *Seeking the Woman in Late Medieval and Renaissance Writings: Essays in Feminist Contextual Criticism* (Knoxville: University of Tennessee Press, 1989): 1–17.

41. Cixous writes, "What happiness for us who are omitted, brushed aside from

the scene of inheritances; we inspire ourselves and we expire without running out of breath, we are everywhere!" Trans. Horer and Socquet, in Marks and de Courtivron, 248.

42. Hrotsvitha's little-known *oeuvre* has been edited most recently by Helen Homeyer, *Hrotsvithae Opera: Mit Einleitungen und Kommentar* (Munich: Schöningh, 1970).

43. Two well-known examples of this work are Elaine Showalter, *A Literature of Their Own* (Princeton: Princeton University Press, 1977), and Sandra Gilbert and Susan Gubar, *The Madwoman in the Attic: The Woman Writer and the Nineteenth-Century Literary Imagination* (New Haven: Yale University Press, 1979).

44. Kolodny, 148.

45. The Latin text is published in Elizabeth A. Francis, *Wace: La Vie de Sainte Marguerite* (Paris: Champion, 1932).

46. Francis, 1932. See also Phyllis Johnson and Brigitte Cazelles, *Le Vain siècle guerpir: A Literary Approach to Sainthood through Old French Hagiography of the Twelfth Century* (Chapel Hill: North Carolina Studies in the Romance Languages and Literatures, 1979).

47. This idea was formulated by Judith Fetterley, *The Resisting Reader: A Feminist Approach to American Fiction* (Bloomington: Indiana University Press, 1978).

48. One of the critics best known for disseminating this interpretation was Denis de Rougemont, *L'Amour et l'occident* (Paris: Plon, 1939).

49. Helen Hazen, *Endless Rapture: Rape, Romance and the Female Imagination* (New York: Charles Scribner's Sons, 1983).

50. Janice Radway, *Reading the Romance: Women, Patriarchy, and Popular Literature* (Chapel Hill: University of North Carolina Press, 1984).

51. Leslie Rabine, *Reading the Romantic Heroine: Text, History, Ideology* (Ann Arbor: University of Michigan Press, 1985).

52. Associated with the critical legal studies movement is Ronald Dworkin, "Law as Interpretation," in *The Politics of Interpretation*, ed. W.J.T. Mitchell (Chicago: University of Chicago Press, 1983), 249–70. Stanley Fish is a key proponent among literary theorists: "Interpretation and the Pluralist Vision," *Texas Law Review* 60 (1982): 495; "Fish vs. Fiss," *Stanford Law Review* 36 (1984):1325; "Pragmatism and Literary Theory: Consequences," *Critical Inquiry* 11 (1985):433.

53. For general overviews of the new field of legal interpretation and literary theory, see James Boyd White, *Heracles' Bow: Essays on the Rhetoric and Poetics of the Law* (Madison: University of Wisconsin, 1985), especially chapter 5, "Reading Law and Reading Literature: Law as Language," and also Richard A. Posner, *Law and Literature: A Misunderstood Relation* (Cambridge: Harvard University Press, 1988), especially chapter 5, "The Interpretation of Statutes and the Constitution." On the increasing trend toward the interdisciplinary in all fields of the humanities and social sciences, see Clifford Geertz, "Blurred Genres: The Refiguration of Social Thought," *American Scholar* 49 (October 1980):165–79.

54. Jacques Derrida, *Marges de la philosophie* (Paris: Editions de Minuit, 1972). See also his "Structure, Sign and Play in the Discourse of the Human Sciences," in *The Structuralist Controversy*, ed. Richard Macksey and Eugene Donato, 1972: 247–65.

55. Michel Foucault, *Archéologie du savoir* (Paris: Gallimard, 1969).

56. Posner, 7–8; John A. Alford and Dennis P. Seniff, *Literature and Law in the Middle Ages: A Bibliography of Scholarship* (New York: Garland Publishing, 1984); R. Howard Bloch, *Medieval French Literature and Law* (Berkeley and Los Angeles: University of California Press, 1977).

57. Posner, 9.

58. Béroul's twelfth-century *Roman de Tristan* pays careful attention to the controversies surrounding adultery laws in its day. See Pierre Jonin, "Le Procès d'Iseut," in *Les Personnages feminins dans les romans français de "Tristan" au XIIe siècle* (Aix-en-Provence: Publication des annales de la Faculté des lettres, 1958), 59–108.

59. An early and rough sketch of the ideas in Chapter 4 was published in Kathryn Gravdal, "Camouflaging Rape: The Rhetoric of Sexual Violence in the Medieval Pastourelle," *Romanic Review* 76 (1985):361–73.

60. Norman N. Holland, *The Dynamics of Literary Response* (New York: Oxford University Press, 1968).

61. As Sheila Fisher and Janet E. Halley note, "feminist criticism of male-authored texts need not rest with alerting us to the mythologizing of women in patriarchy. Feminist readings of these texts can also explore implications about women's power, perceived or actual, that these writings attempt to submerge" (*Seeking the Woman in Late Medieval and Renaissance Writings*, 5).

62. Joplin shows that in Ovid's myth of Philomela and Tereus, "the political anxieties that fuel the myth are transformed into erotic conflicts" (33).

63. Hazen, *passim*. In an analogous twist of logic, the structuralist or "mechanistic" view of rape as narrative motor in *Clarissa* tends to generate literal-minded judgments of Clarissa as a woman who wants to have sex but is too prudish to acknowledge her desire. Dorothy Van Ghent pours her scorn on this insufferable tease and declares that, in being raped, "Clarissa keeps her cake while eating it" (cited in Sue W. Doederlein, "Clarissa in the Hands of the Critics," *Eighteenth Century Studies* 16 [Summer 1983]:411–12).

64. Molly Haskell, "The 2,000-Year Old Misunderstanding—'Rape Fantasy'," *MS* 5 (November 1976):84–86, 92, 94, 96, 98.

65. Radway makes a similar suggestion about the function of attempted rapes in modern popular romance (216).

66. Posner, 9.

67. Posner, 210.

68. White, 95.

69. Susan Estrich, *Real Rape* (Cambridge: Harvard University Press, 1987). See also Catherine MacKinnon, "Feminism, Marxism, Method and the State: Toward Feminist Jurisprudence," *Signs* 8 (1983):635–58, and Camille E. LeGrand, "Rape and Rape Laws: Sexism in Society and the Law," *California Law Review* 61 (1973): 919–41.

70. Natalie Zemon Davis, *Fiction in the Archives: Pardon Tales and Their Tellers in Sixteenth-Century France* (Stanford: Stanford University Press, 1987), 105.

71. Guido Ruggiero, *The Boundaries of Eros: Sex Crime and Sexuality in Renaissance Venice* (Oxford: Oxford University Press, 1985). See also his *Violence in Early Renaissance* (New Brunswick: Rutgers University Press, 1980). For English law see

John Marshall Carter, *Rape in Medieval England: An Historical and Sociological Study* (Lanham, Md.: University Press of America, 1985).

72. M. G. Dupont, *Le Registre de l'Officialité de Cerisy 1314–1457*, in *Mémoires de la Societé des antiquaires de Normandie*, 3rd ser., 10 (1880):271–662.

73. L. Tanon, *Registre criminel de Saint-Martin-des-Champs*, in *Histoire des Justices des Anciennes Englises et Communautés Monastiques de Paris* (Paris: Larose et Forcel, 1883).

74. It is ironic that Susan Estrich reaches the same conclusion in studying twentieth-century America, which, she argues, views "male aggressiveness as desirable and forced sex as an expression of love" (100).

Chapter 1

1. It is not possible to go through the steps involved in these complex developments here, but I send readers to Rosemary Radford Ruether, especially "Misogynism and Virginal Feminism in the Fathers of the Church," in her *Religion and Sexism: Images of Woman in the Jewish and Christian Traditions* (New York: Simon and Schuster, 1974), 150–83. In the same volume, see also Eleanor Commo McLaughlin, "Equality of Souls, Inequality of Sexes: Woman in Medieval Theology," 213–66. For an excellent discussion of the exclusion of medieval women from Church life see Suzanne Fonay Wemple, *Women in Frankish Society: Marriage and the Cloister, 500 to 900* (Philadelphia: University of Pennsylvania Press, 1981), 127–48.

2. Paul wrote: "For I would that all men were even as I myself. . . . But if they cannot contain, let them marry: for it is better to marry than to burn" (1 Cor. 7:7,9). This canonical statement stands almost diametrically opposed to the attitude of the Hebrew Bible in Genesis: "So God created man in his own image, in the image of God created he him; male and female created he them. And God blessed them, and God said unto them, Be fruitful and multiply" (Gen. 1:27–28a). It is worth noting that Paul's first letter to the Corinthians is a master example of the transformation of difference into subordination: "But I would have you know, that the head of every man is Christ; and the head of the woman is the man; and the head of Christ is God. . . . For the man is not of the woman; but the woman of the man. Neither was the man created for the woman; but the woman for the man" (1 Cor. 2:3, 8–9).

3. Wemple, 189.

4. Wemple, 188; Ruether, 165.

5. Joan Kelly, "Did Women Have a Renaissance?" in her *Women, History, and Theory* (Chicago: University of Chicago Press, 1984), 19–50.

6. Jane Tibbetts Schulenberg, "Female Sanctity: Public and Private Roles, ca. 500–1100," in *Women and Power in the Middle Ages*, ed. Mary Erler and Maryanne Kowaleski (Athens and London: University of Georgia Press, 1988), 102–25. "Saints' lives, in their edifying intention, are rich in fantasy and contradiction. Until approximately the past two decades, scholars have generally discredited the historical value of the vitae of saints. With the growing interest in social history and the history of mentalities, however, scholars are beginning to take a serious second look at hagiography" (Schulenberg, 103). The classic work on the *vita* as literary form is Hippolyte Delehaye, *Les Passions des martyrs et les Genres littéraires* (Brussels, 1921).

7. André Vauchez, *La Sainteté en Occident aux derniers siècles du moyen âge*

(Rome: Bibliothèque des Ecoles françaises d'Athènes et de Rome, 1981). See especially "Typologie de la sainteté médiévale," 243–448.

8. McLaughlin, 213–66.

9. McLaughlin, 216–21.

10. Saints' lives are found in J. Bollandus and G. Henschenius, *Acta sanctorum: Editio novissima*, ed. J. Carnandet et al. (Paris: Palmé, 1863). Saint Lucia is threatened with rape and prostitution by the consul, Pascasius. When God protects Lucia from rape, Pascasius has her thrown in boiling oil until she dies. Saint Daria is delivered to a house of prostitution, where a lion protects her. When a man is sent to rape Daria, the lion prevents him. Daria achieves martyrdom when she is stoned to death. The legend of Saint Anastasia includes the story of the attempted rape of her three servants, Agape, Chionea, and Irene. The prefect of Rome tries to possess them, but a spell is cast over him and he fails. Euphemia twice undergoes an attempted rape, first by Priscus, the Roman judge, who fails and then sends all the young libertines of the city to perpetrate a collective rape. Instead, they convert. Euphemia is next hung by the hair, then imprisoned, attacked by wild beasts, and finally stabbed to death. On the symbolic link between hanging and rape, see Eva Cantarella, "Dangling Virgins: Myth, Ritual and the Place of Women in Ancient Greece," *Poetics Today* 6 (1985):91–101.

11. Agatha provokes the desire of Quintianus, who tries to force her to become his mistress. When he fails, he delivers the virgin to a prostitute, who promises to corrupt the virgin, with violence if necessary, but does not succeed. Quintianus has Agatha imprisoned and tortured, pulling off her breasts. Her death is surrounded by miracles. In the story of Agnes, the powerful Roman Simphronius falls in love with the virgin but cannot persuade her to marry him. The young man's father tortures Agnes, even sends her to a brothel and tries to have her stripped and raped, all to no avail. Agnes finally achieves martyrdom.

12. Crisart is a young man who refuses to renounce Christ; Solimius has him locked up with five beautiful young girls ordered to seduce him. With God's help, he remains a virgin and later achieves martyrdom. The Roman Aquilinus asks the 15-year-old Eugenia to marry him. But she has read Saint Paul and escapes to a male monastery where she becomes Brother Eugene. A matron, Melanie, tries to seduce Brother Eugene; unsuccessful, she falsely accuses the brother of attempted rape. This *vita* offers an inversion of the paradigm and becomes a cautionary tale against women who cry rape. In the *vita* of Justine, the saint inflames Cyprian with burning love. He resorts to magic in order to possess her. But even the devil is helpless in his attempts to rape her. Justine is eventually decapitated. The story of Saint Theodora is an exception to most patterns: the chaste wife actually yields to the blandishments of a witch and commits adultery with her seducer. She then spends the rest of her life in a monastery, living as Brother Theodore.

13. In the legend of Saint Margaret, the prefect of Antioch, Olimbrius, falls in love at first sight of her. He captures, tortures, and imprisons her, but cannot persuade her to marry him. The devil himself joins in tempting her, and tries to have her raped, but without success. She finally dies joyfully. Saint Petronille escapes Flaccus, who wants to marry her, by dying. The story of the eleven thousand vir-

gins tells how the chief of the Huns tries to marry Saint Ursula. When she refuses, he kills her.

14. The parents of Alexis contract a marriage for him, but the young Christian escapes on the night of his wedding to save his virginity. He goes on to live in abject poverty until he dies in total humility, following the example of Christ. *La Vie de Saint Alexis*, ed. Christopher Storey (Geneva: Droz, and Paris: Minard, 1968).

15. Sandro Sticca, "Sin and Salvation: The Dramatic Context of Hrotswitha's Women," in *The Roles and Images of Women in the Middle Ages and Renaissance*, ed. Douglas Radcliff-Ulmstead (Pittsburgh: University of Pittsburgh Publications on the Middle Ages and Renaissance, 1975), 3–18. On the topos of Christ's temptation, see pp. 11–12.

16. Ruether, 167–68. See, for example, Jerome: "Let the secret retreat of your bedchamber ever guard you. Ever let the Bridegroom hold converse with you within. When you pray, you are speaking with your Spouse. When you read, he is talking to you, and when sleep comes upon you, He will come behind the wall and He will put His hand through the opening and will touch your body. You will arise, trembling, and will say: *I languish with love*" (*Epistola* 23 ["Ad Eustochium"], in *The Letters of St. Jerome*, trans. Charles C. Mierow [London: Newman Press, 1963], 158).

17. Medieval women writers seized with ingenuity upon the devotional and visionary genres for the exploration of female sexuality and autoeroticism. Hadewijch of Brabant, for example, an early thirteenth-century mystic, describes an experience that certainly resembles an orgasm in a Eucharistic vision in which Christ comes to her: "With that he came in the form and clothing of a Man, as he was on the day when he gave us his Body for the first time, looking like a Human Being and a Man, wonderful, and beautiful, and with glorious face, he came to me as humbly as anyone who wholly belongs to another. . . . He came himself to me, took me entirely in his arms, and pressed me to him; and all my members felt his in full felicity, in accordance with the desire of my heart and my humanity. So I was outwardly satisfied and fully transported" (*Hadewijch: The Complete Works*, trans. Mother Columba Hart [New York: Paulist Press, 1980], 49). On eroticism in the writing of female mystics, see *Medieval Women's Visionary Literature*, ed. Elizabeth A. Petroff (Oxford: Oxford University Press, 1986), 13–18.

18. Ruether, 157–58, 167. The violent diatribes of the Church fathers on the wicked seductiveness of women are well documented. In his famous letter to Eustochium, Jerome writes: "There are women who makes themselves conspicuous in public by their walk and draw a throng of young men after them by furtive winks. . . . Let them have but a little purple in their dress and a head loosely bound, so that the hair may fall, tawdry sandals, and over their shoulders a fluttering little cloak, tight sleeves clinging to their arms, and a loose-kneed manner of walking: this is all such a person's virginity amounts to" (Mierow, 145–46). For a wider range of examples, see R. Howard Bloch, "Medieval Misogyny: Woman as Riot," *Representations* 20 (1987):1–15.

19. On this point I draw on the research of Magdalena Elizabeth Carrasco, "An Early Illustrated Manuscript of the Passion of Saint Agatha (Paris, Bibl. Nat., MS

lat. 5594)," *Gesta* 24 (1985):19–32. I am grateful to Cynthia Hahn for bringing this information to my attention.

20. Wemple, 179–87.

21. Wemple, 187–88.

22. Mary Marguerite Butler, *Hrotsvitha: The Theatricality of Her Plays* (New York: Philosophical Library, 1960), 52. Anne Lyon Haight, *Hroswitha of Gandersheim: Her Life, Times, and Works, and a Comprehensive Bibliography* (New York: The Hroswitha Club, 1965), 9.

23. Ferruccio Bertini, *Il "Teatro" di Rosvita: Con un saggio di traduzione e di interpretazione del "Callimaco"* (Genoa: Tilgher, 1979), 9.

24. All citations are from Helen Homeyer, *Hrotsvithae Opera: Mit Einleitungen und Kommentar* (Munich: Schöningh, 1970). Homeyer's edition is based on the Saint Emmeran manuscript in Regensburg (Bayerische Staatsbibliothek, clm 14485). English translations of passages from the *legenda* are from Sister M. Gonsalva Wiegand, *The Non-Dramatic Works of Hrosvitha*, Ph.D. dissertation, Saint Louis University, 1936. See also the older edition of Karl Strecker, *Hrotsvithae Opera* (Leipzig: Teubner, 1930).

25. Homeyer, 233. As Peter Dronke has pointed out, Hrotsvitha also draws a bold parallel between herself and John the Baptist, *ego vox clamantis* (*Women Writers of the Middle Ages* [Cambridge: Cambridge University Press, 1984], 55–83).

26. Dronke, 70; Katharina Wilson, *Hrotsvit of Gandersheim: The Ethics of Authorial Stance* (Leiden: Brill, 1988), 146.

27. Wilson, 145–51; Dronke, 65–77.

28. Joseph von Aschbach, "Roswitha und Conrad Celtes," *Kaiserlichen Academie der Wissenschraften, Sitzungsberichte* 56 (Vienna, 1867), cited in A. Daniel Frankforter, "Sexism and the Search for the Thematic Structure of the Plays of Hrotsvitha of Gandersheim," *International Journal of Women's Studies* 2 (1979):223. It is only fair to add that such hoaxes actually did occur in early modern French literature and were uncovered in the nineteenth century. I am grateful to Joan DeJean for making this point clear to me.

29. Dronke, 55; Wilson, vii.

30. Wilson, 72–86.

31. Kolodny, 148.

32. Frankforter, 225.

33. My analysis of the plays of Hrotsvitha owes an important debt to Sue-Ellen Case, "Rev-Viewing Hrotsvit," *Theater Journal* 35 (December 1983):533–42, an article that confirmed my early intuitions about this corpus. Case brings modern feminist theory, and especially the work of Luce Irigaray, to bear on Hrotsvitha's theater, in order to highlight its protofeminist agenda.

34. As Luce Irigaray writes of the exchange of women's bodies, "what if these 'commodities' refused to go to 'market'?" ("Commodities Among Themselves," in *This Sex Which Is Not One*, trans. Catherine Porter [Ithaca: Cornell University Press, 1985], 196).

35. Frankforter, 226.

36. Ruether, 156–63.

37. Ruether, 163–65.

38. Case observes, "The most striking difference between the plays of Hrotsvit and those of Terence, is that in her plays women are at the center of the action and it is their response to male aggression which determines the development of the plot. Hrotsvit places her heroines in the context of objectification, use and violence, but offers them an alternative" (536).

39. In the epic history of Gandersheim, commonly referred to as the *Primordia*, verses 315–60 relate the story of Gerberga II, a noblewoman destined to become an abbess of the convent. Engaged to Bernard against her will, Gerberga will not break her vow of virginity. In a dramatic confrontation, Bernard swears by his sword and by Gerberga's neck that when he returns from battle he will ravish her. But the strength of Gerberga's faith prevails: Bernard immediately dies in the battlefield (Homeyer, 462–63).

40. In the version of the Agnes legend codified by Jacobus de Voragine, the famous thirteenth-century hagiographer, Hrotsvitha's articulate heroine is a little girl, walking home from school. Voragine composed the medieval *Legenda aurea sanctorum*. The thirteenth-century Italian author's "Golden Legend" was a Latin compilation of 186 *récits* of saints' lives, moments in the life of Christ and Mary, and explanations of feast days (Jacques de Voragine, *La Légende dorée*, 2 vols., trans. J.-B.M. Roze [Paris: Garnier-Flammarion, 1967], 1:140).

41. Wilson, 16–27. Conversely, as Wilson points out, "The paradigmatic quality of heroism introduced in the legends is thus transferred from male to female and vice versa in the dramas. What characterizes male heroism, Hrosvitha seems to suggest, is what characterizes female heroism as well" (26).

42. Dronke, 56–57.

43. John Boswell, *Christianity, Social Tolerance, and Homosexuality* (Chicago: University of Chicago Press, 1980), 200.

44. Sticca, 9.

45. "Drusiana asks Christ to help her to die, so she may escape her dilemma. Christ complies with her wish immediately. Women have the power to petition and to succeed" (Case, 537).

46. The English translations of the plays are from Larissa Bonfante, *The Plays of Hrotswitha of Gandersheim* (New York: New York University Press, 1979). See also the first modern English translation by Christopher St. John (male pseudonym of Christabel Marshall), *The Plays of Roswitha* (London: Chatto & Windus, 1923; rpt., New York: Benjamin Blom, 1966).

47. "Hrotsvit has dramatized the essence of the passive victim and of the objectification of patriarchal desire. Unlike Terence, who ultimately resolves it as natural, she has staged it as perverse" (Case, 537).

48. Case, 537.

49. This expression, "to mix the playful with the serious," refers to the "Christian style" or the medieval practice of combining jest and earnest in serious genres, as opposed to the "classical style," in which the comic and the sublime registers are strictly segregated according to genre. See Ernst Curtius, "Jest and Earnest in Medieval Literature" (and especially part 4, "Jest in Hagiography"), in *European Literature and the Latin Middle Ages*, trans. Willard Trask (Princeton: Princeton University Press, 1953), 417–35.

50. Voragine's version of this episode is somewhat drier: "Elles étaient chrétiennes et refusaient obstinément d'obéir aux avis du préfet de Rome; celui-ci les fit enfermer dans une chambre où l'on serrait les ustensiles de cuisine. Or ce préfet, qui brûlait d'amour pour elles, les alla trouver afin d'assouvir sa passion. Il fut alors frappé de folie, et croyant s'en prendre aux vierges, il embrassait les casseroles, les pot-au-feu, les chaudrons et autres ustensiles de cuisine. Quand il fut rassasié, il en sortit tout noir, sale et les vêtements en lambeaux" (Roze, 74).

51. "The women watch Dulcitius and giggle. . . . the women dominate the rapist. The male dramatic perspective has been reversed" (Case, 537).

52. Patricia K. Joplin makes a similar observation about classical myth, "as Ovid has it, the chaste woman's body is fatally seductive," and about Shakespeare, "The chaste woman [Lucrece] is a tease even in her sleep" ("The Voice of the Shuttle Is Ours," *Stanford Literature Review* 1 [Spring 1984]:33).

53. Elizabeth A. Francis published the Latin text in her edition of Wace, *La Vie de Sainte Marguerite* (Paris: Champion, 1932). See page xxxi of her Introduction.

54. The aestheticization of the violence of rape appears even more clearly in Voragine's version of the life of Saint Margaret, a more succinct rendition than Wace's. Furthermore, Voragine interpolates a direct commentary discounting the version used by Wace. The thirteenth-century Voragine reports the mysterious devoration scene only to deny that the symbolic rape or swallowing ever took place: "Et ecce draco imamissimus . . . apparuit qui dem eam devoratur . . . signum cruas edidit et ille evanuit. De ut alibi legitur os super caput eius ponens et linguam super calcaneum por rigens eam promnus deglutivit. Sed dum eam absorbere vellet signo crucis se munivit. Et ideo draco virtute cruas crepuit et virgo illesa exivit. Istud autem qui dicitur de draconis devoracom et ipsius crepacone apocrifum et frivolum reputamia." (Behold a terrifying dragon appeared to her who was about to devour her. [She] . . . made the sign of the cross, and the monster disappeared. Elsewhere we read that he put his mouth on her head and his tongue on her heel and swallowed her quickly. But while he wanted to swallow her she armed herself with the sign of the cross, which made the dragon tremble, and the virgin came out. But that which is said about the dragon who devoured her is held to be apocryphal and of little worth. [English translation mine.])

55. Can we recognize in the Latin version a curious analogy with historical practice? Wemple notes that in early medieval history many victims of sexual violence blamed their rapes on devils or demons, in an effort to avoid the shame of going to court or the trauma of accusing a man (41).

56. Schulenberg, 104; Wemple, 127–48; Vauchez, 315–18.

57. Wace, *La Vie de Sainte Marguerite*. All English translations are mine.

58. "Dulcitius wants [the three sisters] because of their beauty, but the guards tell him they will resist seduction. He responds 'Then I shall woo in another fashion—with torture!' The latent relationship in such a patriarchal society between desire and dominance becomes literal" (Case, 536).

59. Phyllis Johnson and Brigitte Cazelles, *Le vain siècle guerpir: A Literary Approach to Sainthood through Old French Hagiography of the Twelfth Century* (Chapel Hill: North Carolina Studies in Romance Languages and Literatures, 1979), 136.

60. Johnson and Cazelles, 136.

61. I am grateful to Laurie Postlewate for making this point clear to me. It is important to note the ease with which twelfth-century romance incorporates the topos of *raptus* followed by forced prostitution in a brothel. It appears in Chrétien de Troyes's *Yvain ou le Chevalier au lion*, in the story of Harpin the giant, and also in Hue de Rotelande's *Ipomédon*, in the episode of the evil pagan knight Leonin. See Roberta L. Krueger, "Misogyny, Manipulation, and the Female Reader in Hue de Rotelande's *Ipomédon*," in *Courtly Literature: Culture and Context*, ed. Keith Busby and Erik Kooper (Amsterdam: Benjamins, 1990), 390.

Chapter 2

1. Paraphrased from Gallen Books's "tipsheet" for contemporary romance writers, cited in Janice Radway, *Reading the Romance: Women, Patriarchy and Popular Literature* (Chapel Hill: University of North Carolina Press, 1984).

2. I.D.O. Arnold and M. M. Pelan, *La Partie arthurienne du Roman de Brut* (Paris: Klincksieck, 1962), vv. 2735–3058. All English translations are mine. See also the earlier edition: Wace, *Le Roman de Brut*, ed. Ivor Arnold (Paris: SATF, 1940), vv. 11288–608. Wace is drawing on Geoffrey de Monmouth's *Historia Regum Britanniae*, ed. E. Faral, *La Légende arthurienne: Etudes et documents*, vol. 3 (Paris: SATF, 1929), Book 10, Parts 3 and 4. Geoffrey's version was more understated than Wace's: "Iste est sceleratissimus ille, qui nuper neptim ducis Hoeli,—pro nefas,—puellam pulcherrimam meque cum illa simul advexit et cum illa concumbere temptans, pondere magnitudinis suae illam oppressit atque morti addixit et hic tumulatam reliquit" (Book 10, 54–58 [Faral, 241]).

3. A recent exception is Antoinette Saly, "La Demoiselle 'Esforciée' dans le roman arthurien," in D. Buschinger and A. Crépin, eds., *Amour, Mariage et Transgressions au Moyen Age* (Göppingen: Kümmerle Verlag, 1984), 215, 216.

4. Janice Radway, in her book on popular twentieth-century romance, demonstrates that "the 'ravishment' of a woman by a man who really loves her is a testimony to her desirability and worth rather than to his power" (216). Such modern feminist studies enable us to recognize the specificity of medieval romance, which uses rape with greater complexity, not in that one simple way.

5. The important link between beauty and ravishment has also been documented by D.D.R. Owen, "Theme and Variations: Sexual Aggression in Chrétien de Troyes," *Forum for Modern Language Studies* 21 (1985):378. For an extensive catalogue of rape scenes in a variety of Old French genres, see Dietmar Rieger's article, "Le Motif du viol dans la littérature de la France médiévale: Entre norme courtoise et réalité courtoise," *Cahiers de civilisation médiévale* 31 (July–September 1988): 241–67.

6. Here and throughout this chapter I have drawn on the psychoanalytic approach elaborated by Norman H. Holland, *The Dynamics of Literary Response* (New York: Oxford University Press, 1968).

7. For a useful discussion of romance diction in medieval French romance, see Nancy Freeman Regalado, "Des Contraires Choses: la fonction poétique de la citation et des exempla dans le *Roman de la Rose*," in *Littérature* 41 (February 1981):62–81, especially 75.

8. Holland studies rape scenes in twentieth-century films such as *The Virgin*

Spring, Through a Glass Darkly, and *L'Année dernière à Marienbad*, to show how the (male) viewer's erotic pleasure is justified either by ponderous moral content or by the challenge of an intellectual and aesthetic problem (165–68): "That preliminary visual pleasure in form combines with a less acceptable source of visual pleasure in content: peeping at some very erotic scenes. The combination of these pleasures from form and from content unbalance and override our usual inhibitions. At the same time, these films displace moral and social inhibition into aesthetic and intellectual demands for 'meaning,' something that intellectuals (at least) find much easier to resolve, and the puzzling quality so provides yet a third source of pleasure" (168). Although Holland is discussing "texts" in another medium and another period, these principles seem highly applicable to medieval literature.

9. Ovid's well-known *Metamorphoses* offer the example of another text built upon the representation of sexual violence. The Latin text depicts the rape or attempted rape of Daphne, Europa, Syrinx, Coronis, Herse, Perimele, Caenis, Arethusa, Philomela, Orithyia, Thetis, Dryope, Chione, Galatea, Pomona, Io, Persephone, and Callisto, among others. During and after each rape, the narrator systematically focuses on the victim's pain, horror, humiliation, and grief. Ovid highlights the cruelty of sexual violation, showing the part of violence and degradation as clearly as the erotic element. Rape is not mystified or romanticized, but presented as a malevolent and criminal action. Chrétien's characteristic strategy is quite the opposite: the medieval author systematically shifts focus away from the literal representation of the female experience of violence, toward the moral, erotic, and symbolic meanings rape holds for male characters. For a useful overview, see Leo Curran, "Rape and Rape Victims in the *Metamorphoses*," *Arethusa* 2 (1978): 213–41. It should be noted, however, that Ovid treats rape in quite different ways in his *Amores* and *Ars amatoria*.

10. Holland, 102.

11. For a study of embedded ambiguities in Chrétien, see Roberta L. Krueger, "Love, Honor, and the Exchange of Women in *Yvain*: Some Remarks on the Female Reader," *Romance Notes* 25 (Spring 1985):302–17.

12. Chrétien de Troyes, *Le Chevalier au Lion*, ed. Mario Roques (Paris: Champion, 1975); *Le Chevalier de la Charrette*, ed. M. Roques (Paris: Champion, 1975); *Cligès*, ed. Alexandre Micha (Paris: Champion, 1975); *Erec et Enide*, ed. M. Roques (Paris: Champion, 1973); *Le Conte du Graal*, ed. Félix Lecoy (Paris: Champion, 1975). All English translations are mine. Examples are grouped neither by romance nor in chronological order, but rather in terms of their various representations of sexual violence.

13. Saly, 220.

14. Entangled with the comic elements, Chrétien embeds the legal codification of rape evidence: the woman fought back, she tried as hard as she could to get away, she resisted—such are the proofs required of the prosecutrix in medieval rape trials. See Danielle Buschinger, "Le Viol dans la littérature allemande au moyen âge," in *Amour, mariage et transgressions au moyen âge*, ed. Danielle Buschinger and André Crépin (Göppingen: Kümmerle Verlag, 1984), 369–88.

15. Owen, 383.

16. This same use of the hero's remorse over an attack is observed by Radway in twentieth-century American and British romance (133).

17. Owen, 385.

18. It is at this moment that Chrétien "signs" his romance. Verse 5233, "Eleinne reçeüe a Troie" (Helen greeted at Troy), is more than an allusion to the Trojan War. "Eleinne" was the rape victim who was avenged by Arthur in Geoffroy de Monmouth's prototypical Arthurian legend. "Troie" is Chrétien's reference to himself. The line can then be read: "the story of Helen reworked by Chrétien de Troyes."

19. The fictional series of abductions and interrupted marriages in *Cligès* is not utterly preposterous, but finds an echo in medieval English history, in the obscure story of the marriages of Joan Plantagenet. See Karl Wentersdorf, "The Clandestine Marriages of the Fair Maid of Kent," *Journal of Medieval History* 5 (1979):203–31.

20. Owen, 378.

21. Owen, 385.

22. The erasure of actual rapes in Chrétien is analogous though not identical to what Janice Radway calls the "promise of patriarchy" in twentieth-century romance: in the popular modern genre, rape is a real, not false threat, but the hero always succeeds in protecting the heroine (133).

23. Radway points to ways, analogous to those of medieval romance, in which rape is "papered over" by the rules of the genre in modern romance (71).

24. For an insightful overview of the conflicting critical interpretations of this challenging text, see Matilda Tomaryn Bruckner, "*Le Chevalier de la Charrete (Lancelot)*," in *The Romances of Chrétien de Troyes: A Symposium*, ed. Douglas Kelly (Lexington: French Forum, 1985), 132–81; and also "An Interpreter's Dilemma: Why Are There So Many Interpretations of Chrétien's *Chevalier de la Charrette*?" *Romance Philology* 40 (1986):159–80.

25. For a reading of the Lovesome Damsel episode as a *mise en abîme* of the relationship between Lancelot and Guenevere as well as that of Chrétien and Marie de Champagne, see Roberta L. Krueger, "Desire, Meaning, and the Female Reader: The Problem in Chrétien's *Charrete*," in *The Passing of Arthur: New Essays in Arthurian Tradition*, ed. Christopher Baswell and William Sharpe (New York: Garland Publishing, 1988), 31–51, especially 39–40.

26. Owen, 379.

27. Norman Holland's chapter "Meaning as Defense" can be applied to Chrétien's work with great profit, especially pp. 182–85. "We take in the fantasy which is an 'hallucinatory gratification.' In literature as in life, such a fantasy will typically both give pleasure and provoke anxiety. To the extent it gives pleasure, we simply get pleasure from it. To the extent it provokes anxiety, it must be modified to reduce the anxiety. Form and meaning are the two agents that control and manage the fantasy, and they in turn may be sources of pleasure in themselves" (181–82).

28. Chrétien de Troyes, *Philomena: Conte raconté d'après Ovide*, ed. C. de Boer (1909; rpt. Geneva: Slatkine Reprints, 1974), vv. 219–33, p. 39. Critics have disputed whether the "Chrétien" who signs *Philomena* is one and the same as Chrétien de Troyes. See Franciscus Zaman, *L'Attribution de Philomena à Chrétien de Troyes* (Amsterdam, 1928). Chrétien also translated Ovid's *Ars amatoria*, as the medieval

poet states in the opening verses of *Cligès*: "Cil qui fist d'Erec et d'Enide, / Et les comandemanz d'Ovide / Et l'art d'amors an romans mist" (*Cligès*, vv. 1–3). Chrétien and Ovid appear to share a fascination with sexual violence, a central issue in much of Ovid's work. See, for example, Leslie Cahoon's cogent analysis of Ovid's interest in rape in his *Amores*: "Raping the Rose: Jean de Meun's Reading of Ovid's *Amores*," *Classical and Modern Literature* 6 (1986):261–85.

29. Ovid, *Metamorphoses*, trans. Frank Justus Miller, 2 vols. (Cambridge: Harvard University Press, 1984), 328–29.

30. Leslie Rabine observed a similar interplay of anxiety and desire in the reader of nineteenth-century romantic literature, in *Reading the Romantic Heroine: Text, History, Ideology* (Ann Arbor: University of Michigan Press, 1985), 180.

31. Radway's study of the modern "supermarket" genre shows that romance deals with the consequences of male aggression without challenging the hierarchy of control on which it is based (216).

32. New compositional tendencies appear in the prolific corpus of thirteenth-century Old French romance. Lengthy romance cycles, extensions of the stories of Arthur and the knights of the Round Table or rewritings of Chrétien's materials, proliferate. Parenthetically we can note that in the first *Continuation du Perceval*, Gauvain, the paradigmatic knight of twelfth-century Arthurian romance, becomes a rapist. In a violent replay of Chrétien's *Perceval*, Gauvain discovers a beautiful virgin asleep in a tent alone and deflowers her (William Roach, ed., *The Continuation of the Old French "Perceval" of Chrétien de Troyes*, vol. 2: *The First Continuation, Redaction of Mss E M Q U*. [Philadelphia: University of Pennsylvania Press, 1950], vv. 13,843–52, 32,191–94).

33. Roberta L. Krueger, "Misogyny, Manipulation, and the Female Reader in Hue de Rotelande's *Ipomédon*," in *Courtly Literature: Culture and Context*, ed. Keith Busby and Erik Kooper (Amsterdam: Benjamins, 1990), 383–97.

34. Krueger, 394.

35. In John Fleming's assessment, "the problem of interpreting the *Roman* begins rather than ends with the unveiling of the surface allegory. The rose quest is a sexual metaphor, slightly less blatant with Guillaume de Lorris than with Jean de Meun but always obvious" (*The Roman de la Rose: A Study in Allegory and Iconography* [Princeton: Princeton University Press, 1969], 6). For Fleming's argument that Jean de Meun's text is parody, see especially 205–6.

36. Guillaume de Lorris and Jean de Meun, *Le Roman de la Rose*, ed. Félix Lecoy, 3 vols. (Paris: Champion, 1975).

37. Leslie Cahoon, "Raping the Rose: Jean de Meun's Reading of Ovid's *Amores*," *Classical and Modern Literature* 6 (1986):261–85.

38. Krueger, 394.

39. "The idea here exemplified [in the concluding lines of the poem], by means of iconographic principles which have little to do with literary realism of whatever social class, is *lechery*. Amant thinks like a lecher, talks like a lecher, and acts like a lecher" (Fleming, 241).

40. According to Cahoon, "The image of the besieged 'fores' [in Ovid's *Amores*] corresponds exactly to and is quite possibly the source of Jean de Meun's besieged Rose, whose castle walls the lover finally breaks down in order to pluck her. Both

the plucking and the breaking in suggest rape rather than seduction" (271). Cahoon further states, "Jean's ironic juxtaposition of the witty narrator's joking military imagery with the cruel reality of sexual violence (for which, see the whole section from line 21,583 to 21,742, where military, architectural, and religious imagery meet in a triumphant tour de force) is a brilliant variation on and imitation of Ovid's achievement" (273).

41. Georges Duby, "*Le Roman de la rose*," in *Mâle Moyen Age*, 83–117. Duby's contention that Jean de Meun is not antifeminist seems curiously contradictory, however, when it leads Duby to complain about that tiresome *mijaurée*, Christine de Pizan, who failed to understand the great fraternal nature of Jean de Meun (117).

Chapter 3

1. References are to Mario Roques's edition (Paris: Champion, 1950–63). Later branches were edited by Ernst Martin, *Le Roman de Renart* (Strasbourg: K. J. Trubner, 1882). A new bilingual edition of certain branches has been translated by Micheline de Combarieu du Grès and Jean Subrenat (Paris: 10/18, 1981). The first twelve branches are dated between 1175 and 1205; the terminus ad quem for the others is fixed as 1250. The later branches contain several allusions to "les amours de Renart et de Hersent": Martin, XI, 1396–1400; Martin, XIII, 1056–9; Martin, XVII, 976–81. All English translations of *Le Roman de Renart* are mine.

2. Philippe de Navarre, for example, remarks on the importance of legal training for members of the feudal elite in *Le Livre de Phillippe de Navarre*, in *Recueil des historiens des croisades* (Paris: Académie des Inscriptions et Belles-Lettres, 1841–1906), Loi 1, 17:569. See also J.S.C. Riley-Smith, *The Feudal Nobility and the Kingdom of Jerusalem, 1174–1277* (London: Macmillan, 1973), 133. I am grateful to James Brundage for familiarizing me with these texts.

3. Richard Posner, *Law and Literature: A Misunderstood Relationship* (Cambridge: Harvard University Press, 1988), argues that in most texts on the subject of law, the legal matter is peripheral to the meaning of the text because "great literature deals with the permanent and general aspects of human nature and institutions" (15). Posner implies that a faithful and detailed representation of law would render a "great book" tedious and local. He concludes that "law as depicted in literature is often just a metaphor for something else that is the primary concern of author and reader" (15).

4. James Boyd White, *Heracles' Bow: Essays on the Rhetoric and Poetics of the Law* (Madison: University of Wisconsin Press, 1985), offers Arnoldian readings of great works of literature that take law as their subject and proposes that they be placed in law school curricula in order to make better lawyers.

5. Robert Weisberg, "The Law-Literature Enterprise," *Yale Journal of Law and the Humanities* 1 (December 1988):3. I am grateful to Daniel Alter for this reference.

6. R. Howard Bloch, *Medieval French Literature and Law* (Berkeley and Los Angeles: University of California Press, 1977). This chapter owes an important debt to the thesis Bloch presents in his Introduction.

7. Bloch, 3.

8. The earliest sources of information on feudal law date from the thirteenth century: *Le Très ancien Coutumier de Normandie*, ed. Adolphe F. L. Tardif (Rouen:

Lestrignant, 1896), part written c. 1199–1200 and another part c. 1220; *Le Grand Coutumier de Normandie*, ed. A.F.L. Tardif (Rouen: Lestrignant, 1896), c. 1230–40; *La Très ancienne Coutume de Bretagne*, ed. Marcel Planiol (Rennes: Plihon & Hervé, 1896), probably written between 1312 and 1325; *Le Livre de Jostice et de Pletz*, ed. P. N. Rapetti (Paris: Firmin Didot, 1850), the customary of Orléans, dated 1254–60. Philippe de Beaumanoir, *Les Coutumes de Beauvaisis*, ed. A. Salmon (Paris: Picard, 1899), perhaps the richest source of information on secular law, was drafted c. 1283. *Les Etablissements de Saint Louis*, ed. P. Viollet (Paris: Renouard, 1881), is a private customary relating practices in Orléans, Touraine, and Anjou, dated November 1272–June 1273. For an overview of secular law at this time, see A. Esmein, *Histoire de la procédure criminelle en France* (Paris: Larose et Forcel, 1882) and also his *Cours d'histoire du droit français* (Paris: Sirey, 1907). For the peculiarities of Normandy, see J. Le Foyer, *Exposé de droit pénal normand au treizième siècle* (Paris: Sirey, 1931).

9. Yvonne Bongert, *Recherches sur les cours laïques du Xe au XIIIe siècle* (Paris: A & J Picard, 1949). A similar study, specifically comparing feudal law to *Le Roman de Renart*, is Jean Graven's *Le Procès criminel du Roman de Renart: etude du droit criminel féodal au XIIe siècle* (Geneva: Librairie de l'Université, 1950). See also Guido Van Dievoet, "Le *Roman de Renart* et *Van Den Vos Reynaerde*, témoins fidèles de la procédure penale aux XIIe et XIIIe siècles?" in *Aspects of the Medieval Animal Epic*, ed. E. Rombauts and A. Welkenhuysen (The Hague: Martinus Nijhoff, 1975), 43–52.

10. On procedure and proof in feudal law see also John W. Baldwin, "The Intellectual Preparation for the Canon of 1215 against Ordeals," *Speculum* 36 (1961): 613–36; Paul Hyams, "Trial by Ordeal: The Key to Proof in Early Common Law," in *On the Laws and Customs of England*, ed. Morris Arnold et al. (Chapel Hill: University of North Carolina Press, 1981), 90–126; Richard M. Fraher, "Preventing Crime in the High Middle Ages: The Medieval Lawyers' Search for Deterrence," in *Popes, Teachers, and Canon Law in the Middle Ages*, ed. James Sweeney and Stanley Chodorow (Ithaca: Cornell University Press, 1988), 212–33.

11. I am grateful to James Brundage for making this point clear to me. For a more detailed discussion, see H.L.A. Hart, *The Concept of Law* (Oxford: Clarendon Press, 1961), 181–207.

12. Nivardus, *Ysengrimus*, ed. Ernst Voigt (Halle, 1884).

13. Lenard Willems's *Etude sur l'Ysengrinus* (Ghent: E. Van Goethem, 1895) remains one of the few studies of this work with a great deal of useful information on the text's sources.

14. Jill Mann, *Ysengrimus: Text with Translation, Commentary and Introduction* (Leiden: E. J. Brill, 1987), 460–61. Mann's volume is a welcome and invaluable contribution to impoverished *Ysengrimus* studies. I am also grateful to Kathy Hardison for her comments and for sharing her translation of Nivardus with me.

15. Léopold Sudre, *Les Sources du Roman de Renart* (Paris: Bouillon, 1893), 21. There is in fact one passing reference to the rape (missed by Sudre) in *Liber* 1:51–52. Sudre's excellent and still useful chapter on the rape episode ("Renart Adultère," 141–58) demonstrates the way in which the French authors of the *Renart* drastically transform a folk tale by investing it with their own cultural preoccupations. Sudre

notes that we recognize a version even more archaic than Nivard's in the *Romulus* or *Fables* of Marie de France. See Marie de France, *Fables*, ed. Harriet Spiegel (Toronto: University of Toronto Press, 1987), 184–85.

16. It is commonly supposed that Pierre de Saint-Cloud was a priest or church official. Doubtless he was a cleric, educated within the Church. See Robert Bossuat, *Le Roman de Renard* (Paris: Hatier, 1967).

17. Gustave Cohen, *La Vie littéraire en France au moyen-âge* (Paris: Tallandier, 1949), 131.

18. Béroul, *Le Roman de Tristan*, ed. Ernest Muret (Paris: Champion, 1974).

19. I have drawn throughout on E. Jane Burns's informative discussion of law and literature in Béroul's *Roman de Tristan*, "How Lovers Lie Together," *Tristania* 8 (Spring 1983):17, 36. On the important and perhaps unexpected parallels between Renart and the character of Tristan, see Nancy F. Regalado, "Tristan and Renart: Two Tricksters," *Esprit Créateur* 16 (1976):30–38.

20. Two critics who have studied the sexual violence in *Renart* are Dietmar Rieger, "Le Motif du viol dans la littérature de la France médiévale: entre norme courtoise et réalité courtoise," *Cahiers de Civilisation médiévale* 31 (July–September 1988):263–65, and Kenneth Varty, "Le Viol dans l'*Ysengrimus*, les branches II–Va, et la branche I du *Roman de Renart*," in *Amour, mariage et transgressions au moyen âge*, ed. Danielle Buschinger and André Crépin (Göppingen: Kümmerle Verlag, 1984), 411–18. Rieger, 263, and Varty, 413, underline the discursive *déplacement* from rape to adultery and its misogynist connotations.

21. Georges Duby, *The Knight, the Lady, and the Priest: The Making of Modern Marriage in Medieval France*, trans. Barbara Bray (New York: Pantheon Books, 1983), 220.

22. Unknowingly reiterating Hersent's strategy following the adultery, Renart himself reintroduces the legal context by mockingly offering to swear that he did nothing dishonest to Hersent: "et por moi et por lui desfandre, / tot par la ou le vodrez prandre, / un sairement vos aramis / au los de voz meillors amis" (VIIa, 5993–96) (To defend my honor and hers, I will take an oath, anywhere you choose, before your closest friends).

23. On the *curia regis* see Bongert, 62–67, 137–48, and Bloch, 129, 136, 138, 231. Rape or *raptus* is classed among the most serious crimes against peace and is judged in royal or high courts (Bongert, 124–26).

24. The council of peers is described in Bongert, 66, 270; and Graven, 21.

25. For a discussion of similar strategies in modern literature, see Weisberg, 35; and Barbara Johnson, "Melville's Fist: The Execution of *Billy Budd*," in *The Critical Difference* (Baltimore: Johns Hopkins University Press, 1981), 79–109.

26. Duby, 221. Studying medieval England, John Marshall Carter shows that royal justice discriminated against rape victims: "However, this same royal justice which helped to maintain order in times of crisis was a great factor in the lessening of women's status in the thirteenth century. Royal justices from distant counties or towns were less concerned about the feelings of an individual female in a county they might not visit again, than they were about law and order, generally, and revenue, specifically. It was much easier to fine a woman for not appearing at an eyre court than it was to pursue the case further" (*Rape in Medieval England: An*

Historical and Sociological Study [Lanham, Md.: University Press of America, 1985], 128–29). Of course, in the fiction of the *Renart*, Hersent is well known to the king since she is the wife of his constable.

27. For examples of the influence of canon on feudal law, see Bloch, 9, 231; and Bongert, 37–38, 181, 201. Readers who seek a thorough survey of these exchanges should consult Harold J. Berman, *Law and Revolution: The Formation of the Western Legal Tradition* (Cambridge: Harvard University Press, 1983), and James A. Brundage, *Law, Sex, and Christian Society in Medieval Europe* (Chicago: University of Chicago Press, 1987).

28. Brundage 1987, 253.

29. On the heaviness of penalties for theft, *La Très ancienne Coutume de Bretagne*, for example, stipulates "que il ait emblé plus de cinq soulz, ou la value, il doit estre jugié a mort par coustume" (Article 117). For further examples, see Chapter 5 and also Graven, 43–44.

30. On the status of the *lex talionis* in the Middle Ages, see Graven, 35–42, and Bloch, 68.

31. James A. Brundage, "Rape and Marriage in the Medieval Canon Law," *Revue de droit canonique* 28 (June–December 1978):62–75. *La Très ancienne Coutume de Bretagne*, c. 1312–1325, states: "Et si aucun forceit famme, pour ce que elle ne fust putain, et il eust sa compaignie par force et oultre sa volonté comme il apparust, ou il la raveist par force, celui qui ce feroit en devroit estre puni comme d'autres crimes. . . . Et auxi ne le devroit justice soustenir contre nulle famme mariée que il ne desut estre puni sans remede" (Article 155).

32. For more general bibliography on Gratian, see Brundage 1978 and 1987, and also my Introduction.

33. Bongert, 103–7; Graven, 53–58; and Bloch, 50, 134–37, describe this aspect of the judge's function. *La Très ancienne Coutume de Bretagne* waxes poetic on the judge's duty to be extremely prudent in sentencing: "Ainczois doit être toute justice plus esmue d'absoudre que de condamner, car homme et femme sont trop forz a nourrir, et ils sont tantôt détruits; et homme vaut plus, pour tant ce qu'il soit bon, de cent et de mille livres. . . . [La cause] doit être plus claire que nulle autre et plus claire qu'étoile au ciel, dont homme est condamné a mort."

34. John Flinn, *Le Roman de Renart* (Paris: Presses Universitaires Françaises, 1963), 35–157. For an argument against reading the *Renart* as satire, see my "1175: Fables and Parodies," in *A New History of French Literature*, ed. Denis Hollier (Cambridge: Harvard University Press, 1989), 46–50. Hans Robert Jauss described the *Roman de Renart* as parody in his *Untersuchungen zur Mittelalterlichen Tierdichtung* (Tübingen: Max Niemeyer, 1959). See also Danielle Buschinger and André Crépin, *Comique, satire et parodie dans la tradition renardienne et les fabliaux* (Göppinger Arbeiten zur Germanistik, no. 391; Actes du Colloque des 15 et 16 Janvier, 1983 [Göppingen: Kümmerle Verlag, 1983]).

35. The difficulty of finding lords willing to act as judges is documented in Bongert, 57–61, and Bloch, 65. See also Georges Duby, *La Société aux XIe et XIIe siècles dans la région mâconnaise* (Paris: Armand-Colin, 1953), 202.

36. "La scène de discussion est traitée avec un réalisme et une attention aux détails qui trahissent une grande connaissance en même temps qu'*un profond respect*

de la part de Pierre de Saint-Cloud pour la procédure de son temps, et sa satire des jugements de Dieu se révèle par conséquent comme *un sincère désir de perfectionner un système auquel il est très attaché.* Les preuves *de son admiration et de son respect* pour les principes fondamentaux et pour les formes de la justice abondent dans la branche II-Va" (Flinn, 39–40 [emphasis added]). Flinn consistently declares that Pierre's descriptions of feudal justice are respectful while his descriptions of the nobility are severely critical. Without justification, however, this seems an arbitrary reading of similar comic techniques. The representation of the king's court can be interpreted as subversive and as disrespectful as the representation of feudal artistocracy.

37. Regalado 1976. See also my *Vilain and Courtois: Transgressive Parody in French Literature of the 12th and 13th Centuries* (Lincoln: University of Nebraska Press, 1989), 81–112.

38. For her persuasive argument on the value of overt misogyny for the female audience of medieval literature, see Roberta L. Krueger, "Misogyny, Manipulation, and the Female Reader in Hue de Rotelande's *Ipomédon*," in *Courtly Literature: Culture and Context*, ed. Keith Busby and Erik Kooper (Amsterdam: Benjamins, 1990).

39. For a general introduction to this branch, see Flinn, 57–58, and also Lucien Foulet, *Le Roman de Renard* (Paris: Champion, 1914), 323–54.

40. Pierre J. Payer, *Sex and the Penitentials* (Toronto: University of Toronto Press, 1984), 117.

41. Varty (1984) and Rieger (1988) were, to my knowledge, the first to point this out.

42. Hincmar de Reims, *De divortio Lotharii regis et Tetbergae reginae*, C. 6, in *Patrologia Latinae*, ed. J. P. Migne (Paris: Garnier, 1844–64), 125:619–77; trans. cited in Burns, 27 n. 2. See also Robert Bartlett, *Trial by Fire and Water: The Medieval Judicial Ordeal* (Oxford: Oxford University Press, 1986), *passim*; F. Carl Riedel, *Crime and Punishment in the Old French Romances* (New York: AMS Press, 1966), 36, 77; and especially Bongert, 216, 223–25, and Graven, 28–29.

43. Cited in Burns, 27 n. 2. For further commentary and descriptions of the trial by glowing iron, see Brundage 1987, 224; Bongert, 216, 221–25; Graven, 28–29; and Riedel, 36.

44. Bongert describes such changes of heart (218).

45. As early as the eleventh century, Ivo of Chartres expressed grave reservations about this type of proof. See Brundage 1987, 224; and Bongert, 218, as well as Baldwin 1961 and Hyams 1981. In 1215, the Latern Council officially prohibited ordeals.

46. Burns, 19–20. Iseut's oath is found in Béroul, ll. 4197–4216. On the rules of the *serment purgatoire*, see Bongert, 205–10; and Graven, 28.

47. Bongert, 188–90, and Graven, 25–27, document the practice of summoning the accused three times. The same rule continued to be observed in the thirteenth and fourteenth centuries, as the legal records studied in Chapter 5 will show.

48. On the nature and history of the *judicium dei*, see Bloch, 18–19, 21–22, 48–49, 63–64; Bongert, 211, 228–52; and Graven, 29–30.

49. It is also possible to speculate that changing attitudes toward women parallel the degeneration of the feudal law system.

Chapter 4

1. Ernst Robert Curtius, *European Literature and the Latin Middle Ages*, trans. Willard Trask (Princeton: Princeton University Press, 1953), 190–93.

2. Pierre Bec defines the genre as "une composition lyrico-narrative, voire dramatique, qui repose sur trois structures poétiques en circulation qui ne sont pas exclusives du genre en tant que tel: 1) la RENCONTRE amoureuse; 2) le DEBAT amoureux; 3) la PLAINTE amoureuse (lyrique). . . . A cela il faut ajouter une certaine atmosphère agreste et bucolique (la scène a lieu en plein air, au printemps, dans un décor champêtre et apaisant) et une certaine tonalité plaisante et moqueuse qui relati-vise, et dédramatise, le heurt psychologique des deux personnages" in *La Lyrique française du moyen âge (XIIe–XIIIe siècle): contribution à une typologie des genres poétiques médiévaux* (Paris: Picard, 1977–78), 120. Paul Zumthor's definition of the genre is structuralist: "un chant narratif de Rencontre, caractérisé par la dénomination de l'objet, PASTOURE, ou TOUSE, ou leurs diminutifs, rarement un autre terme de même sens, ou un prenom à connotation paysanne, selon le registre de la bonne vie. Le sujet JE est en général référé au term CHEVALIER" (*Essai de poétique médiévale* [Paris: Seuil, 1972], 302).

3. The Provençal corpus consists of approximately thirty texts. See Jean Audiau, *La Pastourelle dans la poésie occitane du moyen-âge* (Paris: De Boccard, 1923). The Old French corpus, dating from the thirteenth century only, contains approximately 160 songs. Jean-Claude Rivière has recently reedited them in *Pastourelles*, 3 vols. (Geneva: Droz, 1974–76). Throughout this chapter citations refer to the standard edition by Karl Bartsch, *Romances et pastourelles françaises des XIIe et XIIIe siècles* (Darmstadt: Wissenschaftliche Buchgesellschaft, 1870; rpt. 1967). I have also consulted William D. Paden's edition and translation of medieval pastourelles in several languages, *The Medieval Pastourelle*, 2 vols. (New York: Garland, 1987).

4. According to my count, rape or attempted rape is represented in Bartsch 2:1, 4, 6, 17, 28, 32, 34, 62, 67, 69, 76, 79; 3:5, 6, 9, 12, 28, 42, 48, 49; Rivière, *Chansonnier de Montpellier*, 84, 85, 86, 88, and *Chansonnier* LC 115, of which the sole text represents a rape. In "Rape in the Pastourelle," *Romanic Review* 80 (May 1989):331–49, William D. Paden presents a different set of figures. The discrepancy is in itself meaningful: the songs are sufficiently ambiguous that one cannot always tell but must surmise whether or not a rape was depicted. Thus Paden counts 18 percent "Rape" and 7 percent "Can't Tell." The latter figure seems at least as important as the former: it cannot be an accident that a category of texts exists in which it is difficult (or impossible) to decide whether a rape occurs. Paden also lowers the total percentage of rapes by including pastourelles of all languages, bringing the number to 13 percent. To do so is to erase a key question: why are the texts of northern France more devoted to the representation of rape than those of any other country or language?

5. W.T.H. Jackson, "The Medieval Pastourelle as a Satirical Genre," *Philological Quarterly* 31 (April 1952):156.

6. Gaston Paris, *Mélanges de littérature française du moyen âge*, ed. Mario Roques (Paris: Champion, 1912), 566. Other, more recent, interpretations of the pastourelle are equally blind to the implications of rape. Michel Zink, in his study *La Pastourelle* (Paris: Bordas, 1972), neatly justifies the sexual violence by arguing that the shep-

herdess is in actual fact the *femme sauvage*, which, for Zink, explains the knight's unbridled sexual aggression. Joel Blanchard, in *La Pastorale en France aux XIVe et XVe siècles. Recherches sur les structures de l'imaginaire médiéval* (Paris: Champion, 1983), describes the later genre, called the *pastorale*, as "le lieu d'une tension où s'exprime un pur vouloir-être. Une mimesis de l'Eros se dessine et se prépare, décrivant une courbe asymptotique qui conduit les bergers vers *l'accomplissment d'un plaisir fou*" (22–23; emphasis added).

7. Joan W. Scott, "Gender: A Useful Category of Historical Analysis," *American Historical Review* 91 (December 1986):1069.

8. The English translation of André is by John Jay Parry, *Andreas Capellanus: The Art of Courtly Love* (New York: Columbia University Press, 1941), 150. Drouart La Vache, *Li Livres d'Amours*, ed. Robert Bossuat (Paris: Champion, 1926), 130. The figure of the expert who advises lovers to use force when all other methods of seduction fail may have been a topos in Old French poetry of this period. It recurs in the thirteenth-century *La Poissance d'amours*, in which the "Maistres," instructing his young protégé in the art of love, teaches him that women are so well-bred that they must be taken by force because they are too ashamed to make their desires known: "Car saciés que femme es si noble et si gentius que trop aroit grant honte de dire a son ami: 'Faites de mi vo volenté'; et pour l'abomination que ses cuers aroit de ce dire, doit hom se compaignie conquerre aussi con par force; car, saciés, puis que femme aime, toutes amistés li plaisent." (Be aware that women are so noble and so well-bred that they would be too ashamed to say to their friend: "Do with me as you will." And to spare her the shame that her heart would experience in saying this, a man should conquer her companionship by force.) The master goes on to explain that only one woman in five hundred does not want to dishonor her body: "poir coi vous soiiés tout a vo pais et tout a seür" (and that is why you should do this with peace of mind and confidence) (*La Poissance d'amours dello Pseudo-Richard de Fournival*, ed. Gian B. Speroni [Florence: La Nuova Italia, 1975], 68–69). I am grateful to Sylvia Huot for this reference.

9. Jackson, 156–70.

10. Scott, 1073.

11. Medieval theoreticians do not mention social class in their definitions of the genre. In *Las Leys Damors*, Guillaume Molinier gives the following definition: "La pastourelle est un ouvrage qui peut avoir six, ou huit, ou dix couplets, ou plus, c'est-à-dire autant qu'il plaît à l'auteur, pourvu qu'il ne passe pas le nombre de trente. On doit y traiter de raillerie pour se réjouir. . . . Car un homme et une femme peuvent jouer et se railler l'un l'autre, sans rien dire ni rien faire de grossier ni de deshonnête." The verse translation of the same definition makes no mention of social class (346–47).

12. Scott, 1074.

13. Paden, "Rape in the Pastourelle," 344. In an earlier conference paper, Paden argued with admirable candor that revisionist interpretations must be countered lest they cause his professional stock to drop: "I feel I have an investment in the pastourelle, and that the culture of readers of medieval poetry has an investment in the genre, too, and I fear that if the pastourelle turns out to be a celebration of rape, this investment will take a nosedive." William D. Paden, "Rape and Genre in the

Pastourelle." Paper presented at Lexington, Kentucky, April 1987. Author's typescript, p. 3. (This passage was eliminated from Paden's *Romanic Review* article.) This critical *jouissance* and this "investment" deserve further investigation.

14. "[Gravdal] admits a copious ambiguity . . . an ambiguity between fact and fiction, between history and imagination" (Paden, "Rape in the Pastourelle," 344). That copious ambiguity, which I do admit freely, stems from my view of ideology as a structure, as Althusser described it: every member of that structure, whether literature, law, politics, economics, the family, religion, the plastic arts, or social practices, including the practice of sexual violence, is related to every other member (Louis Althusser et al., *Reading Capital*, trans. Ben Brewster [London: New Left Books, 1970], 186–89).

15. Paden 1989, 23–24.

16. Sigmund Freud, *Jokes and Their Relation to the Unconscious*, trans. James Strachey (New York: Norton, 1963), 97–101.

17. Freud, "Creative Writers and Daydreaming," in *The Freud Reader* ed. Peter Gay (New York: W. W. Norton, 1989), 443.

18. In Norman Holland's view, "To summarize, form can only be understood as managing fantasy content. Form in the larger sense of structure or sequence manages content by controlling what we are aware of at any given moment. . . . Form in the smaller sense of particular rhythms, rhymes, and sounds manages content in more detailed ways" (*The Dynamics of Literary Response* [New York: Oxford University Press, 1968], 157), Holland discusses the psychoanalytic meanings of rape scenes in literature, primarily in modern texts, such as A. R. Gurney, Jr.'s play, *The Rape of Bunny Stuntz* (69–70), but also in medieval literature (43) and particularly in Chaucer's Wife of Bath's tale (12–25). Holland's work consistently posits a male subject (reader, dreamer, writer). The advantage of this male-centered theory is that it matches medieval literature quite perfectly: it excludes the female as subject, relegating her to the object position. To the obvious objection that medieval audiences were doubtless mixed, I would reply that for female listeners the rape scenes may well have constituted not a *wish-fulfillment* fantasy, but rather an anxiety fantasy. In contemplating fictional constructions of sexual violence, women could enjoy allaying their fears about sexual violence and rehearse what the analyst calls "anxiety mastery."

19. "In effect, the literary work dreams a dream for us. It embodies and evokes in us a central fantasy; then it manages and controls that fantasy by devices that, were they in a mind, we would call defenses, but, being on the page, we call form" (Holland, 75).

20. Here and throughout I draw on the work of Holland despite the fact that his book does not discuss the medieval pastourelle. "Thus, form in the narrower sense of rhythm and rhyme and sound matches form in the larger sense of structure. Both serve to manage the fantasy content of the lines" (142).

21. Other examples can be found in Bartsch 2:8, 13, 17, 20, 21, 37, 38, 62, 67, 76; 3:3, 6, 48.

22. Paden 1989, 12, 21.

23. The shepherdess remains faithful in Bartsch 2:27, 43, 45, 50, 56, 61, 63, 64, 71; 3:1, 13, 25, 40, 42, 43, 48, 50, 52; Rivière 3:77, 78, 81, 87, 93.

24. The shepherdess yields to verbal seduction in Bartsch 2:31, 34, 35, 38, 40, 51, 69, 79; 3:19, 41, 45, 49; Rivière, 3:84.

25. The knight attempts to bribe the shepherdess with gifts in twenty-six of the Old French texts; the shepherdess accepts them in more than half of the pastourelles.

26. The knight promises marriage in three texts: Bartsch 2:19; 3:1 and 35.

27. Voltaire, *Romans et Contes* (Paris: Garnier-Flammarion, 1966), 185.

28. In the Provençal corpus, only one pastourelle stages a rape. For the poets and public of the Midi, rape is, obviously, not at the heart of the genre. In light of that fact, it is worth noting that the Provençal corpus includes a parody of the genre, "Porquiera" (Audiau, poem no. 24) and that in that parody no rape occurs. The inversion and distortion focus on the ideals of feminine physical beauty rather than on sexual violence (Audiau 1923, 128–32).

29. Holland extends his thesis that "Form manages content" (142) to music ("Music is entirely the management of fantasy" [159]); and his observations can be applied to the medieval pastourelle, which is, above all, a musical song (Holland, 150–59).

30. Guillaume Molinier, *Las Leys Damors*, in *Monuments de la littérature romane*, ed. Adolphe Gatien-Arnoult (Toulouse: J.-B. Paya, 1841), 347. See also Zink 1972, chap. 2, "Le rôle de la musique," 17–24, and Bec, 1977–78.

31. Holland describes the ways in which "purely" formal devices "serve to modify defensively the unconscious content of the poem" (131–32). We can with profit juxtapose Holland's insights to the findings of Eglal Doss-Quinby, who demonstrated that the use of the refrain is greater, more developed, and more varied in the pastourelle than in other lyric forms of medieval poetry (*Les Refrains chez les trouvères du XIIe siècle au début du XIVe* [New York: Peter Lang, 1984], 85–86, 108–10, 232–35, 245, 276). This elaborate, formal use of the musical refrain cannot be unrelated to the fact that of all the forms Doss-Quinby examines, the pastourelle ("le gene par excellence qui s'actualise sous forme de chansons avec des refrains" [109]) is the only genre that regularly represents rape.

32. Joan Ferrante makes this key point: "Yet the peasant actually speaks in too polished a way and with too much knowledge of courtly traditions and literature to be anything but a figure for the courtly lady; and the courtly lady, when finally allowed to speak for herself, is more than a match for her would-be lover" ("Male Fantasy and Female Reality in Courtly Literature," *Women's Studies* 11 [1984]:70). I would add that the courtly lady, when finally allowed to speak for herself, is raped.

33. The eloquence and wit of the courtly lady are attributed to the shepherdess character in Bartsch 2:55, 57, 61, 65, 66, 71, 72, 97; 3:1, 8, 13, 19, 20, 45, 50.

34. Zink, "Etat de la question," 42–52.

35. See the Introduction on the ambiguous figure of the *domna* in courtly love literature.

36. Part 3 of Bartsch's edition, "Pastourellen von namhaften Dichtern," contains texts authored and signed by a king (4), a duke (9), and two counts (1 and 3).

37. Brundage, "Rape and Seduction in the Medieval Canon Law," in *Sexual Practices and the Medieval Church*, ed. Vern Bullough and James Brundage (Buffalo: Prometheus, 1982), 146–47.

38. Susan Estrich, *Real Rape* (Cambridge: Harvard University Press, 1987), 69.
39. Brundage 1982, 143.
40. *Decretum Gratiani*, Case 36, question 1, *Corpus iuris canonici*, ed. E. Friedberg (Leipzig, 1879–81).
41. Brundage 1982, 147.
42. Hostiensis, *Lectura* X, 5.16.2 (1581 edition, folio 52rb).

Chapter 5

1. See the Introduction for an overview of rape law in medieval France.
2. James A. Brundage, *Law, Sex, and Christian Society in Medieval Europe* (Chicago: University of Chicago Press, 1987), 250. See also Brundage's "Rape and Marriage in the Medieval Canon Law," *Revue de droit canonique* 28 (June–December 1978):62–75, and his "Rape and Seduction in the Medieval Canon Law," in *Sexual Practices and the Medieval Church*, ed. Vern L. Bullough and James Brundage (Buffalo: Prometheus Books, 1982), 141–48.
3. Brundage 1987, 250.
4. John Marshall Carter, *Rape in Medieval England: An Historical and Sociological Study* (Lanham, Md.: University Press of America, 1985), 132.
5. Carter, 154. On rape in English Common Law, see Sue Sheridan Walker, "Common Law Juries and Feudal Marriage Customs in Medieval England: The Pleas of Ravishment," *The University of Illinois Law Review* 3 (1984):704–18.
6. Barbara Hanawalt, *Crime and Conflict in English Communities, 1300–1348* (Cambridge: Harvard University Press, 1979), 104–5.
7. Guido Ruggiero, *The Boundaries of Eros: Sex Crime and Sexuality in Renaissance Venice* (Oxford: Oxford University Press, 1985), chaps. 1 and 5. See also Ruggiero's earlier book, *Violence in Early Renaissance Venice* (New Brunswick: Rutgers University Press, 1980), especially chap. 10.
8. Dietmar Rieger, "Le Motif du viol dans la littérature de la France médiévale: Entre norme courtoise and réalité courtoise," *Cahiers de civilisation médiévale* 31 (July–September 1988):241–67. Pages 242–46 offer a summary of medieval rape law with special reference to Germany.
9. Danielle Buschinger, "Le Viol dans la littérature allemande au moyen âge" (*Amour, mariage et transgressions au moyen âge*, ed. Buschinger and Crépin [Göppingen: Kümmerle Verlag, 1984]. Pages 369–73 give a brief overview of German rape law in the Middle Ages.
10. Buschinger, 372.
11. Philippe de Beaumanoir writes: "Fame esforcier si est quand aucuns prent a force charnel compaignie a fame contre la volenté de la fame et seur ce qu'ele fet son pouoir du defendre" (No. 829, p. 130); "Quiconques est pris en cas de crime et atains du cas, si comme de murtre, ou de traïson, ou d'homicide, ou de fame esforcier, il doit estre trainés et pendus et si mesfet quanqu'il a vaillant, et vient la forfeture au seigneur dessous qui li siens est trouvés et en a chascuns sires ce qui en est trouvé en sa seignourie" (No. 824, p. 129; in *Coutumes de Beauvaisis*, ed. A. Salmon [Paris: A. & J. Picard, 1899–1900; rpt. 1970]).
12. I am grateful to James Brundage for making this point clear to me.
13. M. G. Dupont, *Le Registre de l'Officialité de Cerisy* 1314–1457, in *Mémoires de la Société des antiquaires de Normandie* 3rd ser., 10 (1880):271–662 (English translations

mine). For a useful study (despite several inaccurate citations) of sexual behavior in the Cerisy records, see Jean-Luc Dufresne, "Les Comportements amoureux d'après le *Registre de l'Officialité de Cerisy*," *Bulletin Philologique et Historique* (1973):131–56.

14. Louis Tanon, *Registre criminel de Saint-Martin-des-Champs*, in *Histoire des Justices des Anciennes Eglises et Communautés Monastiques de Paris* (Paris: Larose et Forcel, 1883), 455–556.

15. "luserant ad palmam supra ecclesiam de Listreyo" (390l); "luderant ad palmam supra monasterium de Listreyo" (394d).

16. Entries 3; 6–7; 150; 188b; 205, 235b & d; 245a & b; 292 & 293; 363k & l; 373l; 383c; 394c.

17. It is hardly surprising that Hanawalt finds the same situation in fourteenth-century England (153).

18. On collective assault as a rite of initiation in the French Middle Ages, see Jacques Rossiaud, "Prostitution, Youth, and Society in the Towns of Southeastern France in the Fifteenth Century," in *Deviants and the Abandoned in French Society*, ed. Robert Forster and Orest Ranum (Baltimore: Johns Hopkins University Press, 1978), 1–46. On collective rapes in medieval England, see Hanawalt, 109, and Carter, 57.

19. The livre or pound was originally a measure of silver weighing one pound. It is impossible to fix the value of these sums in the High Middle Ages, but one pound (*livre tournois*) was worth approximately 20 sous (although a *livre parisis* was worth 25 sous). One sou was worth 12 deniers, and one denier was worth two mailles, a small brass coin. For a comparison of fines for rape in England to the price of grain, see Carter, 122–23, 129.

20. Hanawalt observes: "In punishing crimes aginst the person the medieval jurors were lenient. Very few rapes were prosecuted (seventy-eight for the eight counties [of Herefordshire, Surrey, Somerset, Essex, Huntingdonshire, Northhamptonshire, Yorkshire, Norfolk]) and of those only 10.3 percent ended in conviction. . . . From these figures one might conclude that medieval jurors put a low value on life and a high value on property. It would seem that jurors wished to discourage property crimes, especially violent ones, but were quite willing to let homicide and rape pass virtually unnoticed" (61). Hanawalt later continues: "The convictions for the various crimes indicated that the taboo against property crimes was greater than against homicide and rape. Not only did jurors convict more people charged with property crimes, but the taboo would be internalized in the society so that fewer property crimes would have been committed" (272).

21. "Clerics, or those claiming to be clerics, formed the largest percentage of rapists. Many apparently sought the jurisdiction of the ecclesiastical courts, because they handed down milder punishments." Carter, 155. Hanawalt makes interesting observations on the high crime rate among English clergy ("The explanation lies in the broad definition of clergy and the abuses of the plea of benefit of clergy" [136]), who often worked in gangs (136–38).

22. Dufresne, 149–53.

23. In his preface, Dupont himself expresses surprise over this case for, "d'après les aveux même des coupables" (by the admission of the convicted themselves), the attackers' sole goal was the rape of the daughter.

24. Dufresne, 143. Dietmar Rieger gives several examples of this tendency to punish the victim and its precedents in Patristic writing (258–60).

25. See Brundage 1978, 63.

26. Dupont, entries 202, 203, 362, 382.

27. Dufresne, 151. For the account of a rape case in fifteenth-century Brittany, curiously settled by the father of the victim, see Jean-Pierre Leguay, "Un cas de 'force' au moyen âge: le viol de Margot Simmonet" (*Mentalités: Histoire des cultures et des sociétés*, vol. 3, *Violences sexuelles* [Paris: Imago, 1989], 13–33). I am grateful to Gabriel Haddad for this reference.

28. Here, too, actual practices in France are similar to those in England during the same period: "In practice few rape cases were tried and those that were ended in acquittal or some concord with the victim such as fine or marriage" (Hanawalt, 104).

29. 13 July 1333; 21 January 1337; 23 February 1338; 20 April 1338; 10 March 1340; 29 September 1342.

30. Henri Duplès-Agier, ed., *Registre criminel du Châtelet de Paris du 6 septembre 1389 au 18 mai 1392* (Paris: Charles Lahure, 1861), 1:42–47. Hanawalt relates a case in England that resembles the tale of Jean Braque. A powerful lord, Hugh Fitz Henry, raped and battered a young girl, "Maud, daughter of Ingreda Scot of Ingelton." Hugh had two of his servants seize Maud and take her to his manor house. "The jurors maintained that once at his house, she voluntarily submitted to him. It is questionable what sort of resistance she could possibly have made in his manor house . . . Obviously, the jurors were afraid to convict a local lord" (108).

31. In addition to the judge's demand for witnesses, two other factors may have caused Eudelot to drop her complaint. Her case was prejudiced by the fact that on the preceding day her mistress, Nicole, wife of Guillaume Damours, was arrested for beating Eudolet in the street, crying out: "Je te veulg seignier en guise de p. . . . . , car tu as fortrait mon mari" (I want to bleed you like a [whore], for you stole my husband [Tanon, 124]). The domestic strife in the Damours household may have cast doubt on Eudelot's motivations in the rape charge. Still more discouraging for Eudelot was the simple fact that servants had little chance to win against their masters in court and may have been more concerned to keep their position than to alienate their employers. See Ruggiero 1985, 107.

32. Carter, 147–48. This is the only case in the Saint-Martin register in which the plaintiff is charged with a false appeal. The question of false appeal arises far more frequently in England. If a victim does not follow exactly the six procedural steps required to appeal a man of rape, or if she cannot prove the guilt of the accused, she is arrested and convicted of false appeal. Given the arrest statistics, it is startling (and rather telling) that modern historians still argue that medieval women frequently tried to profit from false rape accusations. In the Berkshire eyre of 1248, 78 percent of the alleged victims were arrested for false appeal; in the Warwickshire eyre of 1221, 62.5 percent of the alleged victims were arrested; in the Wiltshire eyre of 1249, 53 percent of the victims were arrested; and in the London eyres of 1244, 1276, and 1321, 50 percent of the alleged victims were arrested (Carter, 98–101). Carter studies at length the famous London case of *Seler vs. Limoges*, in 1321, in which a Frenchman was charged with raping eleven-year-old Joan, the daughter of

Eustace the Saddler (*London Eyre of 1321*, 2:88.) Even though the little girl, injured and bleeding, had the presence of mind to raise the hue and cry immediately, to chase the rapist through several London wards, to report the crime to ward officials, then to the sheriffs, and then to the Coroners at the Tower of London, the French merchant was acquitted and Joan was charged with false appeal (Carter, 142–45).

33. Hanawalt, 105, Carter, 170.

34. "Hugo tried to rape Agnes but was not able to complete coitus because he was not able to penetrate the vagina of a seven-year-old girl. Although there was intromission, she was not deflowered and, according to the thinking of the time, Hugo was not convicted of rape" (Carter, 147–48).

35. *Enfouissement*, or burial alive, is the official penalty for repeated larceny; but it is applied to women only. See Tanon's Introduction, xciii–xcvi.

36. 11 August 1340; 7 December 1340; 11 December 1340; 12 September 1342.

37. Ruggiero reaches similar conclusions in studying Renaissance Venice (Ruggiero 1985, 108).

38. Hanawalt, 105.

39. Susan Estrich, *Real Rape* (Cambridge: Harvard University Press, 1987), 32, 48.

40. Hanawalt, 64.

41. Natalie Zemon Davis, *Fiction in the Archives: Pardon Tales and Their Tellers in Sixteenth-Century France* (Stanford: Stanford University Press, 1987), 105. Davis looks at the rhetorical crafting of pardon letters and also compares them to literary texts of the sixteenth century.

42. Ruggiero 1985, 90.

43. It is not until Guillemete de Costentino marries one Colin Osmont that she comes forward to tell her story, a factor that may have weakened her case.

44. Carter, 81.

45. Perhaps Hanawalt was thinking here of medieval England's very popular writer, Geoffrey Chaucer, who in addition to being court poet was also a controller of customs, clerk of the works, diplomatic attaché, court exchequer, subforester, justice of the peace, and commissioner of walls and ditches. His literary rapes in the Wife of Bath's Tale and the Merchant's Tale might be contextualized anew in view of the fact that Chaucer himself was charged with *raptus*. The 1380 case involved Cecily Champain, a baker's daughter. As witnesses, Chaucer called in some of his most powerful acquaintances: Sir William Beauchamp, Lord Abergavenny, Sir John Philipot, Admiral William Neville, Sir John Clanvowe, and Richard Morel. Cecily called in one Richard Goodchild, cutler, and one John Grove, armorer. Martin M. Crow and Clair C. Olson, eds., *Chaucer Life-Records* (Austin: University of Texas Press, 1966), 343–47. The commentary of one well-known medievalist is enlightening. John Gardner, in *The Life and Times of Chaucer* (New York: Knopf, 1977), introduced his discussion of the case with a smirk: "It seems possible, if not downright likely, that into his busy schedule of 1379 or '80 Chaucer managed to fit at least one pretty wench" (251). Gardner dismisses the argument that *raptus* may have meant abduction and seems to hope that it meant forcible coitus: "But there are reasons for taking a darker—or perhaps more cheerful—view" (252). Gardner

closes with his own touch of poetry: "But the fact that Lewis was almost certainly not Cecily's son is no proof that Chaucer, now forty years old, rich and powerful, more often away from his wife on business for the king than not, never *slipped into bed with a pretty and soft baker's daughter*" (253; emphasis added). What interests me most is the language scholars use to mystify rape, whether in the literary or the legal text, such as Gardner's "slipping into bed" with "a pretty wench." See also the article of the legal historian, T.F.T. Plucknett, entitled "Chaucer's Escapade," *Law Quarterly Review* 64 (1948):33–36.

46. Karl Bartsch, ed., *Romances et pastourelles françaises des XIIe et XIIIe siècles: Altfranzösische Romanzen und Pastourellen*, 2 vols. (Leipzig, 1870; rpt. Darmstadt: Wissenschaftliche Buchgesellschaft, 1967).

47. The garment mentioned here and frequently in the pastourelles, *mantel de brunete*, is a luxury item, made of an expensive fabric, tinted not quite black. Godefroy points out that it was worn by "gens de qualité," and that Councils frequently prohibited the wearing of a "mantel de brunete" by monks. Frédéric Godefroy, *Dictionnaire de l'ancienne langue française* (Paris, 1880; rpt. 1961), 1:747. Ironically, the men of Cerisy promise their vicitm a coat of *burelli*, or rough burlap.

48. Davis, 4.

49. Hanawalt, 108–9.

50. Carter points out the rich stylistic detail in the secular records of the itinerant judges (or their scribes) beginning in the thirteenth century (139).

51. The setting is reminiscent of the scene in an English case already mentioned, in which Hugh Fitz Henry "was passing through the village of Ingelton one day when he saw Maud standing in her mother's doorway" (Hanawalt, 108).

52. In the pastourelle excerpts I have deliberately omitted the comic or euphoric verses that often follow the representation of rape in order to highlight the violence in the description of the attacks. See for example Bartsch 3:42, 28–36: "Mult longuement l'alai proiant, / que riens n'i conquis; / estroitement tout en riant / par les flans la pris: / sus l'erbe la souvinai, / mult en fu en grant esmai, / si haut a crie / 'bele douce mere de, / gardez moi ma chastee.' " (I went on pleading with her for a very long time without getting anywhere. Laughing, I took her tightly by the thighs and laid her back on the grass. She was in great dismay and cried aloud: "Noble and sweet Mother of God, save my chastity.")

53. Michel Foucault, "Introduction" and "Les régularités discursives," in *L'Archéologie du savoir* (Paris: Gallimard, 1969), 1–101.

Conclusion

1. Joan Kelly, "Did Women Have a Renaissance?" in *Women, History and Theory* (Chicago: University of Chicago Press, 1984), 22. For a slightly different critique of Kelly's article, see Sheila Fisher and Janet E. Halley, *Seeking the Woman in Late Medieval and Renaissance Writings*, 7–10.

2. See, for example, M. G. Dupont, *Le Registre de l'Officialité de Cerisy 1314–1457* (*Mémoires de la Société des antiquaires de Normandie*, vol. 10 [1880]). Entries 363k and 363l tell the story of Bertin Quenet and Alicia Hoquet. Bertin was fined five sous for raping Alicia. Alicia was then fined fifteen sous for allowing a man to have carnal knowledge of her.

3. Hincmar of Reims, *De coercendis raptu viduarum, puellarum et sanctimonialum*, C. 4, in *Patrologia Latina*, ed. J. P. Migne, 221 vols. (Paris: Garnier, 1844–64), 4:1019–20. See also Georges Duby, *The Knight, the Lady and the Priest*, trans. Barbara Bray (New York: Pantheon, 1983), 32–34.

4. *Decretum Magistri Gratiani*, in *Corpus Iuris Canonici*, ed. Emil Friedberg, 2 vols. (Leipzig, 1879–81; rpt. Graz, 1955), C. 36.

5. Hostiensis, *Lectura* X, 5.16.2 (1581 edition). See also James Brundage, "Rape and Seduction in the Medieval Canon Law," in *Sexual Practices and the Medieval Church*, ed. Bullough and Brundage (Buffalo: Prometheus, 1982), 143–47.

6. Christine de Pizan, *Le Livre de la cité des dames*, ed. Maureen Curnow, Ph.D. dissertation, Vanderbilt University, 1975, 2:885–87; in English, *The Book of the City of Ladies*, trans. Earl J. Richards (New York: Persea Books, 1982), 161–62.

7. Sylvana Tomaselli, Introduction, in *Rape: An Historical and Social Enquiry*, ed. Sylvana Tomaselli and Roy Porter (Oxford: Blackwell, 1986), 3. Tomaselli also makes the point that the European Middle Ages gave a good deal of attention to the issue of sexual violence.

8. Tomaselli writes: "It may indeed be the case that in a world in which women are treated principally as means rather than ends, as objects rather than subjects, or in which they are primarily members of households deriving their status only through their membership of such social units rather than as individual political beings in their own right, men protected them from theft and violence, from abduction and rape, for reasons of their own self interests. If this holds true we must be open to the possibility that such incentives might no longer hold good in a world in which the position of women is being radically changed. The relative modern silence, or if you wish the relative modern 'male' silence, on rape may point in this direction. . . . Only recently has the issue been brought back into public debate, and this is strictly owing to successful efforts by the feminism of the seventies and early eighties, a feminism which unlike its predecessors made rape the prime focus of its campaign" (5). Is it possible that rape, understood in the Middle Ages as a problem for men, has today been marginalized as a woman's issue?

9. I borrow the words from Peter Brown's reference to the history of early Christianity in the conclusion to *The Body and Society: Men, Women, and Sexual Renunciation in Early Christianity* (New York: Columbia University Press, 1988), 447.

Bibliography

Alford, John A., and Dennis P. Seniff. *Literature and Law in the Middle Ages: A Bibliography of Scholarship*. New York: Garland, 1984.

Althusser, Louis, et al. *Reading Capital*. Trans. Ben Brewster. London: New Left Books, 1970.

Andreas Cappelanus. *The Art of Courtly Love*. Trans. John Jay Parry. New York: Columbia University Press, 1941.

Arnold, I.D.O., and Margaret M. Pelan. *La Partie arthurienne du Roman de Brut*. Paris: Klincksieck, 1962.

Audiau, Jean. *La Pastourelle dans la poésie occitane du moyen-âge*. Paris: De Boccard, 1923.

Baldwin, John W. "The Intellectual Preparation for the Canon of 1215 against Ordeals." *Speculum* 36 (1961):613–36.

Bartsch, Karl. *Romances et pastourelles françaises des XIIe et XIIIe siècles*. Darmstadt: Wissenschaftliche Buchgesellschaft, 1870; rpt. 1967.

Basdevant, Jules. *Les Rapports de l'église et de l'état dans la législation du mariage du Concile de Trente au Code Civil*. Paris: Société du Recueil général des lois et des arrêts et du Journal du Palais, 1900.

Beaumanoir, Philippe de. *Les Coutumes de Beauvaisis*. Ed. A. Salmon. Paris: Picard, 1899.

Bec, Pierre. *La Lyrique française du moyen âge (XIIe–XIIIe siècle): contribution à une typologie des genres poétiques médiévaux*. Paris: Picard, 1977–78.

Bellamy, John G. *Crime and Public Order in England in the Later Middle Ages*. London: Routledge and Kegan Paul, 1973.

Benton, John F. "Clio and Venus: An Historical View of Medieval Love." In *The Meaning of Courtly Love*. Ed. F. X. Newman. Albany: SUNY Press, 1968.

Bergman, Mary Bernardine. *Hrosvithae Liber Tertius*. Ph.D. dissertation, Saint Louis University, 1942.

Berman, Harold J. *Law and Revolution: The Formation of the Western Legal Tradition*. Cambridge: Harvard University Press, 1983.

Béroul. *Le Roman de Tristan*. Ed. Ernest Muret. Paris: Champion, 1974.

Bertin, Ernest. *Les Mariages dans l'ancienne société française*. Paris: 1879 (rpt. Geneva: Slatkine Reprints, 1975).

Bertini, Ferruccio. *Il "teatro" di Rosvita: Con un saggio di traduzione e di interpretazione del "Callimaco."* Genoa: Tilgher-Genova, 1979.

Bibliotheca sanctorum. 12 vols. Rome: Instituto Giovanni XXIII della Pontificia Universita Lateranense, 1961–69.

Blanchard, Joel. *La Pastorale en France aux XIVe et XVe siècles. Recherches sur les structures de l'imaginaire médiéval*. Paris: Champion, 1983.

Bloch, R. Howard. *Medieval French Literature and Law*. Berkeley: University of California Press, 1977.

———. "Medieval Misogyny: Woman as Riot." *Representations* 20 (Fall 1987):1–15.

Bollandus, J., and G. Henschenius. *Acta sanctorum . . . editio novissima*. Ed. J. Carnandet et al. Paris: Palmé, 1863.

Bonfante, Larissa. *The Plays of Hrotswitha of Gandersheim*. New York: New York University Press, 1979.

Bongert, Yvonne. *Recherches sur les cours laïques du Xe au XIIIe siècle*. Paris: A & J Picard, 1949.

Bossuat, Robert. *Le Roman de Renard*. Paris: Hatier, 1967.

Boswell, John. *Christianity, Social Tolerance, and Homosexuality: Gay People in Western Europe from the Beginning of the Christian Era to the Fourteenth Century*. Chicago: University of Chicago Press, 1980.

Bridenthal, Renate, and Claudia Koonz, eds. *Becoming Visible: Women in European History*. Boston: Houghton Mifflin, 1977.

Brown, Peter. *The Cult of Saints: Its Rise and Function in Latin Christianity*. Chicago: University of Chicago Press, 1981.

———. *The Body and Society: Men, Women, and Sexual Renunciation in Early Christianity*. New York: Columbia University Press, 1988.

Brownmiller, Susan. *Against Our Will: Men, Women and Rape*. New York: Simon and Schuster, 1975.

Bruckner, Matilda Tomaryn. "*Le Chevalier de la Charrete (Lancelot)*." In *The Romances of Chrétien de Troyes: A Symposium*. Ed. Douglas Kelly. Lexington, Ky.: French Forum, 1985; 132–81.

———. "An Interpreter's Dilemma: Why Are There So Many Interpretations of Chrétien's *Chevalier de la Charrette*?" *Romance Philology* 40 (1986):159–80.

Brundage, James A. "Carnal Delight: Canonistic Theories of Sexuality." In *Proceedings of the Fifth International Congress of Medieval Canon Law*. Ed. Stephan Juttner and Kenneth Pennington. Vol. 6 (1980), 361–85. Vatican City: Biblioteca Apostolica Vaticana, 1963–85.

———. "Rape and Marriage in the Medieval Canon Law." *Revue de droit canonique* 28 (1978):62–75.

———. "Rape and Seduction in the Medieval Canon Law." In *Sexual Practices and the Medieval Church*. Ed. Vern Bullough and James Brundage. Buffalo, N.Y.: Prometheus Books, 1982, 141–48.

———. *Law, Sex, and Christian Society in Medieval Europe*. Chicago: University of Chicago Press, 1987.

Bullough, Vern L. "Medieval Medical and Scientific Views of Women." *Viator* 4 (1973):485–501.

Bumke, Joachim. *Höfische Kultur: Literatur und Gesellschaft im hohen Mittelalter*. 2 vols. Munich: Beck, 1986.

Burns, E. Jane. "How Lovers Lie Together." *Tristania* 8 (Spring 1983):15–30.

Burns, E. Jane, and Roberta L. Krueger, eds. *Courtly Ideology and Woman's Place in Medieval French Literature. Romance Notes* 25:iii (1985).

Buschinger, Danielle. "Le Viol dans la littérature allemande au moyen âge." In

Amour, mariage et transgressions au moyen âge. Ed. Danielle Buschinger and André Crépin. Göppingen: Kümmerle Verlag, 1984, 369–88.

Buschinger, Danielle, and André Crépin, eds. *Comique, satire et parodie dans la tradition renardienne et les fabliaux*. Göppinger Arbeiten zur Germanistik, no. 391, Actes du Colloque des 15 et 16 Janvier, 1983. Göppingen: Kümmerle Verlag, 1983.

Butler, Mary Marguerite. *Hrotsvitha: The Theatricality of Her Plays*. New York: Philosophical Library, 1960.

Bynum, Caroline Walker. *Holy Feast and Holy Fast: The Religious Significance of Food to Medieval Women*. Berkeley: University of California Press, 1987.

Cahoon, Leslie. "Raping the Rose: Jean de Meun's Reading of Ovid's *Amores*." *Classical and Modern Literature* 6 (1986):261–85.

Cantarella, Eva. "Dangling Virgins: Myth, Ritual and the Place of Women in Ancient Greece." *Poetics Today* 6, nos. 1–2 (1985):91–101.

Carrasco, Magdalena Elizabeth. "An Early Illustrated Manuscript of the Passion of Saint Agatha (Paris, Bibl. Nat., MS lat. 5594)*." *GESTA* 24 (1985):19–32.

Carter, John Marshall. *Rape in Medieval England: An Historical and Sociological Study*. Lanham, Md.: University Press of America, 1985.

Case, Sue-Ellen. "Re-Viewing Hrotsvit." *Theater Journal* 35 (December 1983): 533–42.

Castle, Terry. *Clarissa's Ciphers: Meaning and Disruption in Richardson's "Clarissa."* Ithaca: Cornell University Press, 1982.

Cazelles, Brigitte, and Phyllis Johnson. *Le vain siècle guerpir: A Literary Approach to Sainthood through Old French Hagiography of the Twelfth Century*. Chapel Hill: North Carolina Studies in Romance Languages and Literatures, 1979.

Chrétien de Troyes. *Les Romans de Chrétien de Troyes: Edités d'après la Copie de Guiot (Bibl. Nat. Fr. 794): Erec et Enide*. Ed. Mario Roques. Paris: Champion, 1973. *Cligès*. Ed. Alexandre Micha. *Le Chevalier de la Charrette*. Ed. Mario Roques. Paris: Champion, 1975. *Le Chevalier au Lion*. Ed. Mario Roques. Paris: Champion, 1975. *Le Conte du Graal*. Ed. Félix Lecoy. Paris: Champion, 1975.

———. *Philomena: Conte raconté d'après Ovide*. Ed. C. de Boer. 1909; rpt. Geneva: Slatkine Reprints, 1974.

Christine de Pizan. *The Book of the City of Ladies*. Trans. Earl Jeffrey Richards. New York: Persea Books, 1982.

Cixous, Hélène. "Le Rire de la méduse." *L'Arc* 61 (1975):39–54.

Cohen, Gustave. *La Vie littéraire en France au moyen-âge*. Paris: Tallandier, 1949.

Combarieu du Grès, Micheline de, and Jean Subrenat, eds. *Le Roman de Renart*. Paris: 10/18, 1981.

Crow, Martin M., and Clair C. Olson, eds. *Chaucer Life-Records*. Austin: University of Texas Press, 1966.

Curnow, Maureen. *The "Livre de la cité des dames" of Christine de Pisan: A Critical Edition*. Ph.D. dissertation, Vanderbilt University, 1975.

Curran, Leo C. "Rape and Rape Victims in the *Metamorphoses*." *Arethusa* 11 (1978):213–42.

Curtius, Ernst Robert. *European Literature and the Latin Middle Ages*. Trans. Willard Trask. Princeton: Princeton University Press, 1953.

Davis, Natalie Zemon. *Society and Culture in Early Modern France*. Stanford: Stanford University Press, 1975.

———. *Fiction in the Archives: Pardon Tales and Their Tellers in Sixteenth-Century France*. Stanford: Stanford University Press, 1987.

DeJean, Joan. "Classical Reeducation: Decanonizing the Feminine." In *The Politics of Tradition*. Ed. Joan DeJean and Nancy K. Miller. *Yale French Studies* 75 (Fall 1988): 26–39.

Delehaye, Hippolyte. *Les Passions des martyrs et les genres littéraires*. Brussels: Société des Bollandistes, 1921.

Derrida, Jacques. *L'Ecriture et la différence*. Paris: Seuil, 1967. *Writing and Difference*. Trans. Alan Bass. Chicago: University of Chicago Press, 1978.

———. *Marges de la philosophie*. Paris: Minuit, 1972.

———. *Eperons: Les styles de Nietzsche*. Paris: Flammarion, 1978.

Doederlein, Sue Warrick. "Clarissa in the Hands of the Critics." *Eighteenth Century Studies* 16 (Summer 1983):401–14.

Doss-Quinby, Eglal. *Les Refrains chez les trouvères du XIIe siècle au début du XIVe*. New York: Peter Lang, 1984.

Dronke, Peter. *Medieval Latin and the Rise of European Love-Lyric*. Oxford: Clarendon, 1968.

———. *Women Writers of the Middle Ages: A Critical Study of Texts from Perpetua to Marguerite Porete*. Cambridge: Cambridge University Press, 1984.

Drouart La Vache. *Li Livres d'Amours*. Ed. Robert Bossuat. Paris: Champion, 1926.

Duby, Georges. "Les Jeunes dans la société aristocratique dans la France du nord-ouest au douzième siècle." *Annales 19 (1964): 835–46*. Rpt. in *Hommes et structures du moyen âge*. The Hague: Mouton, 1973.

———. *La Société aux XIe et XIIe siècles dans la région mâconnaise*. Paris: Armand-Colin, 1953.

———. *Le Chevalier, la femme et le prêtre: le mariage dans la France féodale*. Paris: Hachette, 1981. *The Knight, the Lady, and the Priest: The Making of Modern Marriage in Medieval France*. Trans. Barbara Bray. New York: Pantheon, 1983.

———. *Mâle Moyen Age: De l'amour et autres essais*. Paris: Flammarion, 1988.

Duckett, Eleanor. *Death and Life in the Tenth Century*. Ann Arbor: University of Michigan Press, 1967.

Dufresne, Jean-Luc. "Les Comportements amoureux d'après le Registre de l'Officialité de Cerisy." *Bulletin Philologique et Historique* (1973):131–56.

Duplès-Agier, Henri, ed. *Registre criminel du Châtelet de Paris du 6 septembre 1389 au 18 mai 1392*. 2 vols. Paris: Charles Lahure, 1861.

Dupont, M. G. *Le Registre de l'Officialité de Cerisy 1314–1457*. In *Mémoires de la Société des antiquaires de Normandie*. 3rd Series, 10 (1880):271–662.

Dworkin, Roger B. "The Resistance Standard in Rape Legislation." *Stanford Law Review* 18 (1966):680ff.

Dworkin, Ronald. "Law as Interpretation." In *The Politics of Interpretation*. Ed. W.J.T. Mitchell. Chicago: University of Chicago Press, 1983, 249–70.

Eagleton, Terry. *The Rape of Clarissa: Writing, Sexuality, and Class Struggle in Samuel Richardson*. Minneapolis: University of Minnesota Press, 1982.

Erler, Mary, and Maryanne Kowaleski, eds. *Women and Power in the Middle Ages*. Athens: University of Georgia Press, 1988.

Esmein, A. *Histoire de la procédure criminelle en France*. Paris: Larose et Forcel, 1882.

———. *Cours d'histoire du droit français*. Paris: Sirey, 1907.

Estrich, Susan. *Real Rape*. Cambridge: Harvard University Press, 1987.

Ferrante, Joan. *Woman as Image in Medieval Literature from the Twelfth Century to Dante*. New York: Columbia University Press, 1975. Durham, N.C.: Labyrinth Press, 1985.

———. "Male Fantasy and Female Reality in Courtly Literature." *Women's Studies* 11 (1984):67–97.

Findlay, Barbara. "The Cultural Context of Rape." *Women Lawyers Journal* 60 (1974):199–206.

Fineman, Joel. "Shakespeare's *Will*: The Temporality of Rape." *Representations* 20 (Fall 1987):25–76.

Fish, Stanley. "Interpretation and the Pluralist Vision." *Texas Law Review* 60 (1984):495–505.

———. "Fish vs. Fiss." *Stanford Law Review* 36 (1984):1325–47.

———. *Doing What Comes Naturally: Change, Rhetoric, and the Practice of Theory in Literary and Legal Studies*. Durham: Duke University Press, 1989.

Fisher, Sheila, and Janet E. Halley. *Seeking the Woman in Late Medieval and Renaissance Writings: Essays in Feminist Contextual Criticism*. Knoxville: University of Tennessee Press, 1989.

Fleming, John V. *The Roman de la Rose: A Study in Allegory and Iconography*. Princeton: Princeton University Press, 1969.

Flinn, John. *Le Roman de Renart dans la littérature française et dans les littératures étrangères au moyen âge*. Paris: Presses Universitaires Françaises, 1963.

Foucault, Michel. *L'Archéologie du savoir*. Paris: Gallimard, 1969.

Foulet, Lucien. *Le Roman de Renard*. Paris: Champion, 1914.

Fournival, Richard de. *La Poissance d'amours della pseudo-Richard de Fournival*. Ed. Gian Battista Speroni. Florence: La Nuova Italia, 1975.

Fraher, Richard M. "Preventing Crime in the High Middle Ages: The Medieval Lawyers' Search for Deterrence." In *Popes, Teachers, and Canon Law in the Middle Ages*. Ed. James Ross Sweeney and Stanley Chodorow. Ithaca: Cornell University Press, 1988; 212–33.

Francis, Elizabeth A. *Wace: La vie de Sainte Marguerite*. Paris: Champion, 1932.

Frankforter, A. Daniel. "Sexism and the Search for the Thematic Structure of the Plays of Hrotsvitha of Gandersheim." *International Journal of Women's Studies* 2 (1979):221–32.

Freud, Sigmund. *Jokes and Their Relation to the Unconscious*. Trans. James Strachey. New York: Norton, 1963.

Gardner, John. *The Life and Times of Chaucer*. New York: Knopf, 1977.

Geertz, Clifford. "Blurred Genres: The Refiguration of Social Thought." *American Scholar* 49 (October 1980):165–79.

Gellinek, Christian. "Marriage by Consent in Literary Sources of Medieval Germany." *Studia Gratiana* 12 (1967):555–79.

Given, James B. *Society and Homicide in Thirteenth-Century England*. Stanford: Stanford University Press, 1977.

Godefroy, Frederic. *Dictionnaire de l'ancienne langue française*. Paris, 1880; rpt. New York: Kraus Reprint Corporation, 1961.

Gold, Penny Schine. *The Lady and the Virgin: Image, Attitude and Experience in Twelfth-Century France*. Chicago: University of Chicago Press, 1985.

Gratian. *Decretum Magistri Gratiani*. In *Corpus iuris canonici*. Ed. E. Friedberg. 2 vols. Leipzig, 1879–81; rpt. Graz, 1955.

Gravdal, Kathryn. "Camouflaging Rape: The Rhetoric of Sexual Violence in the Medieval Pastourelle." *Romanic Review* 76 (1985):361–73.

———. *Vilain and Courtois: Transgressive Parody in Old French Literature of the Twelfth and Thirteenth Centuries*. Lincoln: University of Nebraska Press, 1989.

———. "1175: Fables and Parodies." In *A New History of French Literature*. Ed. Denis Hollier et al. Cambridge: Harvard University Press, 1989, 46–50.

Graven, Jean. *Le Procès criminel du "Roman de Renart": etude du droit criminel féodal au XIIe siècle*. Geneva: Librairie de l'Université, 1950.

Hadewijch of Brabant. *Hadewijch: The Complete Works*. Trans. Mother Columba Hart. New York: Paulist Press, 1980.

Haight, Anne Lyon. *Hroswitha of Gandersheim: Her Life, Times, and Works, and a Comprehensive Bibliography*. New York: The Hroswitha Club, 1965.

Hanawalt, Barbara A. *Crime and Conflict in English Communities 1300–1348*. Cambridge: Harvard University Press, 1979.

Hart, H.L.A. *The Concept of Law*. Oxford: Clarendon Press, 1961.

Haskell, Molly. "The 2,000-Year-Old Misundertanding: 'Rape Fantasy.' " *MS* 5 (November 1976):84–86, 92, 94, 96, 98.

Hazen, Helen. *Endless Rapture: Rape, Romance and the Female Imagination*. New York: Charles Scribner's Sons, 1983.

Higgins, Lynn, and Brenda Silver, eds. *Rape and Representation*. New York: Columbia University Press, 1991.

Hincmar of Reims. *De coercendis raptu viduarum, puellarum et sanctimonialium*. C. 4. In *Patrologia Latina*. Ed. J. P. Migne. 221 vols. Vol. 125 (1855), 1019–20. Paris: Garnier Fratres, 1844–64.

———. *De divortio Lotharii regis et Tetbergae reginae*. In *Patrologia Latina*. Ed. J. P. Migne. 221 vols. Vol. 125 (1855), 619–772. Paris: Garnier Fratres, 1844–64.

Holland, Norman N. *The Dynamics of Literary Response*. New York: Oxford University Press, 1968.

Homeyer, Helena, ed. *Hrotsvithae Opera*. Munich: Schöningh, 1970.

Hostiensis. *Lectura*. 5 vols. Turin: Bottega d'Erasmo, 1963.

Hyams, Paul. "Trial by Ordeal: The Key to Proof in Early Common Law." In *On the Laws and Customs of England: Essays in Honor of Samuel E. Thorne*. Ed. Morris Arnold, Thomas Green, Sally Scully, and Steven White. Chapel Hill: University of North Carolina Press, 1981; 90–126.

Irigaray, Luce. *Spéculum de l'autre femme*. Paris: Minuit, 1974. *Speculum of the Other Woman*. Trans. Gillian C. Gill. Ithaca: Cornell University Press, 1985.

———. *Ce sexe qui n'en est pas un*. Paris: Minuit, 1977. *This Sex Which Is Not One*. Trans. Catherine Porter. Ithaca: Cornell University Press, 1985.

Jackson, W.T.H. "The Medieval Pastourelle as a Satirical Genre." *Philological Quarterly* 31 (April 1952):156–70.

Jacobus de Voragine. *Legenda Aurea*. Ed. T. Graesse. Osnabruck: O. Zeller, 1965.

———. *The Golden Legend of Jacobus de Voragine*. Trans. Helmut Ripperger and Granger Ryan. New York: Arno Press, 1969.

———. *La Légende dorée*. Trans. Jean-Baptiste M. Roze. 2 vols. Paris: Garnier-Flammarion, 1967.

Jauss, Hans Robert. *Untersuchungen zur Mittelalterlichen Tierdichtung*. Tübingen: Max Niemeyer, 1959.

Jerome. *The Letters of Saint Jerome*. Ed. James Duff. Dublin: Browne and Nolan, 1942.

———. *The Letters of Saint Jerome*. Trans. Charles Christopher Mierow. London: Newman Press, 1963.

Johnson, Barbara. "Melville's Fist: The Execution of *Billy Budd*." In Barbara Johnson, *The Critical Difference: Essays in the Contemporary Rhetoric of Reading*. Baltimore: Johns Hopkins University Press, 1981; 79–109.

Johnson, Phyllis, and Brigitte Cazelles. *Le vain siècle guerpir: A Literary Approach to Sainthood through Old French Hagiography of the Twelfth Century*. Chapel Hill: North Carolina Studies in Romance Languages and Literatures, 1979.

Jones, W. Powell. *The Pastourelle: A Study of the Origins and Tradition of a Lyric Type*. Cambridge: Harvard University Press, 1931.

Jonin, Pierre. *Les Personnages féminins dans les romans français de Tristan au XIIe siècle*. Aix-en-Provence: Publication des annales de la Faculté des lettres, 1958.

Joplin, Patricia Kleindienst. "The Voice of the Shuttle Is Ours." *Stanford Literature Review* 1 (Spring 1984):25–53.

Kalifa, Simon. "Singularités matrimoniales chez les anciens Germains: Le rapt et le droit de la femme à disposer d'elle-même." *Revue historique de droit français et étranger*, 4th Series, 48 (1970):199–225.

Kelly, Amy. *Eleanor of Aquitaine and the Four Kings*. Cambridge: Harvard University Press, 1963.

Kelly, Joan. *Women, History, and Theory: The Essays of Joan Kelly*. Chicago: University of Chicago Press, 1984.

Kolodny, Annette. "Dancing Through the Minefield: Some Observations on the Theory, Practice, and Politics of Feminist Literary Criticism." In *The New Feminist Criticism*. Ed. Elaine Showalter. New York: Pantheon, 1985, 144–67.

Krueger, Roberta L. "Love, Honor, and the Exchange of Women in *Yvain*: Some Remarks on the Female Reader." *Romance Notes* 25 (Spring 1985):302–17.

———. "Misogyny, Manipulation, and the Female Reader in Hue de Rotelande's *Ipomédon*." In *Courtly Literature: Culture and Context*. Ed. Keith Busby and Erik Kooper. Amsterdam: Benjamins, 1990.

———. "Desire, Meaning, and the Female Reader: The Problem in Chrétien's *Charrete*." In *The Passing of Arthur: New Essays in Arthurian Tradition*. Ed. Christopher Baswell and William Sharpe. New York: Garland, 1988, 31–51.

Labalme, Patricia H., ed. *Beyond Their Sex: Learned Women of the European Past*. New York: New York University Press, 1980.

Leach, Eleanor Winsor. "Ekphrasis and the Theme of Artistic Failure in Ovid's *Metamorphoses.*" *Ramus* 3 (1974):102–42.

Leclercq, Jean. *Monks and Love in Twelfth-Century France: Psycho-Historical Essays.* Oxford: Clarendon Press, 1979.

Le Foyer, J. *Exposé de droit pénal normand au treizième siècle.* Paris: Sirey, 1931.

LeGrand, Camille E. "Rape and Rape Laws: Sexism in Society and the Law." *California Law Review* 61 (1973):919–41.

Leguay, Jean-Pierre. "Un cas de 'force' au moyen âge; le viol de Margot Simmonet." In *Mentalités: Histoire des cultures et des sociétés.* Vol. 3: "Violences sexuelles." Paris: Imago, 1989, 13–33.

Lemercier, Pierre. "Une curiosité judiciaire au moyen âge: la grâce par mariage subséquent." *Revue Historique de droit français et étranger*, 4th Series, 33 (1955):464–74.

Lepointe, Gabriel. *Droit romain et ancien droit français: Régimes matrimoniaux, libéralités, successions.* Paris: Editions Montchrestien, 1958.

Levine, Mortimer. "A More than Ordinary Case of 'Rape': 13 and 14 Elizabeth I." *American Journal of Legal History* 7 (1963):162–63.

MacKinnon, Catherine. "Feminism, Marxism, Method and the State: Toward Feminist Jurisprudence." *Signs* 8 (1983):635–58.

Macksey, Richard, and Eugene Donato, eds. *The Structuralist Controversy.* Baltimore: Johns Hopkins University Press, 1972.

Mann, Jill. *Ysengrimus: Text with Translation, Commentary, and Translation.* Leiden, New York, Copenhagen, Cologne: E. J. Brill, 1987.

Marie de France. *Fables.* Ed. Harriet Spiegel. Toronto: University of Toronto Press, 1987.

Martin, Ernst. *Le Roman de Renart.* Strasbourg: K. J. Trubner, 1882.

Miller, Nancy K. *Subject to Change: Reading Feminist Writing.* New York: Columbia University Press, 1988.

———. "Arachnologies: The Woman, the Text, and the Critic." In *Poetics of Gender.* Ed. Nancy K. Miller. New York: Columbia University Press, 1986; 270–95.

———. *The Heroine's Text: Readings in the French and English Novel 1722–1782.* New York: Columbia University Press, 1980.

Molinier, Guillaume. *Las Leys Damors.* In *Monuments de la littérature romane.* Ed. Adolphe Gatien-Arnoult. Toulouse: J.-B. Paya, 1841.

Monmouth, Geoffrey de. *Historia Regum Britanniae.* Ed. Edmond Faral. In *La Légende arthurienne: Etudes et documents.* Vol. 3:71–303. Paris: Société des anciens textes français, 1929.

Newnan, Eva May. *The Latinity of the Works of Hrotsvit of Gandersheim.* Chicago: University of Chicago Libraries, 1939.

Nivardus. *Ysengrimus.* Ed. Ernst Voigt. Halle: Verlag der Buchhandlung des Waisenhauses, 1884.

Noonan, John T. "Marital Affection in the Canonists." *Studia Gratiana* 12 (1967):479–510.

Ovid. *Metamorphoses.* Trans. Frank J. Miller. 2 vols. Cambridge: Harvard University Press, 1977.

Owen, D.D.R. "Theme and Variations: Sexual Aggression in Chrétien de Troyes." *Forum for Modern Language Studies* 21 (1975):376–85.

Paden, William D. "Rape and Genre in the Pastourelle." Paper presented at 40th Annual Kentucky Foreign Language Conference, Lexington, Kentucky, April 24, 1987.

———. *The Medieval Pastourelle*. 2 vols. New York: Garland, 1987.

———. "Rape in the Pastourelle." *Romanic Review* 80 (May 1989):331–49.

Paris, Gaston. *Mélanges de littérature française du moyen âge*. Ed. Mario Roques. Paris: Champion, 1912.

Parry, Hugh. "Ovid's *Metamorphoses*: Violence in a Pastoral Landscape." *Transactions and Proceedings of the American Philological Association* 95 (1964):268–82.

Payer, Pierre. *Sex and the Penitentials: The Development of a Sexual Code. 550–1150*. Toronto: University of Toronto Press, 1984.

Petroff, Elizabeth Alvilda. *Medieval Women's Visionary Literature*. Oxford: Oxford University Press, 1986.

Philippe de Navarre. *Le Livre de Philippe de Navarre*. In *Receuil des historiens des croisades*. 16 vols. Paris: Académie des Inscriptions et Belles-Lettres, 1841–1906.

Planiol, Marcel, ed. *La Très ancienne Coutume de Bretagne*. Rennes: Plihon & Hervé, 1896.

Plucknett, T.F.T. "Chaucer's Escapade." *Law Quarterly Review* 64 (1948):33–36.

Posner, Richard A. *Law and Literature: A Misunderstood Relation*. Cambridge: Harvard University Press, 1988.

Rabine, Leslie. *Reading the Romantic Heroine: Text, History, Ideology*. Ann Arbor: University of Michigan Press, 1985.

Radway, Janice. *Reading the Romance: Women, Patriarchy and Popular Literature*. Chapel Hill: University of North Carolina Press, 1984.

Rapetti, P. N. *Le Livre de Jostice et de Pletz*. Paris: Firmin Didot, 1850.

Regalado, Nancy F. "Tristan and Renart; Two Tricksters." *Esprit Créateur* 16 (1976):30–38.

———. "Des Contraires Choses: la fonction poétique de la citation et des exempla dans le *Roman de la Rose*." *Littérature* 41 (1981):62–81.

Riedel, Frederick Carl. *Crime and Punishment in the Old French Romances*. New York: AMS Press, 1966.

Rieger, Dietmar. "Le motif du viol dans la littérature de la France médiévale: Entre norme courtoise et réalité courtoise." *Cahiers de civilisation médiévale* 31 (July–September 1988):241–67.

Riley-Smith, J.S.C. *The Feudal Nobility and the Kingdom of Jerusalem, 1174–1277*. London: Macmillan, 1973.

Rivière, Jean-Claude. *Pastourelles*. 3 vols. Geneva: Droz, 1974–76.

Roach, William. *The Continuations of the Old French "Perceval" of Chrétien de Troyes*. 5 vols. Philadelphia: University of Pennsylvania Press, 1949–83.

Robinson, Lillian. "Treason Our Text: Feminist Challenges to the Literary Canon." In *The New Feminist Criticism*. Ed. Elaine Showalter. New York: Pantheon, 1985, 105–21.

Roques, Mario, ed. *Le Roman de Renart: Branches I–XIX*. Paris: Champion, 1950–63.

Rossiaud, Jacques. "Prostitution, Youth, and Society in the Towns of Southeastern France in the Fifteenth Century." In *Deviants and the Abandoned in French Society*. Ed. Robert Forster and Orest Ranum. Baltimore: Johns Hopkins University Press, 1978; 1–46.

Rougemont, Denis de. *L'Amour et l'occident*. Paris: Plon, 1939; rpt. 1972.

Ruether, Rosemary Radford, ed. *Religion and Sexism: Images of Woman in the Jewish and Christian Traditions*. New York: Simon and Schuster, 1974.

Ruggiero, Guido. *Violence in Early Renaissance Venice*. New Brunswick: Rutgers University Press, 1980.

———. *The Boundaries of Eros: Sex Crime and Sexuality in Renaissance Venice*. Oxford: Oxford University Press, 1985.

St. John, Christopher. *The Plays of Roswitha*. New York: Benjamin Blom, 1966.

Saly, Antoinette. "La Demoiselle 'esforciée' dans le roman arthurien." In *Amour, mariage et transgressions au moyen âge*. Ed. Danielle Buschinger and André Crépin. Göppingen: Kümmerle Verlag, 1984.

Schneebeck, Harold. "The Law of Felony in Medieval England from the Accession of Edward I until the Mid-Fourteenth Century." Ph.D. dissertation, University of Iowa, 1973.

Schulenberg, Jane Tibbetts. "Female Sanctity: Public and Private Roles ca. 500–1100." In *Women and Power in the Middle Ages*. Ed. Mary Erler and Maryanne Kowaleski. Athens and London: University of Georgia Press, 1988, 102–25.

Shahar, Shulamith. *The Fourth Estate: A History of Women in the Middle Ages*. London and New York: Methuen, 1983.

Shorter, Edward. "On Writing the History of Rape." *Signs* 3, 2 (1977):471–82.

Smith, Cyril J. "History of Rape and Rape Laws." *Women Lawyers Journal* 60 (1974):188–91, 207.

Sticca, Sandro. *The Latin Passion Play: Its Origins and Development*. Albany: SUNY Press, 1970.

———. "Sin and Salvation: The Dramatic Context of Hrotswitha's Women." In *The Roles and Images of Women in the Middle Ages and Renaissance*. Ed. Douglas Radcliff-Umstead. Pittsburgh: University of Pittsburgh Publications on the Middle Ages and Renaissance, 1975, 3–22.

Stimpson, Catharine R. "Shakespeare and the Soil of Rape." In *The Woman's Part: Feminist Criticism of Shakespeare*. Ed. Carolyn Ruth Smith Lenz, Gayle Greene, and Carol Thomas Neely. Urbana: University of Illinois Press, 1980.

Strecker, Karl. *Hrotsvithae Opera*. Leipzig: Teubner, 1930.

Sudre, Léopold. *Les Sources du Roman de Renart*. Paris: Bouillon, 1893.

Sweeney, James Ross, and Stanley Chodorow, eds. *Popes, Teachers, and Canon Law in the Middle Ages*. Ithaca: Cornell University Press, 1989.

Tanon, Louis. *Registre criminel de la Justice de Saint Martin des Champs à Paris au XIVe siècle*. Paris: Léon Willem, 1877.

Tardif, Adolphe F. L., ed. *Le Très ancien Coutumier de Normandie*. Rouen: Lestrignant, 1896.

———. *Le Grand Coutumier de Normandie*. Rouen: Lestrignant, 1896.

Tomaselli, Sylvana, and Roy Porter, eds. *Rape: An Historical and Social Enquiry*. Oxford: Basil Blackwell, 1986.

Van Dievoet, Guido. "*Le Roman de Renart* et *Van Den Vos Reynaerde*, témoins fidèles de la procédure pénale aux XIIe et XIIIe siècles?" In *Aspects of the Medieval Animal Epic*. Ed. E. Rombauts and A. Welkenhuysen. The Hague: Martinus Nijhoff, 1975.

Varty, Kenneth. "Le Viol dans l'*Ysengrimus*, les branches II–Va, et la branche I du *Roman de Renart*." In *Amour, mariage et transgressions au moyen âge*. Ed. Danielle Buschinger and André Crépin. Göppingen: Kümmerle Verlag, 1984, 411–18.

Vauchez, André. *La Sainteté en Occident aux derniers siècles du moyen âge d'après les procès de canonisation et les documents hagiographiques*. Rome: Bibliothèque des Ecoles Françaises d'Athènes et de Rome, 1981.

Viollet, P., ed. *Les Establissements de Saint Louis*. Paris: Renouard, 1881.

Vodola, Elisabeth. *Excommunication in the Middle Ages*. Berkeley and Los Angeles: University of California Press, 1986.

Voltaire. "Candide." In *Romans et contes*. Paris: Garnier-Flammarion, 1966.

Wace. *Le Roman de Brut*. Ed. Ivor Arnold. Paris: Société des anciens textes français, 1940.

Walcot, Peter. "Herodotus on Rape." *Arethusa* 11 (Spring and Fall 1978):137–48.

Walker, Sue Sheridan. "Violence and the Exercise of Feudal Guardianship: The Action of *Ejectio Custodia*." *The American Journal of Legal History* 16 (1972): 320–33.

———. "Common Law Juries and Feudal Marriage Customs in Medieval England: The Pleas of Ravishment." *University of Illinois Law Review* 3 (1984): 705–18.

Warner, William Beatty. "Reading Rape: Marxist-Feminist Figurations of the Literal." *Diacritics* 13 (Winter 1983):12–32.

———. *Reading "Clarissa": The Struggles of Interpretation*. New Haven: Yale University Press, 1979.

Weisberg, Robert. "The Law-Literature Enterprise." *Yale Journal of Law and the Humanities* 1 (December 1988):1–77.

Wemple, Suzanne Fonay. *Women in Frankish Society: Marriage and the Cloister, 500 to 900*. Philadelphia: University of Pennsylvania Press, 1985.

Wemple, Suzanne, and Jo Ann McNamara. "The Power of Women Through the Family in Medieval Europe: 500–1100." *Feminist Studies* 1 (1973):126–41.

White, James Boyd. *Heracles' Bow: Essays on the Rhetoric and Poetics of the Law*. Madison: University of Wisconsin Press, 1985.

Wiegand, Mary Gonsalva. "The Non-Dramatic Works of Hrotsvitha." Ph.D. dissertation, Saint Louis University, 1936.

Willems, Lenard. *Etude sur l'Ysengrinus*. Ghent: E. Van Goethem, 1895.

Wilson, Katharina M. *The Dramas of Hrotsvit of Gandersheim*. Saskatoon: Peregrina, 1985.

———. *Hrotsvit of Gandersheim: The Ethics of Authorial Stance*. Leiden, New York, Copenhagen, Cologne: E. J. Brill, 1988.

Zink, Michel. *La Pastourelle*. Paris: Bordas, 1972.

Zumthor, Paul. *Essai de poétique médiévale*. Paris: Seuil, 1972.

Index

University of Pennsylvania Press
NEW CULTURAL STUDIES SERIES

Joan DeJean, Carroll Smith-Rosenberg, and Peter Stallybrass, Editors

Alex Owen. *The Darkened Room: Women, Power and Spiritualism in Late Victorian England*. 1990

Barbara J. Eckstein. *The Language of Fiction in a World of Pain: Reading Politics as Paradox*. 1990

Jonathan Arac and Harriet Ritvo, editors. *Macropolitics of Nineteenth-Century Literature: Nationalism, Exoticism, Imperialism*. 1991

Kathryn Gravdal. *Ravishing Maidens: Writing Rape in Medieval French Literature and Law*. 1991

This book has been set in Linotron Galliard. Galliard was designed for Mergenthaler in 1978 by Matthew Carter. Galliard retains many of the features of a sixteenth century typeface cut by Robert Granjon but has some modifications which gives it a more contemporary look.

Printed on acid-free paper.

Franklin Pierce College Library
00063077